Emperor William the Second congratulating
Prince Bismarck on his 80th birthday
in the grounds of Friedrichsruhe.

KAISER AND CHANCELLOR

THE OPENING YEARS OF THE REIGN OF KAISER WILHELM II

BY
KARL FRIEDRICH NOWAK

TRANSLATED BY
E. W. DICKES

NEW YORK
THE MACMILLAN COMPANY
1930

SET UP BY BROWN BROTHERS LINOTYPERS
PRINTED IN THE UNITED STATES OF AMERICA
BY THE FERRIS PRINTING COMPANY

The illustrations in this book are reproduced by permission from originals in the private collection of Kaiser Wilhelm II. The Publishers desire to express their grateful acknowledgements for the use of the pictures and for the descriptive titles in the Kaiser's own handwriting. These are printed in facsimile.

FOREWORD

THE sources relied on for this and the succeeding volumes are manifold and are not in evidence at a glance. Emperor William II contributed substantial material by placing at the disposal of the author numbers of confidential memoranda, giving him written material for important sections of the work and accounts of the course of various events, answering in precise terms every question that the author put to him, and assisting to make the material clear in the course of countless conversations at Doorn. The notes taken of every talk were regularly gone through on the following day, when the Kaiser made sure that they accurately reproduced what he had said, and made any further explanations or additions needed.

That, apart from the various historical works published, and the collections of documents, which can only be a guiding thread for the thirty years of rule of the last of the German Emperors, and apart from the documents inspected and studied in the archives, was the first stage in the preliminary work. Then began the checking of the Kaiser's statements: dates had to be compared, inconsistencies between his statements and those of other persons or the documents had to be noted and removed beyond cavil. Often a subject was dealt with five, six, ten times over. Even this was not enough for the author.

Numbers of statesmen, Ambassadors and persons who in one way or another had been associated with the Kaiser in his work, were visited by the author: they contributed material out of their recollection, their diaries, their own actual experience. This material also was noted down there and then—so far as it was not supplied to the author in written form. The new material was transmitted or handed by the author to the Kaiser—complete, exactly as communicated, with all the unpleasant things for the Kaiser that were to be found here and there in the manuscripts. The Kaiser left the unpleasantnesses untouched, confirmed what was accurate, made necessary corrections on points of fact. Then, where there were points of doubt, the author once more consulted his informants.

At last the material was sufficiently cleared up and freed from the mass of the relatively trivial and the purely legendary to stand out plainly in its true contours and interconnected detail, so that the author could proceed to write this first volume. The Kaiser had not insisted to the author that he must read the manuscript before publication. He had made no demand of any sort; on the contrary, when, several years ago, the author's constant intercourse with the ex-Kaiser began, it was he, the author, who insisted that two things were indispensable if his work was to take shape: the author must have the certainty that he would be able to speak always alone with the Kaiser and correspond with him without any sort of interposition on the part of the court entourage or any court intermediaries; and, further, there must be no attempt to influence the shaping and presentation of the material.

Emperor William not only at once agreed that both conditions should be complied with, but when, shortly before publication, the author passed the manuscript to him, as a matter of tact, for perusal, he refrained from any sort of objection to its contents. Yet the chapter "The

Young Master," for instance, could scarcely have been pleasant reading for him: he said to the author,

"One charge it will certainly be impossible for anyone to level against you—that of obsequiousness. You are not servile!"

The German edition of the present volume appeared in the autumn of 1929, and naturally produced storms. Enthusiastic assent alternated with bitter attacks. It was a work dealing with a ruler who had lost his throne and his power; accordingly the attacks predominated. The historic side of the matter, which was all the author was concerned with, was disregarded, and it was discussed from political standpoints. The socialistically inclined, the party democrat turned against the author for not reviling the fallen, where there was nothing to revile if one was concerned only to let simple justice speak. The conservatively minded and those rooted and held fast in the tradition of the founding of the Empire in 1870 turned in fury against the author for the opposite reason: he had not only seen weaknesses as well as qualities in Emperor William II, but had presumed to see weaknesses or defects in Bismarck, the elect, the chosen of the Lord. Recognized authorities abroad bore witness at once and unreservedly to the plain intention of impartiality in the work; in Germany it was for many months a centre of contention. Ultimately the contending parties appealed to the arbitrament of authorities whose standing was above all criticism; and the result was a scientific imprimatur of the work, its bases, its presentation, its general historic scheme, its accuracy of detail. Such has been the judgment delivered by Dr. Friedrich Thimme, the editor of the German Foreign Ministry's great collection of documents, *Die Grosse Politik der Europäischen Kabinette,*

1871-1914, whose expert authority is uncontested, by Professor Joseph Redlich, the famous historian of the Universities of Vienna and Cambridge (Mass.), and by the *Rector Magnificus* of Vienna University, Professor Hans Uebersberger, the joint editor of the comprehensive and admirable collection of Austrian official documents, whose researches in the field of Eastern European history have won international recognition.

In Britain and America it will be possible for the work to be read with a critical calm and impartiality which to this day are beyond the reach of many Germans in approaching its subject, since it concerns their own experiences and destinies too closely and too deeply. The Anglo-Saxon reader will appreciate and recognize the unquestionable genius, the almost superhuman capacities of a statesman who was, for all that, deeply in error in the systems of statesmanship by which he sought to maintain abroad and at home the realm which he had founded. He will see a human personality of immense strength, and yet all-too human in its limitations; at issue with a young prince who was not always perfect in outward form, was often dominating and inconsiderate, and yet was on a solid basis of right in his struggle for his independence and for freedom to pursue his own not ignoble ideas. Placing over against one another these two characters, with their motives and settled convictions, amid their environment and the conditions and limitations of their time, to which they were inevitably subject in all that they did, the detached British or American reader will without doubt himself realize the fact that it has been the endeavour of this volume to bring out—the inexorability of the process of history.

KARL FRIEDRICH NOWAK.

Berlin, August 19, 1930.

CONTENTS

CONTENTS
ILLUSTRATIONS

ILLUSTRATIONS

xiii

KAISER AND CHANCELLOR

CHAPTER I

THE HEIR TO EMPIRE

WITH no hope left, brought home in agony from San Remo, the Emperor Frederick lay tortured and dying. He was no longer fighting for his life, only enduring its pain, heroically, to the end.

The whole country was torn by the controversy between the doctors; most of them favoured operating and believed that it might yet save the patient's life, but the doctor in whom he placed his trust had stood firm, up to the moment when the Emperor was plainly collapsing, against any sort of operation as unnecessary. The truth concerning the Emperor, if it was the truth, was only whispered about the country, amid the grief over the passing away of William I and the general unrest of the changing times—the old and outworn weariedly sinking, the new unable to lift itself up, and everything lying in the lap of a future impenetrably obscure.

Prince Bismarck still stood at the helm. But the Chancellor was no longer in all men's eyes far above criticism, an infallible archangel of the Empire. Unfamiliar currents of opinion, strange forces hitherto ignored, were beginning to claim the right to exist and have their domicile on German soil as elsewhere. Since the Chancellor had allowed free play to the secret ballot, a new power had asserted itself in public life alongside the bourgeoisie, not yet with fiery insistence on its demands, but for all that in a tone that was not customary, a tone, indeed, that had never before been ventured on, and often in provocative terms—the Social Democracy.

The Empire which had been created and irradiated by glorious victories at arms under William I had shared the Emperor's ideals and political conceptions so long as he lived; but now it stood face to face with big internal change and new departures: this, in hope or fear, every party in Germany knew, and every citizen, whether at the desk or bench.

When a young soldier the old Emperor had been present at Waterloo. To him Metternich's statecraft of long since was no mere tradition of the past, magnified by history into monstrous proportions. To him it had retained the actuality of things seen, things in which, for a time, he had taken part. At that time he had beaten down the Revolution which had been too strong for him as Prince of Prussia. His fabulous rise to power had been accompanied by nothing but popular enthusiasm and applause, never by popular demands. Nothing in his lifetime had as much as laid a finger on the inmost convictions of the Emperor, to which he had held fast in spite of every concession to the people of Prussia and Germany, in spite of the Constitution which had actually been granted, in spite of the powers of the Chancellor and the innovation of Ministerial responsibility—his belief in sovereignty with its rights and duties. As a boy of fifteen he had fought against the Holy Alliance in the Wars of Liberation. Their memory stirred the patriarch to his dying day. His successor had to move forward almost a century.

Now, however, there was still hope that the new

Emperor would make no break with tradition: the tempestuous onset of death was plainly allowing him no time for it. It was a hope that greatly disturbed one side—a challenge to all the freedom-loving and progressive thinkers who had long praised the Crown Prince and claimed him as their leader in a new ordering of the State with new freedoms imperially protected. All these now feared for their Emperor. They anticipated that the grandson would continue in the old Emperor's footsteps, though they were not sure of it. But all the world knew what to expect if the Emperor and Empress Frederick remained on the throne.

The prospect, however, was full of uncertainty. The Emperor was a lost man. Yet he would suddenly drive out from Charlottenburg to the palace in Berlin. Or he would attend a parade of the three regiments of the Crown Prince's brigade, which the Prince would himself march past him. Whenever the Empress appeared in public or in any large company, she was seen to be in good spirits. The gravity of the truth about the Emperor, if it was the truth, was only whispered in the country.

In the Charlottenburg Palace, however, and finally in the "New Palace" at Potsdam, the closing scenes were being enacted in a prison solitude over which the Empress kept rigid watch. During the ninety-nine days of the Emperor's rule the Empress Frederick dominated all, through her energy and love of power, and commanded the respect of all in her agonized fear for the patient's life and the bitter disappointment that was breaking in on her. She had now been struggling for two years, up to the threshold of the end of his inconceivable torture, for the life of her consort and for her dreams of succession with him to the throne.

This blond giant of a Prince, the unexpected apparition

of whose splendid frame had astonished and impressed the Empress Eugénie in the Tuileries, had been the choice of the merry, laughing Princess Victoria, Princess Royal of Great Britain, from pure affection. In her new homeland it had been plain to all the world that she simply idolized her husband. Her happiness had filled her with a perpetual radiance, but even as Princess Royal she had been aware that one day she would wear the Imperial crown, had calculated on it, and had made it a condition. It had ·been her intention to wear it in her own proud way, inherited from her British forbears, with the self-confidence born of her faith in British traditions. In ruling she would be able to apply the knowledge won from her intimate and painstaking collaboration with her father, the Prince Consort, and all the ability united with the imperious nature and the passionate earnestness of her mother Queen Victoria, who would scarcely brook denial at any time, but knew, on the other hand, very much better than the daughter how quietly to get her way by means of an effective gesture of majesty or a shrewd decision. She had endured with impatience her long wait for her Crown Prince. She had been dominated by her ambition to present to the new country in which she was destined to live and work the western idea of liberty which was second nature to her, the British belief in democratically limited monarchy, which had been accepted unquestioningly in the past and was to be in the future.

But everywhere she had found herself obstructed by the contrast between ideal and actuality. She loved the bright green English sward, and when she looked for it she found only the sand of Brandenburg. She thought of the British Earls and Viscounts in whose comfortable and well-kept

One of the last photos taken
of Emperor William the Great
in the uniform of the First
Regiment of Cuirassiers.
(First Life-Cuirassiers bearing
the name of the Great Elector)
This regiment escorted Marlborough
through Flanders & distinguished
itself under his command at
Oudenarde and Malplaquet —

Prince Fredrick William of Prussia,
later Emperor Fredrick, as First-
Lieutenant of the First Foot Guard,
in the year of his confirmation

palaces she had passed her youth; now, when she sought out her noble relatives, she found only Junkers. Manners in her new country were not only different, they were rough. She had always been for toleration, for the axiomatic equality of human rights; here she found nothing but narrowness, provincialism, and obsolete ideas that fought furiously for survival. She had imagined a statesman who would help her in constructive work, a Gladstone, perhaps, or a Disraeli; she found facing her Prince Bismarck, a broad-shouldered, formidable being, in his cuirassier's boots the very symbol of all that she hated, passionate as herself, unbending as herself, but more powerful. In all the years of her life as Crown Princess she had gained nothing, no influence over the old Emperor, none over the business of government. Never was her advice sought, or even that of the Crown Prince, whom she believed she had largely inspired with her own views. Her consuming ambition had gradually turned to a bitterness which revealed itself in her letters to England. Still, one day the hour would strike for which she had always hoped—the hour of accession to the throne. She knew that there were limits to the kindliness and the warm humanity of the Crown Prince's attitude to life, limits set by the traditions of Prussian royalty amid which he had grown up, and by his sense of his mission as a Monarch and a Hohenzollern. But she knew that almost always he could be led, and his beautiful, passionate consort knew above all how to lead him. Distant as the day of power might be, it must come—even though the Chancellor scarcely concealed his hatred of this Englishwoman any longer; even though he dared to open her letters and Queen Victoria's replies; even though in the end, in order to ensure safe transmission, the Queen and the Crown Princess had to correspond through their Ladies-in-Waiting. All these humiliations, which her pride had allowed no outward sign to admit, would end with the ascent of the throne, before which the whole of this old and effete period, thick with the dust of prejudice, would fall with its standardbearers —and perhaps its Chancellor.

Suddenly, in January, 1887, in the midst of all these plans for the future, which she had so often discussed with her husband, there came a ghastly shock: the Crown Prince was attacked, with no warning, by a mysterious malady. His voice acquired an unnatural hoarseness. It resisted all the efforts of the specialists. The German doctors at once took a grave view of the affection and pronounced it malignant; but the carcinoma could, they considered, be extirpated without danger to life by an operation on the larynx. The hoarseness would remain, but there would be no further development. The Crown Princess Frederick had listened mutely to the verdict, and in the end had assented; but afterwards, when preparations were already under way for the operation, she stood out against it. She had been nearly thirty years in her new homeland, and herself held German medical science in high esteem, but now she sent out a cry for help to England, which had always been her refuge in distress and her counsellor in indecision. In any case she was determined that an English doctor should be called in before the Crown Prince actually went under the knife. Wonderingly Queen Victoria asked:

"Why an Englishman, when you have such good German doctors?"

When Queen Victoria's physician, Sir John Reid, heard the name of the chosen doctor, Morell Mackenzie, his comment was:

"My God! here in England we have never heard of the man!"

One of the German doctors had mentioned Mackenzie to the Crown Princess as an authority. Mackenzie's pronouncement brought hope; he promised that the patient would recover, and confidently dismissed the suggestion of malignancy. The Crown Princess decided to rely entirely on him. Even the hoarseness, he said, would disappear. The Prince would be able to speak again in a loud voice, to address an army corps, to deliver lectures and addresses. The Crown Princess decided against operation.

Then the last torturing pilgrimage began. The Crown Prince sought health in the Isle of Wight, in Scotland, in the Pustertal, and finally harassed and exhausted, in San Remo. Here his voice disappeared altogether. He was still a man of heroic stature, with the frame and features of a Siegfried; but the impression he conveyed was uncanny: the giant had become dumb, only his eyes spoke.

Finally, at the Villa Zirio, in San Remo, Mackenzie abruptly revised his diagnosis, and admitted that the patient was incurably afflicted with cancer. He himself found that the disease had suddenly become much worse. He himself now asked that the specialists should be summoned. Schrötter, the Viennese laryngologist, made the definite pronouncement that the Crown Prince had another eighteen months to live. He said this in the presence of the patient, from whom he considered that the knowledge of his condition should not be withheld. The only possible operation would be of doubtful efficacy. The Crown Prince must himself decide whether he would undergo it or not. Summoning all her resolution, and showing herself so at her finest, the Crown Princess supported him through the ordeal of the pronouncement. The patient decided against the operation.

"Well," he wrote in his diary, "I shall evidently have to put my house in order."

He had finished with the things of this world. Yet, four months later, the hour of her supremacy struck for the Crown Princess. The old Emperor had died in Berlin, tired and used up; his life, prolonged amid heavy cares, had slowly faded out like a lamp consumed. The succession had not come as the laughing Princess Royal had imagined it, or the Crown Princess amid the hostility and the woundings in this atmosphere so alien to her, though for these she was sure of her revenge. Still, her hour had come, and the new Empress had her opportunity. She had prevented up to then any leakage of the hopeless secret of the Villa Zirio. There were whisperings at home, but nothing was known. Now the royal train was carrying her, the bearer of supreme power, to Germany. She knew exactly for how long, at most, she would wield it. But if she had no more than an hour, she was nevertheless now the ruler. The power which at last she had found in her hands was to be hers entirely. The new Emperor would exercise his brief rule, through her alone. Inexorably, with icy hardness, she sealed off the death chamber from the outer world. No one had access to it unless she herself brought him to the bedside of the sick man, who for a long time now had only spoken with pencil and paper. Even Prince William of Prussia, the new heir to the throne, could see little of his father.

"Why don't you come oftener?" the Emperor wrote on one occasion.

The Pss Royal & Pce Frederick William of
Prussia.

Jan: 29 1858.

Prince Fredrick William of Prussia
and his bride Princess Victoria after
their engagement.
Taken in the Quadrangle of Windsor
Jan. 29ᵗ 1858

SOMMER 1866
HERINGSDORF
ODER
ERDMANNSDORF.

Crownprince + Crown Princess with
Pr. William, Pr. Henry, Pruss: Charlotte,
Pruss: Victoria at Heringsdorf 1866

"I am always turned away. I'm always told you are asleep, or something of the sort."

The Empress heard, but made no sign. She remained as always—icy, inscrutable, unapproachable during all this time. If Dr. Mackenzie was hovering about the Emperor his reporters would peer into the sickroom. The Empress permitted it: it was left to Prince William to close the door against them while he spoke to his father. But Crown Prince William above all others had to be kept away from any conversation with the Emperor. For it was he above all others whom she hated.

Perhaps she had only loved her eldest son in the moment of his birth, as she came out of the anæsthetic and over-heard and understood the Latin of the doctors. They had been considering sacrificing the child in order to save his mother.

"On no account!" she had cried out. "I would rather die."

At that long distant date the doctors had had poor success in the home of the Crown Princess Frederick. They had not ventured to break through the rules of the etiquette which prescribed that even in the hour of confinement an English Princess could not be exposed to the sight of the doctors, and at the critical moment their efforts were impeded. The Prince paid the penalty in an injury to his left arm. Nor did the young mother ever entirely recover from her confinement. Moreover, the injury to the Prince was not remarked and treated at once. From that moment the Crown Princess, whose enthusiasms were all for beauty and æsthetic harmony, was hard, hostile, bitter, whenever she recalled the coming of the Prince into the world.

She had had no share herself in the bringing up of Prince

William: she had merely supervised it; and from his earliest childhood she had insisted on two things as indispensable —strictness and discipline. Her own childhood and youth had been a time of brightness and merriment, but there was nothing of either in Prince William's first ten years, nothing in his whole boyhood and youth. His father was full of kindness for all else in the world, but it was a rare thing for him to give a kindly word or a smile to his son. He would do so when they were alone, but never if the mother entered the room: his son found him stricken dumb in her presence. She had entirely approved the methods adopted by the tutor who took the boy under his care at ten years, Dr. Georg Ernst Hinzpeter, a dogmatic Spartan from Bielefeld, who considered laughter as superfluous an element in boyhood as the Crown Princess had considered it in Prince William's nursery. It was difficult to say which of the two parents sinned the more in the bringing up of their son. The mother applied unrelenting severity as a means of ripening and strengthening the frail boy, with his super-sensitiveness, his pride and emotionality and tenderness that went far beyond those of an ordinary healthy child. The father stood aside, left her to do as she would. Sorrowfully he accepted the fact of the mother's unconcealed repugnance; he made no effort to combat it. The tutor, on the contrary, had his own positive ideals, stiff and bony as himself, built up on the ethics of his day, misunderstood; these latest improvements in educational methods, inhumanly applied, he tried out on a pupil whom he hoped to set before the world as a model of princely training.

Hinzpeter had no notion of the fact that to make a child work and to give him no praise for his effort is to rob him of the sun in his sky. Humourless, strict with himself, a

dry idealist who became a pedant the moment he began to
set his ideas in order, he reduced all morality to two things,
duty and abstention. His face had no life in it, his sharp-
cut features damped down all enthusiasm in advance and
made a dogma of dour correctness. In their long solitary
walks together he set Prince William the task of delivering
extempore addresses, and urged him to exercise the art of
original thinking. But seldom can a teacher have brought
less imagination to the training of an imaginative child. He
was incapable of directing the Prince's fancifulness at the
right moment along the right lines: he cut short his fancies
if he was unable to follow them. He suppressed every
impulse to get away from the sober and pursue the picturesque. Since they must study psychology, he found it a
sufficient exercise to set Prince William and his brother
Henry to watch the faces of the passers-by in the Tiergarten
and work out their characters. If he took them to see works
of the old masters in the museums he would weary them
with the dry bones of history. When they came to the sculp-
tures the history would recommence. Not a word would
be spoken about the period of the artist, his technique, his
subject, his intention.

At home Prince William sat from seven in the morning
to ten at night, filling his head with Latin and Greek, English and French, mathematics, physics, geography and history. In the midst of it all the Doctor would readily agree
to the Prince applying some of his scanty leisure to "thinking out" some religious composition. But his enjoyment
of his composition rarely extended beyond the first lessons.
Long before he got well into it his pleasure was destroyed
by the reduction of the subject to dullness, by persistent
repetitions of wrong-headed criticism, by this pedagogue's

rage for finding fault and picking holes. He would throw
the composition aside: a flower picked to pieces, robbed
of the last vestige of beauty. His interest in the subject had
been killed and he longed to pass on to something else.
His ideas had deserted him.

The Hinzpeter period was full to overflowing with subjects and programmes of work and supervision of work.
But Hinzpeter himself spoiled everything for the Prince.
Up to the end of his seven years' tutorship, in a myriad subjects, in every field he made his company repulsive to the
Prince. He accepted no responsibility if Prince William
were to fail to develop into a model of manhood. When
the Prince escaped to become a student at Bonn, the Doctor
was satisfied with the results of his instruction. Yet this
trainer of youth did not mind saying occasionally in confidence that his pupil had never learned to work, without
feeling the need to ask himself how much in that case he
had really been doing for his charge during all those seven
years. It scarcely ever dawned on Hinzpeter that his whole
method of teaching pupils through carping and faultfinding
was bound in the end to produce exasperation, however
much the Prince might lean on his tutor; that to be for ever
pointing to inadequacies could only depress his pupil and
in the end defeat any natural incentive. In his pedantic
way Hinzpeter had an appreciation of humane ideas, of
the pains of the worker, of the need for constructive social
development the world over. But this humanitarianism did
not begin at home. To take from the child—a child by no
means pampered—a present of fine fruit sent by a tender
aunt, in order to chasten him by letting him see it without
being allowed to taste it; to invite little guests to enjoy it
without stint, only their little host going without; to allow

him no joy, to visit an unexpected joy with immediate destruction, standing glumly by; never to admit that the lesson had been done, much less well done—all this was Hinzpeter's neo-Spartan method, approved by the mother, acquiesced in by the father, applied in the unconscious bigotry of infallibility to shatter a childhood.

If, in spite of all this, the sun shone on occasion in Prince William's youth, it was only from afar. His English grandmother spoke of him always tenderly, and spoke tenderly to him when she saw him. His grandparents were kind to him when they had him with them. But the sun's rays were counted out, and were almost always dangerous. Even the Crown Prince was displeased if Queen Victoria went so far as to have her grandson, for whom she had evident affection, to tea. And for the good fortune of the kindness of the old Emperor and Empress he paid with the ill-humour of his mother: he had been pert—just because he had answered questions; he had pushed himself into everyone's view—when in truth he had been brought there.

No one could read the face of Crown Prince William as his father lay dying. Dr. Hinzpeter's experiments in education belonged then to the distant past. The public knew little about the Crown Prince; what little it had learned was of recent date and quite indefinite. He had pursued the career of almost all heirs-presumptive, had commanded his regiment, later his brigade, had been living in modest Court state in Potsdam, had married while quite young the Princess Augusta Victoria of Schleswig-Holstein. He had been entrusted with Court missions by the old Emperor—to Queen Victoria, to Tsar Alexander III at St. Petersburg. Once the public had pricked up its ears, when his name had been mentioned in connexion with a plan of social service—the proposed Berlin City Mission. Count Waldersee, the Quartermaster General, known to be a friend of the Prince, had wanted to start this mission in collaboration with Stöcker, a Court preacher, a man of all-too pronounced political views and all-too little tolerance in questions of race and religion; the two had proposed to spread the organization throughout the Empire as a means of educating the people to Christian Socialism. Then the effort had been given up. At the head of his troops Prince William had shown energy; he had so far overcome the weakness of his left arm that it was no longer very noticeable. His voice had the officer's tone. His manner was impenetrable; often he seemed reticent, sometimes sharp. He alone knew that he was full of grief and bitterness and disillusionment.

Everywhere, even if he tried entirely to forget his childhood and tutelage, there had been endless pinpricks in the sad period of nearly two years which was now reaching its end in the great tragedy of the Emperor's death. Always and everywhere in his parents' house he had met with disapproval. The old Chancellor had proposed that he should be withdrawn from a purely military environment and purely military ways of thinking, and brought to the Foreign Ministry, to be gradually initiated into the administrative side of political control; his father had replied in wounding terms from Porto Fino:

"In view of the immaturity and inexperience of my eldest son, together with his tendency to vanity and conceit, I can only describe it as absolutely dangerous to bring him so soon into contact with foreign affairs."

Always, though he neither spared effort nor wanted to, whether he showed his ambition or checked it, there was

Prince William of Prussia
aetus 3 years. 1862

Queen Victoria 1862.
Gift by H. M. to her grandson
on his visit with parents after
the death of his grandfather.

nothing for him but condemnation and reproach. When he was first entrusted with a political mission, that to the Tsar, he had demurred from fear of his parents; only to find them deeply irritated at the suggestion that he should be so engaged, and suspicious that the suggestion had proceeded from him. When Sir Morell Mackenzie gave his alarming diagnosis at San Remo the Prince had hurried to his grandfather, full of anxiety about his father, to whom he secretly clung in affection and concern, in order to see whether anything could still be done to save him by the highest authorities on his case. He was blamed then for interference and presumption, and again when he went to San Remo.

There was no denying that at many points Prince William's views of political and social and constitutional questions, his conceptions of State and people and ruler, differed radically from his mother's. She had never forgotten that she was an English Princess; he never forgot that he was a Prince of Prussia. To him Bismarck had always been a mighty paladin wearing the crown of superhuman exploits. What Bismarck had achieved was in the Prince's eyes above criticism and on no account to be touched. But his mother dreamed of a new democratic German realm, and this she meant to achieve at all costs; she would impose Liberalism with the iron will of a despot. For her, Bismarck was an abomination; yet this evil spirit had her own son's willing allegiance. Had mother and son discussed their differences it might have proved that he was for progress no less than she, even, perhaps more than she, only he was not for a complete break with tradition and with things that in his eyes seemed of immemorial sanctity —at least, he would spare established rights and institutions sanctioned by history. But the Princess evaded discussion. Only once did her grief, or the deepest emotion within her, that she took to be grief, break through her reserve. At San Remo she had wanted once more to get rid of this son who was forever thrusting himself upon her. Let him go quietly on to Rome straightaway—that, she supposed, was his destination. Only a chance meeting with his father, who caught sight of him on the stairs and spoke to him in his ghostly whisper, and then embraced him, silently weeping, had enabled him to get permission to stay. After that a gentler feeling seemed suddenly to have sprung up between mother and son. The Crown Princess herself sent the Prince to Professor Schrötter—who had hurried to San Remo from Vienna—to discuss his father's state with him. And it was during a walk with her son just after this that she excitedly said to him, abandoning all restraint:

"When I think of how all the plans which I had worked out with Papa will collapse, because I shall be robbed of power—I shall never come to power—"

Never had the Prince dreamed of an outburst of that sort; he exerted himself to the utmost to remain collected. The Villa Zirio was surrounded by reporters day and night, watching every sign of life, dogging the steps of every guest; there were reporters now behind mother and son. The Crown Princess was shaking with emotion, her nerves were visibly giving way; with difficulty she supported herself, hanging on her son's arm. Never had she spoken so plainly of her invincible suspicion that her own son intended to drive his dying father from the throne by a *coup d'état* and completely ignore her rights. That she had these ideas the Prince knew, but until then she had only given distant indications of them, in cryptic innuendos. For his part, if ever

Coburg

Her Majesty the Queen, Empress
Fredrick, Duke of Connaught
Duke of Saxe-Coburg Gotha
German Emperor, Prince of Wales

Prince William of Prussia
ætas 1 year 1860

the mad suggestion came to his ears that now that the Emperor had lost his speech and could not hold a Crown Council or command troops, he would be incapable of ruling, the Prince had openly and emphatically rejected it. On one occasion he had said to Count Waldersee:

"Constitutionally it makes no difference whether the Emperor can speak or not. He can write down his commands."

He did not know that the Count had noted down the exact opposite of this in his diary, and had retailed the story in that sense. He tried now to soothe the agitated Crown Princess, to set her mind completely at rest by an unequivocal assurance:

"But, Mama!" he began, still in English, in which they had been conversing in the busy street in which they were walking—"Dear Mama, all that is laid down by the Constitution. The King of Prussia cannot be deposed at all. Besides, he can give his commands in writing . . . Only in the event of his suffering from mental trouble is a regent appointed for him."

Only slowly did the Crown Princess regain composure. For some seconds it seemed as though the two might come closer together. But her unapproachability, her icy coldness had returned when she looked again at the Prince.

Then, in the midst of the days of sickness in Charlottenburg, there had come the unfortunate plan for the marriage of the Empress's daughter Victoria, a plan which had the Empress's approval. While the old Emperor was still alive the marriage of the Prussian Princess to Prince Alexander of Battenberg had been proposed; the Chancellor had raised objections to it. The young Prince had been offered their throne by the Bulgarians. He had accepted it, against the wish of the Tsar. The proposed marriage could not but annoy the Tsar, even if the Prince had now renounced his throne in deference to the Tsar's feelings. Bismarck had absolutely opposed the marriage; the old Emperor had given way, and Prince William now supported Bismarck. At this time Queen Victoria was once more staying with the Emperor Frederick; she agreed with her grandson and Bismarck, to the annoyance of the Emperor and Empress. Prince William could never do right: his every thought and word, whatever he touched on, whatever he advocated, was ill-advised. In his parents' house there was nothing but irritation with him.

He was now living in the Palace in Berlin. An Order in Council of the Emperor's had instructed him to sign papers as the Emperor's representative. He signed patents of nobility, appointments of officials, promotions of officers. Of serious discussions or decisions of any importance he learned nothing. General von Winterfeld, Adjutant General to the Emperor, might tell him something of the labours of the Committee which the Emperor had set up to revise the out-of-date orders for army exercises, but save for such occasional pieces of information he learned nothing of military affairs. He had just to sign papers which the adjutant on duty brought, and took away again. He set his teeth and secretly tested the serviceability of the new exercise regulations, so far as he was acquainted with them, with his regimental commanders.

But for all his powerlessness a change had begun to be noticeable in those around him. Not, indeed, in Field Marshal Count Moltke: the old Marshal, absent-minded and reticent as always, far ahead of all others in his ideas of strategy and on technical papers, gave the Prince the same reception as ever when he saw him. General von Albedyll, faithful confidant of Emperor William I, was also outwardly little changed. (On one occasion the Prince had been violently at issue with the General, who had disagreed with an order issued by the Prince as regimental commander forbidding his officers to visit a certain club of doubtful repute! While standing guard during the night for the old Emperor, when he collapsed in Salzburg on his last homeward journey from Gastein, they had buried their quarrel.) But all the other visitors to the Prince had for weeks past been showing a markedly increased deference. Reports were eagerly and obsequiously presented. Advice offered unasked was most humbly submitted.

In all this bitter period the Prince devoted himself entirely to military work. He exercised daily with his regiments on the Tempelhofer Feld. He rode at the head of his troops up to the Brandenburg Gate, ordered the battalions to march past, a popular spectacle, had the old historic marches of his own choosing played, instead of the operetta music which had been customary, to set the step; then he would ride into the Palace. The papers for signature had to wait. It did not disturb him to find himself beginning to be more and more frequently attacked by a section of the Press as all-too militaristic, or, if Mackenzie had shown the attacks to the Empress Frederick, to hear her talk cuttingly of "drilling to curry favour with the mob." His officers wanted to prevent the attacks; he told them to ignore them: the venom would pass away. He did not want to spoil the pleasure of the Berliners who came marching in crowds alongside the regiments. But the venom did not pass away. In the end the Quartermaster General, Count Waldersee, himself felt compelled to mention the

matter. He asked for an audience with the Prince. It was
granted at once, for the General was very welcome at all
times. The Quartermaster General opened with lengthy
assurances:

"All officers in Berlin, senior and junior alike, rejoice
in your Imperial Highness's military keenness, which fills
them with confidence and hope for the future. But there
are other quarters in which your Imperial Majesty is
regarded with hostility, especially those in which hopes
were entertained of an era of Liberalism under your
Imperial Highness's parents; an era in which your critics
counted on playing an active part. The articles in the Left-
wing Press containing attacks on your Imperial Highness
proceed from these quarters, whose connexion with Charlottenburg is evident, if the articles are not actually inspired
by Charlottenburg."

The General paused. The Crown Prince was silent.
Waldersee proceeded:

"In all loyal quarters, military and civil, there is extreme
irritation over the petticoat rule which is being exercised
indirectly through the sick Emperor from Charlottenburg
over Prussia and Germany—an experience never before
suffered in Prussia. Consequently all eyes are fixed on your
Imperial Highness in the full hope that you will not allow
this petticoat rule to have injurious effects. Emperor Frederick has but a short time left to live, and consequently this
régime will not be prolonged. Nevertheless, there is time
for a good deal of harm to be done. Your Imperial Highness must therefore not take the Press vulgarities seriously
or be annoyed by them; but it is also unnecessary for your
Imperial Highness to carry out the commands sent from
Charlottenburg on the part of His Majesty the Emperor

Morell Mackenzie

Crownprince with Prince William
at Balmoral

to your Imperial Highness—considering that it is well known what is the true source which inspires them;—you could quietly leave them unfulfilled and set them on one side. Once your Imperial Highness is at the helm you will be able to do and leave undone what you will, and you must not unnecessarily commit yourself in advance."

The Crown Prince had listened with growing astonishment. The General had enjoyed the special confidence of the old Emperor. Count Moltke described him as the ablest of those who would come after him. He himself had thought him until then the most reliable of friends. For some time the Crown Prince was entirely at a loss. Count Waldersee waited, and now remained perfectly silent. At the Prince's first words he paled.

"Recently," the Prince replied, "at the head of my brigade, with my officers and grenadiers and fusiliers, I swore on our standards the military oath of loyalty to my father. To that, come what may, I shall adhere! That obviously implies strict execution of every command of His Majesty the Emperor coming from Charlottenburg. Even if such a command were to run, say: 'Having attempted to seduce the brigade commander of the 2nd Infantry Brigade of the Guards into disobedience to his Emperor and breach of his military oath, Count Waldersee is to be placed in front of a sandheap and shot,' I should execute the command to the letter—with pleasure."

The Crown Prince turned his back on the General. The audience was over. Count Waldersee departed without another word. The Prince, horrified, remained. It was not in mere romanticism that he built on honour and loyalty. It was not even his genuine, implicit faith in Providence and its laws that made him shrink from the breach of an oath

as a mortal sin. Officers were officers. Everything was
reduced to chaos if the oath to the supreme head of the army
was to become a subject for exegesis. If such a proposal
was made by such a General as Count Waldersee, there
must be others still more misguided and unreliable.

He could have nothing more to do with this friend and
adviser. He was living in a sombre world. He could not
pretend that his feeling was not now one of longing for an
end to it all. He was the Prince who had learnt nothing,
who had been capable of nothing, who did everything ill;
who yet itched for popularity, and sought it by demagogic
methods; who was perpetually in conflict with his parents.
He was thoughtless, heartless. Certainly he had his faults;
but after all he thought it strange if he could do nothing
but give offence to everybody, if he had nothing but faults.
He would gladly have given proof that in the main he was
very different to that. But even if he could put out of his
mind all the unpleasant things that seemed to be said against
him, and could completely master the intrigues which had
had their culmination in these weeks, here was his main
pillar of support, on which he had counted for the future,
in ruins. He grieved over his loss. Scarcely a soul knew
him as he really was. There grew and overtopped his grief
a sense of loneliness.

The days passed greyly. The sick Emperor had been
brought to the New Palace in Potsdam. Everything there
proceeded under a veil, in obscurity; scarcely any Government business was transacted. Only von Puttkamer, Minister of the Interior, was suddenly dismissed, and the Minister of Justice, Friedberg, who had the ear of the Empress,
secured assent to a Bill prolonging the life of Parliament,
extending the period for which Deputies were in future to

be elected. This was a restriction of the power of the Government. From then onwards the representatives of the people had a longer-continued say, and in consequence greater influence, in regard to legislation. It looked as if it had been the Empress Frederick who secured the dismissal of von Puttkamer (who had opposed the Bill), in order to get rid of the defender of a system which she hated and wanted to abolish; but the dismissal had been the Chancellor's own work. He had been equally opposed to the Bill, but perhaps it would be easier for him to make his peace with the Empress if he made, on his own initiative, a sacrifice which would bring her satisfaction.

Then, on June 15, 1888, the end came. The officers in the New Palace changed their tone entirely. Now they all recognized only "the young master." Hussars galloped up and surrounded the Palace. The "young master" knew that once more he was incurring disapproval. But this was the final act of a past against which he had at last jumped to the defensive. The hussars came, however, too late. Mackenzie's English colleagues had all the time been quietly, though not unnoticed, carrying away from the Palace bags and portfolios filled with documents. No one could now leave the Palace, but most of Emperor Frederick's documents had already been got away. Beside his deathbed there stood the widowed Empress, majestic, her head high, voicing nothing of her grief—her grief over her consort and over her future and her life's aims that had died that day with him.

The power was now in the hands of Emperor William II.

CHAPTER II

THE HOUR OF INHERITANCE

THE succession to the throne was uneventful. Shortly before the death of Emperor Frederick, Friedberg had informed Crown Prince William of a remarkable document which was to be laid before the new ruler immediately after his succession. The document, which had slumbered in the secret archives, was signed by Frederick William IV, and contained a suggestion to his successor to rescind the Constitution that had been wrung from him. It had been placed before Emperor William I at the outset of his reign. Emperor Frederick III had had it in his hands. Both had had it replaced in the secret archives. Now it was the turn of William II to read this ancestral letter. He tore it up.

The troops were sworn in in allegiance to the new ruler. Emperor William II issued his first messages to army and navy. Prince Bismarck ought, perhaps, to have advised preparing the message to the German people for issue at the same moment. Nothing was more natural than that a soldier's first challenge should also be that of the supreme commander, to whom army and navy were the plainest outward symbol of the power entrusted to him; but the world beyond Germany's borders, to which he was a new and unknown factor, was likely to be disturbed by it. Bismarck, however, said nothing. He agreed with the course taken. As for public opinion in Germany, it paid a warm tribute to the personality of the new ruler, a tribute in which all parties joined. Meanwhile Emperor William gave orders for the new Court appointments.

He made his choice, as he had determined to do while still Crown Prince, among those whom he had found reason to trust, taking the advice of General von Versen, his former brigade commander. The General was one of the few who had often had kind things to say of the Prince. Now he was the Emperor's adviser in the first big decisions that faced him.

Count August Eulenburg became Marshal of the Court. He was a man of polished manner and of wide knowledge, cautious in his political judgments, and a man of the attractive, intellectual, cultured type to which all the Eulenburgs belonged. The Emperor retained his Master of the Household, von Liebenau. This officer had done good service in the war of 1870, but had had a certain amount of nervous trouble since then. He supervised the Court arrangements with more brusqueness than the Prince had been aware of or realised now as Emperor, combined with an unnecessary and not wholly justified sense of his own virtues. Hermann von Lucanus, Under-secretary of State, became the new Head of the "Civil Cabinet," the Kaiser's secretariat for civil affairs, with the agreement of Prince Bismarck. The Chancellor had formed a high opinion of the Under-secretary's capacity in the Ministry of Religious Affairs; in the time of Prussia's *Kulturkampf* he had showed tact and shrewdness in opening up and maintaining Bismarck's relations with the Vatican. As a voice always at the ear of the new ruler Bismarck felt that he would be useful and even important, and he counted on his readiness to be of service. Von Versen had recommended General Adolf von

Wittich as Adjustant-General, describing him as reliable and modest and absolutely loyal. But of all Adjutants-General the new Head of the "Military Cabinet," General von Hahnke, a great friend of Emperor Frederick in the past and a man of striking appearance, was the strongest and intellectually the most outstanding personality. He was a master of lucid statement, and a man of exceptional military knowledge: he had been on the Crown Prince's General Staff in 1870. His minutes were distinguished by brilliant style and mastery of their subject. His house was open to all who valued the things of the mind: material luxuries it was beyond him to offer, for he had no private means. He was of an unusual type for Germany; there was something of the Spartan or Roman about him, with his pitch black moustache, his stern features, his olive complexion. Sometimes the Emperor would say to him, laughingly, "I know how many there are who are afraid of you." Of more importance was the General's unchanging, inflexible sense of justice. He hated favouritism and back-stairs influence.

The *"maison militaire,"* the Court military establishment of Emperor William I, which had remained in existence under Emperor Frederick, was disbanded. The household of Emperor Frederick ceased to exist. The new Court arrangements were rapidly completed.

The Chancellor had one more question:

"Does your Majesty desire a coronation?"

"I do not intend to have one," replied the young Emperor, "as my grandfather once more laid special emphasis in his coronation on the principle of monarchy by divine right."

"I thank your Majesty," declared Bismarck, who agreed with the Emperor, "in the name of the Ministry and of the

Empress Fredrick 1888

Emperor William the Great at the grand Manoeuvres. next to the carriage the Master of the Horse Herr von Rauch, next to him Aide-de-Camp General Count Lehndorff; on his left Aide-de-Camp General von Albedyll Chief of the Military Office, brother in law to the late Duchess of Manchester. behind the Emperor General Count Waldersee

German people, whom you have spared the expense of a coronation."

The cost would have been ten million marks; this remained in the exchequer.

The first important duty of his reign, one which Emperor William felt impelled to undertake without delay, was the fulfilment of a mission entrusted to him by his dying grandfather, the nonagenarian Emperor William I. The old Emperor had very slowly slipped away from life, growing constantly weaker but retaining all his faculties. His grandson could still picture the final scene. For two hours he had supported his grandfather with his arm, so that the sick man lay half sitting up. The Empress Augusta had been brought in her bath chair and sat on the Emperor's right, holding his hand. Next her was the Grand Duchess of Baden. He himself had been at the other side of the bed. The Emperor had his eyes closed. He spoke of the political problems of the Empire. The doors into the next room were open, and the Court had assembled; Adjutant General von Albedyll was there, and Wilmowski, Head of the Emperor's Civil Cabinet, and many others. The Emperor spoke in the style of one giving audience and issuing instructions long ago formulated. Prince Bismarck was called in. He stood behind the Court physicians, von Lauer and Leuthold, at the foot of the bed. He spoke not a word, but stood silently weeping.

The Emperor spoke of the fostering of good relations with Russia. The friendship with Austria-Hungary must not be disturbed, but every effort must be made to remain on good terms with Russia. He returned constantly to this subject, repeating his very words. His tired eyelids he kept closed. Then the voice grew fainter. At last the Emperor seemed to sleep. He did not wake.

Emperor William II resolved that the courtesy of the first visit which he made as a ruler should be paid to the Tsar. His English grandmother asked, almost commanded, that her grandson should make his first visit to his mother's country; but he refused to be deterred by the thought of her annoyance. The Chancellor was irritated, and wanted to have an end of the interference of "English aunts"; the Emperor soothed him, and wrote himself to the Queen. He was not, he said, simply her grandson, for all his respect and love and honour for her; his first duty was to fulfil the obligations of the German Emperor, imposed on him in this instance by a sacred trust. To Bismarck's surprise, Queen Victoria replied at once not only acquiescing, but renewing her invitation to her grandson to come soon to England, in a letter of undiminished cordiality. So the Emperor carried the day: he would go to Russia.

Germany's relations with the Russian Empire had long been a matter of grave concern to him. The Tsar had given the young Prince a very friendly reception in St. Petersburg some time before, but at his second visit to him at Brest-Litovsk he had been deliberately allowed to come away with disturbing impressions, and in the end very clear ones. St. Petersburg's cordiality had cooled off; the Russian officers had become almost hostile. He had at once sent word home of his experience in Brest-Litovsk: the unpopularity of the Germans, the lavish and ostentatious expenditure on the army, the enormous military equipment which the Tsar had displayed to him amid the thunder of the batteries of the fortress. On that occasion Prince Bismarck had

sent him to Brest to offer the Tsar Constantinople. The
Tsar had replied testily to the Prince that he did not need
Prince Bismarck's permission; if he made up his mind to
have Constantinople he would take it when he chose——

*"Si je veux avoir Constantinople, je le prendrai quand
il me plaira, je n'ai point besoin de la permission du Prince
de Bismarck!"*

As early as that the Prince had been unable to fathom
the Chancellor's policy. It seemed to him to create complications rather than do away with them. Prince Bismarck
was, he knew, an unsurpassed master of the highest statecraft; he had implicit trust in Bismarck's judgment. Yet
the longer he thought over the Russian problem, the more
intricately involved it seemed to him.

The Prince had often talked about the subject with the
Chancellor. In their conversations they had wandered back
as far as the Congress of Berlin. Bismarck had explained
to the Prince that he had aimed at producing causes of
friction, even of conflict, between Russia and England. He
was coolly working to bring the two strongest powers in
Europe to blows with one another.

"But, your Serene Highness," the Prince had asked,
"what exactly have you had in mind? Why, if that is your
policy, did you call together the Congress of Berlin?"

"I had no desire for a general war," the Chancellor had
always replied; "the German Empire was too young for it."

Bismarck's policy had been to do everything possible to
maintain peace in Europe. In his view Germany would
have been drawn into any general war if it had come, and
as yet she was too weak to face it. But it was always a mystery to the Prince why, in that case, the Chancellor wanted
not only to let the differences between Britain and Russia

The Prince Consort, Grandfather
of Prince William. Gift by the
Queen to her Grandson for his
confirmation

Wild boar shooting, H.I.M. with Herr von Krosigk - Rathmannsdorf

continue but to accentuate them. In Gastein, when Bismarck entrusted him with the mission to Brest, he had felt the inconsistency of the Chancellor's policy even more strongly. Prince Bismarck must have been well aware that Austria-Hungary had intentions on Salonica, and meant to acquire control of that port before long; the Emperor Francis Joseph had himself told Bismarck of his views. Not only that, but Bismarck had done everything to give the Austrian Emperor the impression that he entirely agreed and entirely approved of his plans, and of Austria-Hungary's establishment in Salonica at the first decent and safe opportunity.

"Your Majesty," Bismarck had finally said to the Emperor, "is a good huntsman. If you see a fine stag coming through the brushwood towards a glade, you will not risk a shot at a venture into the copse; you wait until the animal comes out into the glade."

Immediately after this he had sent the Prince to Brest-Litovsk to convey to the Tsar the Chancellor's express consent if Russia now really intended to march on Constantinople. Bismarck had discussed this question with Francis Joseph, but the Emperor—Germany's ally—had refused to entertain the idea at any price, had rejected it as unthinkable.

"If, your Serene Highness," Prince William had asked again, puzzled, "if you are ready to give the Russians Constantinople, why did you summon the Berlin Congress? The Russians were as good as in Constantinople! They were at the gates of the city and had sacrificed a hundred and eighty thousand lives for it; your Highness drove them away!"

The withdrawal from the city, perhaps on the eve of

its capitulation, had, as the Prince realized, been a bitter humiliation for Russia and the Russian army. The Chancellor's reply was now to describe the Berlin Congress as "a triumph of Disraeli and Austria over Russia." Plainly he now wanted to reverse his course.

The offer to be made at Brest-Litovsk clearly involved a departure from straight dealing with Austria. But perhaps the Chancellor was thinking once more mainly of widening the gulf between Russia and Britain. He must certainly know quite well what he was about; up to now he had shown unchanging mastery in his play with the rising and falling apples of discord in Europe, even if the Prince was not entirely sure how it would all end. However, he recalled a phrase of Emperor William's about Bismarck. The old Emperor had been upset at the Chancellor's persistent adherence to his own view on a point over which the two were at issue. After the audience General von Albedyll had said, in his rather free way:

"Throw him out, your Majesty!"

"I cannot," the old Emperor had answered—"*I* can't juggle with five balls and keep three of them always up in the air!"

Then the ill-humour at Brest-Litovsk and the reply made by Alexander III had shown that Bismarck's calculation must be out somewhere. Not until the Tsar's visit to Berlin later in the year had the trouble been more or less smoothed away in discussion, and some sign given that the Russian irritation was beginning to pass away. The Chancellor was in high spirits at the improvement and volubly welcomed it. At the great farewell dinner, however, to the Tsar, the Court Chamberlain had placed Prince Bismarck, to his utmost indignation, among the princes of the blood, at an infinite distance from the centre table. The honour meant nothing to the Chancellor, while the impossibility of even a moment's conversation with the Tsar maddened him. He had hoped to sit opposite him, instead of entirely out of reach of him. He had his suspicions of the intention behind the Chamberlain's arrangement. At the moment the public was keenly observing every movement, every glance between Tsar and Chancellor. Perhaps the object was precisely to delude the public into supposing that the two had parted and would have nothing more to do with one another.

The Tsar looked towards the Chancellor and smilingly lifted his glass. The giant sprang up from the table, and with his left hand deliberately pushed his chair back and upset it, with a tremendous crash. The glasses clattered on the table, the waiters started, the guests were struck dumb. Prince Bismarck, drawing himself up to his full gigantic stature, his face beaming, drank to the Tsar—a demonstration of the reconciliation. It had been impossible for anyone to fail to observe the gesture. Alexander III did in fact depart in friendship. After this the Chancellor had been a still more convinced believer in a coming rapprochement between Russia and Germany.

He was very ready to agree to Emperor William II going not to England, not to Francis Joseph, but first of all to St. Petersburg, to the Tsar.

There was a great deal to do in Russia, all the more, and all the more easily, since the Russian attitude was much more friendly than it had been a year before. De Giers, the Russian Chancellor, was full of apprehension over the possibility of Austro-Hungarian intervention in Serbia. That country had been in turmoil over the quarrel between King

Milan and Queen Natalie, both claiming possession of the little Crown Prince Alexander; the quarrel was approaching settlement, but it was possible that Count Kálnoky, the Austro-Hungarian Foreign Minister, intended to seize the opportunity for a military move. As for Bulgaria, Prince Alexander of Battenberg had gone, but in his place in that country (which was always regarded in Russia as a sphere of influence and almost as a dependent State) there now reigned Prince Ferdinand of Coburg; he had recently been invited to their throne by the Bulgarians themselves, but, in the Chancellor's view, was undoubtedly supported by Austria-Hungary. He had served in the Austro-Hungarian army, and though now in Greek orthodox Bulgaria, remained a Catholic. Prince Alexander of Battenberg had not asked the Tsar's permission before accepting the Bulgarian crown, and Prince Ferdinand had been equally remiss. A Bulgarian mission had entered into informal negotiations with the Prince; shortly afterwards he had received the formal offer from the Bulgarians while in the light-hearted company of his brother officers in the Hotel Imperial, Vienna—an ordinary telegram, not in code. He read it unconcernedly. "We shall see how long it lasts," he commented. Then he had set off. Russia looked on in ill-humour.

The Chancellor sent his son, Count Herbert Bismarck, the Secretary of State for Foreign Affairs, who was familiar with all State business, precise instructions as to his proceedings during the visit. He was to accompany the Emperor not only for ceremonial reasons; any political conversations of any sort on which the Russians might embark were to be his business and his only. The Chancellor's "*Aide-mémoire* for His Majesty the Emperor for any dis-

Emperor Wilhelm I at the historical corner window
in the year of his death.
drawn by an Englishman from the crowd.
Sent to His Majesty after his accession
to the throne

*Victoria Crownprincess of Prussia
and her eldest son William.
taken at Norderney in 1869*

cussion with the Emperor of Russia" advised Emperor William not himself to embark on political discussions:

"I am strongly of the opinion that His Majesty's first visit must be one of friendship and neighbourliness, with no political motive; that is what is needed for it to have the best political effect. Any attempt to stamp it as political, to assign it the task of achieving an immediate and tangible political success, would damage the political success which it can and should have; it would damage it not only on the generally accepted basis of psychological valuations in human intercourse but especially and above all on account of the peculiar character of Tsar Alexander, who is habitually very responsive to an open friendly approach but easily upset in any sort of political dealings and even suspicious of any friendly advance for which he has given no opening."

Before this the Chancellor had declared his opinion unchanged with regard to Russia's acquisition of Constantinople: Russia would "not be strengthened but weakened, both intrinsically and through British enmity, and would in any case become less dangerous." He gave a warning against excessive political complaisance, or even the mere show of it: "Any particular readiness to meet Russia would, with the Russian tendency to exaggeration, be interpreted as implying that we sought Russia's goodwill because we feared her, and that, accordingly, we could be made use of."

Count Herbert Bismarck implicitly followed the lines laid down by his father. He explained to Emperor William the Chancellor's line of thought. Where Bismarck's memorandum contained indications as to the handling of particular questions he interpreted them as referring only to his own conversations. The Emperor accepted Bismarck's advice as thoroughly sound. He determined to win the Tsar's confidence purely by his personal approach, by frankness and cordiality, with no attempt to push through any business. Count Herbert Bismarck had a thorough discussion with the Russian Chancellor, in the unconcerned tone prescribed to him—not an easy task for the Secretary of State, who preferred to be forthright and emphatic; but this had been the Chancellor's instructions, and it was not without effect on the Russian Chancellor. The Count tried to allay his fears for Serbia. As to Bulgaria, he was very ready to give friendly consideration to any proposals the Russian Chancellor might have to make for the restoration of "legitimate conditions," though, he said, no one could expect Germany to have ideas of her own as to the sort of conditions that it was in Russia's interest to introduce in Bulgaria. The Secretary tried to smooth away the fears of undisclosed Austrian activities in the Balkans; the Monarchy was surely being watched from too exclusively Russian a standpoint. Germany fully shared Russia's hopes for a tariff agreement; and even if it failed to eventuate there would be no reason why the fact should embitter their political relations.

The Secretary of State had fulfilled his task with great success. The Russian Chancellor had been able to have his say over all sorts of things, but nothing had been really discussed, nothing had been asked, even the Russian movements of troops against Austria-Hungary had not been seriously touched on, while the Secretary had been able to lay some stress on the fact of Austria's alliance with Germany without any disturbance of the pleasant tone of the discussion. All had passed off in a friendly way.

The Tsar himself sent for Count Bismarck. The Count gossiped tactfully; the Tsar learned for the first time, under the seal of secrecy, about the tragedy of poor Emperor Frederick, and the deep gulf between mother and son. The last of the shadows cast by the "Affaire Battenberg" seemed to be passing away. The Secretary of State had many kind things to say about his young Sovereign during the conversation. He knew, he said, that the Kaiser's English uncle had recently been blackening his character to the Tsar. But when the Prince of Wales left Berlin with Queen Victoria (who was always full of affection for her grandson) he had been in an ill humour. He had had no success in his advocacy of the claims of the house of Cumberland; the young Emperor had been unable to agree to them.

"I have known your Emperor for a long time," said the Tsar at the end of a talk that had pleased him; *"c'est un caractère franc et ouvert*—uncommonly to my taste." At the end of the audience he added: "Tell your Emperor to come as often as he likes; I shall always be very pleased to see him; you are entirely right in saying that trust is the first of all essentials."

So Emperor William's visit to St. Petersburg on his accession had passed off in the pleasantest possible way and in perfect harmony, entirely as he had hoped. The Secretary of State was not generally fastidious in his style of writing, but his two reports to his father, written in an exalted frame of mind, had a more literary character than usual. He kept the Austro-Hungarian Embassy in St. Petersburg informed of the details of his conversations in Russia, though in his conversation with Counsellor of Embassy von Aehrenthal he did not admit having talked to the Tsar on certain subjects of the closest concern to the

Counsellor—on Austria-Hungary and Bulgaria. At the end of the visit he was satisfied with every phase of it. The German Ambassador at the Court of the Tsar, General von Schweinitz, was also able to report that there had been nothing but the best of impressions created, and the greatest cordiality between host and guests.

Emperor William returned home. He returned with pleasant feelings. He was still unconvinced of the sincerity of Russia's policy. He had no intention of smothering his doubts of her diplomatists and her military leaders. But he felt that he had introduced more friendliness into his personal relations with the Tsar. Prince Bismarck seemed thoroughly content.

Some time later Count Hatzfeldt sent from London a detailed report on the Emperor William's visit which contained information of a different nature. The Prince put it for the time being in a drawer in his desk.

Home politics in Germany were still controlled at this time by the "Cartel," the union of Conservatives, National Liberals, and the Reich party. The Cartel had ranged itself round Prince Bismarck since its cooperation in the great and successful fight for the Septennat of 1887. Up to the death of Emperor Frederick, Chancellor and Government had had no difficulty in carrying their Bills and Estimates and meeting all the requirements of the State, thanks to the loyal support of the majority of the Cartel parties; but almost immediately after William II ascended the throne rifts and cleavages began to appear in the citadel of the Cartel. The Chancellor found it more and more difficult to come to terms with the Conservatives, especially the extremists of the Right, the *"Kreuzzeitung"* party. This group of extreme reactionaries, intolerant of any other shade of opinion, unprepared to allow any other views but their own to exist on this earth, frequently made life difficult for him. But the Chancellor was not without some share in the responsibility for this, since his own highhandedness, his wild rage against any opposition, were vented in violent invective against all who differed from his views, and especially, should they venture to do so, against men whose whole tradition was to regard the absolute security of the State and unquestioning loyalty to the man at the helm as an obvious duty—he himself would have said a sacred one. It would have been difficult to say whether the Chancellor or the Conservatives were the more conservative.

The new Emperor proceeded more softly and more cautiously in examining the political terrain than might have been expected from his evident tendency to quick decisions and his general youthfulness. However close might be the association of the Hohenzollerns with Prussia, the parties came from South as well as North Germany, and the Reichstag spoke for the whole nation. The Emperor discussed the aims and claims and the case for the existence of each of the various parties with von Benda, a National Liberal Deputy whom he had known for years and respected as a politician. He sent for Rudolf von Bennigsen, leader of the National Liberals. His purpose in asking him to come was not only to get information; he wanted also to make his own views more widely known. He admitted that his friend Count Douglas had worked up into a speech a good deal of his expressed views; this speech [1] the Count had prepared for the electoral campaign, without definitely

[1] See page 238.

committing the Emperor to its contents even in speaking to persons on a confidential footing. The Emperor advised the Conservatives to work closely with the National Liberals, the principal Cartel party; that party was not too remote from their own ways of thinking, and could form a useful bridge for an understanding with the more democratic, more emotional Catholic parties of South Germany.

As a rule the Emperor was chary of expressing his views in official conversation or during negotiations. Where negotiations had a political character, he sought for compromises. He made Rudolf von Bennigsen Governor (*Oberpräsident*) of the province of Hannover. At the same moment, in order to avoid wounding the Conservatives, he appointed a man from their ranks, von Maltzahn, to be Secretary of the Treasury. Disregarding the anger of the orthodox Evangelicals, he brought Professor von Harnack, the great theologian and church historian, a man placed far above political controversy by his achievements in research and the broadness of his views, to the University of Berlin. The Chancellor might hit out all round, in the Press, against the Press, elections or no elections, wherever he found opponents; he himself only wanted to let it be seen that he intended to show respect and toleration for every shade of opinion up to the limit where State and Crown were involved. More than that did not seem to him to be permissible. Public opinion expressed scarcely any objection to this policy. Democratic opinion was concerned with the commencement of an epoch in which government would perhaps become possible by representatives of the people. The whole of the public, from the Conservatives past the Liberals very nearly to the extreme Left, had greeted the young Monarch in the profusely loyal verbiage of the period. Nearly all felt that the Emperor was anxious not to disappoint them; nearly all counted on his having something to give in many directions.

He proceeded with more energy and freedom in the constructive task which he found reserved for himself personally as ruler. Everything around him was long out of date. Those members of the staff of his grandfather's *"maison militaire"* and Emperor Frederick's household who were still keen to remain on the active list and were usable, he had transferred to other posts or to army service. The rest, with all possible consideration, he had dismissed. But he knew that the out-of-date was not removed merely by being removed from his sight, by changes in his immediate retinue. Emperor William I had lived to enjoy long years of honourable fulfilment. The whole of his old guard were still in harness. They had fought under him on three battlefields; his paladins had stood around him in the Hall of the Mirrors at Versailles. After that they had continued at duty almost for two decades. Those who under Emperor William I had been young in the young Empire, progressive, looking forward to an era of reform, had rallied to the ideas and ideals which had been associated with the names of Emperor and Empress Frederick. They had all held themselves ready. But in a rule that lasted only ninety-nine days it was impossible for programmes to be carried through, workers to be found for them, or even their ideas adumbrated. The plans that Emperor and Empress Frederick had conceived for Germany were new to that nation and, no doubt, not all practicable at the outset. But those who stood around Emperor Frederick's coffin were men suddenly disinherited, fighters for a future for which they had long waited and which, in the moment of realization, had deceived all their hopes of advance and activity, and plunged all their ideals into sudden and undreamed-of annihilation. Emperor Frederick had not gone alone; a whole generation had departed with him. That generation still lived, but its fires had been extinguished. A whole generation had been robbed of florescence and fruition. It was shelved, doomed to decay and pass.

With the new Emperor there came a new world. His outlook was unknown to the disinherited; all that they knew was that it was different from that of his parents. While Emperor Frederick had been Crown Prince, and then during the tragedy of his reign, his contemporaries had been waiting to bear the standards of the future. The heir was supposed to have been at issue with his parents, and that was enough to assure him the hostility of the rest of them. They could no longer work out their ideas; the sudden turn in events had put an end to their effort and their hope of service. They no longer even had the desire to serve. The Empire was full of seed sown in Emperor Frederick's long years as Crown Prince, but when the time of fulfilment came the seed was swamped by the rains or scattered by the wind. Either the new Emperor must try single-handed to raise the seed, or the whole earth must be ploughed up and sown anew. In either case he must look around him for helpers. All he had was the soil. One human signpost stood, wide-armed, gigantic, a Titanic monster: the Chancellor, Prince Bismarck. Bismarck had achieved enormous feats; he must have enormous strength. He would hold fast to Bismarck, would lean on him; he owed his Empire and his throne to him, to all that he had endured for his, Emperor William's sake. With him he would forge ahead. A genius could overleap a generation of progress: time

could set no bounds to genius. The Emperor was determined to carve himself a place: this he felt to be plainly
due to him. But he wanted Bismarck's partnership: that
also seemed the obvious thing. For the rest, the old guard
had served their time: he would throw open the gates to
the active spirits who would work for the new times, for
Germany's future.

The Emperor placed a considerable number of old Generals on the retired list: grey-headed soldiers who had done
good service in Germany's campaigns, but were ripe now
for repose. He did them honour in their retirement, conveying the thanks of their supreme commander. He retired,
with every mark of veneration, the ninety-year-old Count
Moltke. The Field Marshal had himself asked to be
allowed to retire: whenever anything of importance happened his advice would continue to be sought before taking
action. He remained President of the Defence Committee,
with undiminished authority. The Emperor made many
new appointments, and various young officers gained unexpected promotions. He wanted the Minister of War, von
Bronsart, to resign. The Minister had been an unwilling
advocate of new artillery estimates which the Emperor had
regarded as in certain respects essential; but that was not
the Emperor's reason. The War Minister belonged to the
old régime: he was all too dogmatic, always resentful of
change, clinging to old traditions, and altogether overweening in language and tone. He was an enormous man, and
in his audiences with the Emperor he spoke from aloft in
every sense, rubbing in his advantage at every chance, with
no doubt whatever of his superiority. It was a style that
recalled to the Emperor the days of his youth and prince-
dom: a style that he would no longer tolerate. He dis-

missed the Minister, and put General von Verdy in his place.

Of all the decisions that the Emperor had to take, none was so difficult as that of the successor to Moltke as Chief of Staff. In recent years the Field Marshal had again and again recommended the First Quartermaster-General. He did so when Emperor Frederick wanted to send Count Waldersee away from Berlin, preferring to give him the command of an army corps far from the capital rather than continue to watch the Count's endless angling for political influence and efforts to make play with it. In the end the Emperor had given way and allowed the old Field Marshal to retain his assistant at his side as he desired. Count Waldersee had won Moltke's entire confidence as a man and a soldier, and the Field Marshal was not the only one whom the General had captivated by the wide range of his knowledge, his abilities and his unbounded amiability. Waldersee had come early to Prince Bismarck's notice, while still a young officer. In the campaign of 1870, during the bombardment of Paris, the Chancellor had declared that Waldersee's was the ablest head in the General Staff —a plain hit at Moltke and Roon. Little progress had been made in the bombardment. "That comes of having such old Generals," Bismarck had shouted. "You ought to make Waldersee Chief of Staff—then there would be a change!"

The Chancellor had so prized Waldersee's diplomatic abilities that after the preliminary peace with France he had sent him to Paris as acting Ambassador. As a diplomat Waldersee was suppler than any other soldier, and the years had gradually developed his gift into mastery. His quick, shrewd glance, controlling every movement of the eyes, could express the whole gamut of feelings, but was never

The newly married couple Prince
Fredrick William and Princess
Victoria of Prussia. In the background Castle and Park of Babels-
berg. The small building close to
the lake is their first home

General Count Waldersee

allowed to reveal his actual thoughts. Count Waldersee's
face had no lines, only surfaces. The chin was undefined,
the skull lofty but with no sharp contours. He sat with his
neck set back and buried deep in his collar, like a badger
in his burrow, with ears pricked up and sly and crafty eyes
ready to blaze out at any moment. The story is told of Garrick that he brought an artist to despair in the attempt
to paint his portrait. Day after day he sketched the head,
but on the actor's return on the morrow there was not the
slightest resemblance between sketch and reality. Lenbach
found his Garrick in Waldersee. For three or four days he
tried in vain to capture the essentials of Waldersee's features, and day after day when the General returned an
entirely strange face looked out at him from the canvas.
Finally the artist threw away his brush.

"I can't make out what's up! It defeats me!"

"Paint him side face," one of Waldersee's confidants
suggested, "in an Uhlan's overcoat."

Then the work succeeded: a fox's head emerged. To
this man's sincere-seeming cordiality, his deep-laid, unob-
served devices, his warmth of phrase almost everyone suc-
cumbed. And great as were his charm and his capacity,
his industry was yet greater. Late at night he would still
be entering in his diary every detail of his day's work.
Everything done, thought, heard, recommended, rejected
he noted down. He took pains to invest every line with
moral fervour and intellectual sublimity. He was conscientious in taking thought for the good impression which his
diaries must some day create. He filled them with pious
and exalted sentiments.

At his desk he would chasten the childlike simplicity
of his soldier's soul with an ample dose of quotations from

Holy Writ; these would give place to brilliant schemes and calculations. Then he would note down, with every sign of carefully faithful reproduction, smart sayings of other men, or witty epigrams, that had had no real existence: as a rule he had himself invented them for some definite purpose in forging his own way ahead. He passed them on to von Bagensky, his adjutant, and this blindly loyal servant retailed them to all the world. This world around him had only two aspects for Count Alfred Waldersee: it was good if it served him, bad if it injured him. In this world he moved with no tolerance whatever for any opposition from below. If *that* came he forgot all his charm: the opposition was "base." When on duty Waldersee loved the tradition of selfless, self-sacrificing devotion to the community. If an idea or a bit of organization happened by some chance to prove a success, it was in accordance with the old Prussian rule that the credit belonged entirely to the leader and commander. He bowed to all the flattery and accepted it with modesty and the implicit admission that honour must be paid where it is due—that is, to him. If an idea or a bit of organization proved a failure he visited it with pedagogical faithfulness on an underling:

"You have made a thorough mess of that."

But, for all his human weaknesses, he was a man of great and rare military gifts. He mastered every situation with lightning rapidity. Problems of army drill, the training of the General Staff, mobilization questions were familiar ground to him as to few of his contemporaries. Waldersee the politician was made bellicose by the soldier. He saw Germany's future threatened by the geography of her neighbour countries. And, geography apart, he was for "the preventive game." Germany's future was "hopeless unless we spread death to right or left." At one time it would be France who must be destroyed, a little later it would be Russia.

"Whom we are to fight," he usually concluded, "is for the Foreign Ministry to say."

The best thing of all, in his view, would be for the day to come when what the Foreign Ministry was to say would be left to him to settle. Occasions for war could always be found. Gradually he came to form a strong opinion that the Chancellor, Prince Bismarck, nowadays had little energy left; he would no longer listen for a moment, for instance, to talk of a preventive war. The old Emperor William had believed up to the last that if he were to take a new war on his shoulders it would mean that he would have himself to mount horse once more. Now there was a young Emperor in his place. It was a good opportunity. The General hoped to be able to bring all his influence to bear on Emperor William. The scene in the Berlin Palace was a forgotten incident. Waldersee evidently did not take it seriously; he had not even entered it in his diary. The Crown Prince must surely have had sense enough to realize at the time that his advice had really been given with the best intentions.

The Emperor did, in fact, appoint Waldersee to be Chief of Staff. Field Marshal Moltke had recommended him with all the weight of his authority. Moltke would no longer continue to serve, for all the Emperor's efforts to persuade him. And, in the Marshal's view, he could not conscientiously propose anyone else as his successor, put any other name before the Emperor, than that of Waldersee. It was a hard struggle that the Monarch had against his inward feelings. His mistrust of the Quartermaster-General

was intensified by the reply which Adjutant-General von
Hahnke gave when he told him of the incident of the
audience:

"His contemporaries and acquaintances," said von
Hahnke, "call him The Badger, because he is so fond of
nosing underground."

Waldersee was an intriguer, said von Hahnke—a man
of eminent military ability, greatly respected as such, and
rightly so, by the General Staff and the army; but not to
be trusted politically. His ambition was unbounded.

After long hesitation the Emperor discovered a way out.
If the Quartermaster-General had really the great qualities
as a soldier which the Field Marshal and the very fair-
minded Adjutant-General attributed to him, if he were
really indispensable to the army as they declared, then the
Emperor would overcome his reluctance and make Waldersee Chief of Staff. In all military matters he would continue to place entire trust in him. And in personal intercourse he would allow no sign of dislike, of the change in
his real feelings towards the General, to be observed. But
politically he would never allow him to open his mouth,
would never listen to a suggestion from him. Among the
statesmen whose advice he might need one man should never
be counted—Count Waldersee.

"May the Almighty," wrote the new Chief of Staff in
his diary on the day of his appointment, "give me the
needed initiative and energy and endurance; there shall
never be any lack of good intention, and I shall endeavour
always to maintain undaunted courage. How wonderful
are God's dispensations!"

The General saw the Emperor's policy already entirely
controlled by his, the General's, brain. He saw himself

already the predestined successor to Prince Bismarck when the day came for the Chancellor to retire. But never had one of Fate's apparent darlings deceived himself more thoroughly as to the circumstances of his advancement and the prospects it opened up. For once the fox's scent had failed him. He did not know that on that same day the Emperor had cast him politically into the outer darkness.

CHAPTER III

KAISER AND KINGS

EMPEROR WILLIAM was making his round of visits on elevation to his throne. The tour had not been given its wide extent merely for political and ceremonial reasons; this was the Kaiser's first journey in entire independence, the first in which he was his own master and could at last give free rein to his long-suppressed desire to see strange cities and countries and Courts. As a Prince he had never been able to decide for himself whether he could leave his garrison or for how long. His purse had been kept poorly filled. His father had made him no grants. Prince William had been dependent almost always, with Crown Prince Frederick, on the head of the house; and Emperor William I was consistently parsimonious in all things, for all that he loved his grandson. The old Emperor preferred to see the Prince doing his regular military duties rather than going on journeys for which he saw no necessity.

Now, however, Prince William had himself become the master. The style of his journeys, the provision made for them, and the programme laid down were of a different order. Their purpose and scale depended entirely on himself. Repressed and kept in the background as he had always been, he was now throwing himself eagerly and almost thirstily into his new opportunities. He had done his best at Peterhof, as his first duty, to fulfil the mission which his grandfather had laid upon him. Then he had sailed his yacht *Hohenzollern* homewards via Stockholm and Copenhagen. He had been delighted with Stockholm and the Swedish royal house; had continued his journey from the Court of Copenhagen in slightly damped enthusiasm. Now he was on his way to the Viennese Court as his next duty. Thither he meant to convey particularly hearty greetings, and thereafter to the King of Italy, partner of the other two Great Powers in the Triple Alliance.

The Emperor travelled via Stuttgart and Munich, in order to visit the King of Württemberg and the Prince Regent of Bavaria, the foremost Princes in Germany. He had already paid a visit to King Albert of Saxony. Formerly, when he had not been travelling on any special mission, Prince William had scarcely been noticed; now all the bells rang. Everywhere he was met with rejoicings; his hymn was intoned; companies of honour stood at attention along a motionless front; ceremonial arches marked his route; the roads were lined with waiting people; troops defiled. He no longer had time enough to note all the changes that had come. He enjoyed all these experiences, the crowds, the scenes. Wherever he arrived the foremost men in the State and its first servants came to bow before their Prince. Princes themselves did honour to him. He exerted every effort to win all hearts. He did not spare himself. His vivacity charmed everywhere. In this way he covered all Europe.

Count Herbert Bismarck accompanied him to Vienna. Once more the Secretary of State had conversations to carry on on lines prescribed by his father, the Chancellor. They were to commit neither side, and he neither asked nor gave any undertakings. In audience with Emperor Francis Joseph he dissipated that Monarch's apprehensions of a possible clouding of the relations between Britain and Germany. Francis Joseph was clearly afraid that influence might continue to be brought to bear on the British royal house by Empress Frederick. The Secretary replied by describing "the tinsel of the so-called English monarchy" as *"une quantité négligeable."* The real relationship between the two Empires was unaffected by any excessive assumptions on the part of that Monarchy. In saying this the Secretary of State was considerably underestimating Queen Victoria's influence on the attitude of her country and its statesmen, but Francis Joseph accepted his assurances. The Secretary touched on Austro-Russian relations in the Balkans, and sought to do something towards reducing the friction there. The Emperor would have nothing to do with partition or the definition of spheres of influence, such as Count Bismarck advocated—the Count had already suggested to Count Shuvalov, the Russian Ambassador in Berlin, that Russia should absorb the Principality of Bulgaria and Austria-Hungary the Kingdom of Serbia. But while the Emperor rejected that proposal, the Secretary heard from the lips of the Austrian Monarch much that it relieved him to hear, and that might be put to good use at the first opportunity at the Court of the Tsar. It was not true that Austria-Hungary was supporting Prince Ferdinand of Coburg in Bulgaria; on the contrary, the Dual Monarchy was "holding aloof." There was not the slightest basis of truth in the allegations of proselytizing in Rome's interest in the Balkans which had disturbed Russia as Protrectress of the Orthodox church. Rome was reaping nothing but disappointments. Emperor Francis Joseph seemed disturbed over Roumania; he considered that King Carol, of whom he had a low opinion, was on the road to ruin, exposing

Austria-Hungary to the danger of the extension of Russian influence to another "dependency." But on the whole there was no critical situation at the moment anywhere on the Continent. So ran Count Herbert's report; Prince Bismarck transmitted it to the Foreign Ministry, without remark, for putting away.

Emperor Francis Joseph gave Emperor William a warmer greeting than was usual with him on such occasions. The winning and almost reverential manner of the German Emperor towards his ally, a man of nearly sixty years, seemed to show a desire to efface the last traces of any impressions remaining from the war year 1866 in the mind of the Habsburg Emperor. Emperor William II had nothing to do with the generation which had brought Francis Joseph the bitterness of Königgrätz. Here again he hoped to bring a changed future. His host was visibly endeavouring to show marked cordiality, though Emperor William was unable entirely to escape the influence of the coldness that emanated from Emperor Francis Joseph even on great occasions. The Austrian Emperor displayed all the overwhelming magnificence of the Habsburgs, dating from Spanish times, to greet the young Kaiser's eyes for the first time. Fifteen years before, the Crown Princess Frederick had taken her son with her to the country palace of Hetzendorf; but the palace had not then been the scene of the turning out of guards and halberdiers who now stood stiffly as statues before the Kaiser, in undreamed-of splendour. They put into the shade the Tsar's household brigade and Queen Victoria's lifeguardsmen. In Vienna the Court sat at table amid groves of orchids. The young Kaiser was astonished, almost dumbfounded, at the profusion of wealth displayed. The Court ceremonies observed

forms that had been preserved for centuries. The Prince
of Wales had told his nephew how on his arrival at the
Hofburg he had found himself suddenly face to face with
a whole company of stately, smooth-shaven gentlemen in
evening dress and buckled shoes. Prince Edward had
bowed low to them. But they were not the diplomatic corps,
as the Prince had supposed, but only some of the Austrian
Kaiser's Court lackeys. For all that, they were of sovereign
distinction. They wore the same solemn, dignified, deadly
depressing air that spread from the Austrian Kaiser himself over his Chamberlain and themselves and every guest
at Court.

Emperor William had his first day in Vienna to himself.
The Austrian Emperor had tactfully left him, on this as on
all subsequent occasions, to devote the first day of his visit
to seeing and talking to anyone he wanted to meet at the
Germany Embassy. There Emperor William gave his big
dinners in Vienna: the gay reception room in the Ambassador's palace would hum with the talk of a hundred guests,
conversing unrestrainedly in the way the young Kaiser
liked. On one occasion when he was on the point of giving
the sign for going in to dinner, the folding doors suddenly
parted, and Emperor Francis Joseph appeared, unannounced. The hum of a hundred guests was abruptly cut
short: the conversation at once ceased entirely. Dumbly
the young Emperor took his soup, and his guests no less
dumbly. Minutes trickled slowly away in an unending,
ice-bound silence. The burden of the silence grew worse
and worse, until at last Emperor Francis Joseph's neighbour, Pauline Princess Metternich, spoke up spiritedly for
all to hear:

"Well, your Majesty, that's as much as I can stand—

King Humbert of Italy & H.I.M.
on a visit to the gunnery-school
of Field-Artillery at Listerbough.

King Humbert of Italy (in Prussian Hussar Uniform) & H.J.M. on a visit to the Gunnery school of Field-Artillery. The General in Lancer-Uniform is Chief of the General-Staff Count Waldersee

will your Majesty permit me to tell one or two funny stories!"

Never had anything like that been ventured on in Francis Joseph's presence. Even his "intimate" family dinners were dreaded affairs, passed in the silence of a family vault. The German Embassy had itself become a vault. But Francis Joseph smiled:

"Of course, with much pleasure, your Highness. Why not?"

Princess Metternich, then in her days of romping high spirits, began to tell stories. Francis Joseph smiled, laughed out, went on laughing. The whole dining room rocked with the general laughter. Neither Emperor William nor anyone else had ever seen Francis Joseph like this. But next morning in the Hofburg the guards were at their posts, and the lackeys who looked like Ambassadors. Emperor Francis Joseph received the German Sovereign, his ally: with more warmth than he usually showed on such occasions, but not allowing his guest entirely to conquer the frigid atmosphere that surrounded him.

But the young Kaiser, in all his lively and captivating charm, had also to meet the Empress Elizabeth, whose train, as a little prince, he had once proudly borne in Hetzendorf —enchanted, child as he was, by her radiant, incomparable beauty. Empress Elizabeth was always a more or less unwilling participant in the cold formalities of Francis Joseph's Court, and her relief was great when any break could come in the traditional ceremonial so punctiliously organized by the Court Chamberlain. She had had her own opinion of the system in force in the Monarchy, she hated the policy of the Prime Minister, Count Taaffe, his whole régime of decisions deferred, his programme of "reconciliation" between the nationalities of the Empire, which was no more than a playing off of race against race. Above all she was averse to the new policy, not even pursued with conviction by the Premier, of fostering Czech influence. Yet the Count was high in favour with her husband. Her hatred of the Premier was shared by Prince Bismarck, who loathed him "as the plague."

It was over Taaffe that the difficulty came which clouded the end of this first visit to Vienna. When the customary distribution of orders was under discussion in the committee hurriedly assembled before the Kaiser started —the Kaiser himself presiding,—the order of the Black Eagle was suggested for Koloman Tisza, Prime Minister of Hungary, and for Count Taaffe. Both were of sufficiently high rank: the order was usually conferred on prominent and distinguished Prime and Foreign Ministers of Great Powers. Count Herbert Bismarck had agreed in regard to Tisza. In regard to Taaffe he replied, with the curtness which he sometimes adopted, simply—"No!" He shared his father's opinion of Taaffe. He had long and persistently disliked everything Austrian, a dislike which he only restrained when he had to. It did not trouble him that to confer the order on the Hungarian Premier and ignore the Austrian would be to inflict an ostentatious insult. He persisted in his refusal, in spite of the consternation of the whole committee.

"My father said he must not have it, and he must not," persisted the Count.

Emperor William gave way. It was uncomfortable to have to face the possibility of inflicting an injury, even, perhaps, mystifying his friend the Austrian Monarch. But he would do as Prince Bismarck wished: the Prince must have his reasons for his open hostility to Taaffe. Emperor Francis Joseph showed his annoyance quite plainly to the Secretary. Count Bismarck swallowed the unpleasantness of his disfavour. He wrote to Holstein, at the Foreign Ministry, that he could not "find terms adequately to describe the pleasant impressions" which he had received during the visit to Vienna. He thought best to confine himself to mentioning the graciousness of Empress Elizabeth. After a state dinner she had called the Secretary to her side: "How glad I am," she had said, "my dear Count, that your Emperor had the courage to abstain from giving the Order to that infamous man Taaffe."

Emperor Francis Joseph let no sign escape him in his guest's presence. He knew who it was who had wanted to strike at Taaffe. Francis Joseph had an inimitable way of ignoring things that he could not alter—even if he never forgave them. How he would stand with the young Emperor when he had got over his first beginnings as ruler must be left for the future to show. He bade his guest farewell in friendly terms, in accordance with the due forms for meetings between rulers and allies.

Emperor William travelled on into Italy. He was to see not only King Humbert but the Pope.

The King of Italy and Crown Prince Frederick had for many years been on terms of real friendship, and a warm welcome therefore awaited Emperor William. It was dictated not only by the personal tie: all Italy had for weeks before the Kaiser's arrival been preparing with southern exuberance for the festal reception which the royal house, the Government, and the city of Rome intended to give "the new Cæsar." When at last he arrived, the piazzas resounded with the *"Evviva!"* of the popular acclamation.

One banquet followed another; there was a grand review
and march past the Kaiser at Centocelle; in the Capitol the
city fathers organized a splendid festival which extended
to the Senate building and all the palaces; the whole scene
had been given unity by means of wooden bridges in the
style of the *palazzi*. The Palatine was decorated by the
municipality with brilliant illuminations. The crowds
thronged the streets, which were thickly hung with flags
and carpets and gaily coloured wreaths in welcome to the
Kaiser. The southerner loves noise and glare and high-
pitched emotions, but "the new Cæsar" had not anticipated
a reception amid all this wild enthusiasm.

He paid court to his Italian ally as he had to the Austrian. He spoke of Italy's future, of the nation's unity; he
drank not only to the health of the King but to "the brave
Italian army." The Triple Alliance had now been in existence for five years. Emperor Francis Joseph had not set
foot during that period on Italian soil: he had feared offending the Pope if he visited the King first, and the King if
he went first to the Vatican, and so he had not gone at all.
Emperor Frederick III, "the invalid," had borne his suffer-
ings on Italian soil. William II had come to Italy three
months after ascending the throne. He spoke of the Italians,
of their destiny, of the greatness and the high gifts of their
nation, in language to which they had not before listened.
For the first time he gave the Italians a sense of being a
Great Power. Intoxicated with their newly discovered,
hitherto unrecognized greatness, and with their new and
powerful friend, they acclaimed him with the enthusiasm
of children.

Here again the Kaiser's feeling was that it was of more
importance to create an atmosphere of friendship than to

talk politics. He was much more attracted by the personality of the aged Francesco Crispi than by all the special questions arising out of the Triple Alliance treaty—which were, in any case, all settled. Crispi was a bald-headed man with a prominent nose and a large white drooping moustache, and big eyes that shone out brightly from under bushy eyebrows, in a face full of thought and character. The Kaiser knew him to be a sincere supporter of the Triple Alliance, and a friend of Bismarck. He admired the Italian statesman's constant and convinced advocacy of western European democracy, of true constitutionalism and of Monarchy of the English type. Towards the end of their long conversation on modern state systems the Kaiser remembered a telegram which had been handed to him just before Crispi's arrival. The Mikado had resolved on the voluntary grant of a Constitution to the Japanese, and a Parliament was to be summoned to Tokio. The news would please this democratic statesman; the Kaiser pulled the telegram out of his pocket and read it to him. Crispi said not a word. The Kaiser remembered what he had been told of Crispi's peculiar habit of listening and even looking his interlocutor full in the face, but meanwhile allowing his thoughts to wander far away. Usually some time would elapse before he would come out of his ruminations and reply. Now, however, Crispi still continued silent, sat motionless, looking past the Kaiser into a far distance. Clearly he had not listened at all. At last the Kaiser picked up the telegram again. He began to repeat its contents, but Crispi suddenly interrupted him—evidently he had heard after all, —remarking, unemotionally,

"Que cet homme est bête!"

He would not say why. But the reply had been the very

opposite of what the Kaiser had expected from Crispi, of all men. The only possible explanation seemed to be the old conflict between theory and practice. He himself, though he had various plans of the most progressive nature, was regarded in many quarters as a ruler with absolutist principles. Crispi went away. In spite of his view of the Mikado he continued entirely loyal to his liberal convictions.

The Kaiser had prepared carefully in Berlin for his visit to the Vatican. He had agreed with his uncle, the Cardinal, on the line to be followed, and before his departure he had also made a point of hearing the advice of Cardinal Kopp, whose services in the settlement of the *Kulturkampf* he had not forgotten—nor had the Vatican. Cardinal Kopp knew Leo XIII well, his character and his policy; nor was he a stranger to the men who surrounded the Pope, the forces and counter-forces, the whole atmosphere of the Vatican. Prince Bismarck had himself made good use of the Cardinal's knowledge and ability and sincere desire to bring concord out of every controversy. The Cardinal gave the Kaiser all the information desired. His advice was—"Talk in private to the Pope, your Majesty —be entirely straight and open with him and let him hear the truth. That does not happen to him too often!" Leo XIII was setting great hopes, the Cardinal added, on the issue of the elections in France; he was counting on a great victory for the church. "The news we receive does not point to that, but the Pope does not know it; he is not kept informed. Neither Cardinal Lavigerie nor Cardinal Richard seems to have let him know how matters really stand. Your Majesty should tell him the true position."

Leo XIII made a deep impression at once on the Kaiser. The Pope was a man of slight and elegant figure, and in

Francesco Crispi
Italian Premier

Crown princess Victoria of Prussia
with Prince William 1861

everything, in face and hands and his whole attitude, spiritualized. He was almost emaciated, and his big, flashing eyes dominated everything. No one who came into his presence could escape from their force, their penetration, their will to command. In the company of Princes, surrounded by the grave magnificence of royal state, he had the dignity of the statuesque in spite of his slightness; he was the equal of the greatest of his predecessors in the Holy See, of the greatest even among all the rulers whose names have been recorded by History. He gave the Kaiser a greeting that was both vivacious and warm. And he seemed entirely filled with the one subject which was now occupying him.

"C'est une grande victoire que nous aurons en France. . . . Rampolla has reported the situation to me, and Cardinal Richard . . . we shall witness a great triumph!"

The Pope read out the messages almost with passion. His eyes sparkled with satisfaction. It was hard for the Kaiser to cast a gloom over those anticipatory rejoicings. But, so far as his information went, there would be no victory for the Pope. He determined to follow the advice which Cardinal Kopp had given him.

"Your Holiness, I doubt whether that information is entirely correct. The situation in France appears to be rather serious—"

"Oh, non, non, non—I have my sources of information!"

"Your Holiness, our information is very precise. The Republic is no friend of the Church, and the prospects of victory are very poor."

The Pope energetically shook his head. He spoke rapidly, full of fire, returning to the charge:

"Non, non, non—the Church's eldest daughter! You will see!"

The Pope retained his own conviction, but he could see that the Kaiser was beyond convincing. He passed to other subjects. He came, of set purpose, to the subject of the *Kulturkampf*. He was anxious to see the last traces of ill-feeling smoothed away. He praised Cardinal Kopp's services. So an hour passed; then Prince Henry of Prussia was announced. The Chamberlain had not wanted to announce him until the Pope had brought the conversation with Emperor William to an end, but had been faced in the anteroom with Count Herbert Bismarck's indignant insistence:

"A Prince of Prussia is not to be kept waiting in the Pope's ante-room!"

The Secretary had protested so loudly that the Chamberlain gave way and conducted Prince Henry to the Pope. So the talk had ended more abruptly than, perhaps, either Pope or Kaiser had wished. The Holy Father bade farewell to Emperor William—in every word, every gesture a Sovereign.

The Kaiser had a conversation with Cardinal Rampolla. The Cardinal had not the Pope's unrestricted breadth and sublimity of view. His caution was evident; there was an element of the lurking in his glance. The Kaiser had brought a precious pectoral for the Cardinal; Rampolla took it with something of a wry smile. Prince Bismarck had decided in favour of the cross because he knew that the Cardinal, who was a little vain of his imposing presence, would have preferred the order of the Black Eagle, to which, as Cardinal Secretary of State, he considered that he had a claim. This was Prince Bismarck's return for unpleasant memories of difficulties made for him in the days of the *Kulturkampf*. The Kaiser could not make an order out of the cross; nor had he any idea of doing so.

Events in France justified Cardinal Kopp and the Kaiser, and not the Holy Father. It was no victory for the Church that the elections brought, but a severe defeat. Rampolla called the cardinals together. He himself and all the cardinals had buoyed up the Pope with false hopes. At last, "The Holy Father must be told," he said.

He asked for an audience.

"You bring me good news, your Eminence?" the Pope began at once—"What is the result?"

The Cardinal Secretary of State concealed his embarrassment only with difficulty. Finally he summoned up resolution enough to say:

"Unfortunately I have to report to your Holiness that our expectations have not been fulfilled."

The Pope started. "Not fulfilled? How is that?"

"We have suffered a severe defeat in France."

There was a pause. Rampolla said no more; the Pope remained silent. But suddenly he burst out passionately, with the unbridled anger of the absolute King against unprofitable servants. He struck the table with his fist:

"So, then, you have been feeding me with false news! The German Emperor is the only one who gives me pure wine."

Days passed before the storm in the Vatican calmed down. Monsignore Montel gave the Kaiser the full story. But by then he had left Rome, King Humbert, and the Pope far behind.

Emperor William had returned to the palace in Berlin. He had issued orders for his first manœuvres. The good effect which his visit to the Viennese Court had had was

shown in the presence at the manœuvres of Field Marshal
Archduke Albert, the victor at Custozza and Austrian Com-
mander-in-chief. He was now of great age and nearly blind,
but still pursued his study of general staff problems, passing
his fingers over maps specially prepared for him in high
relief. Now he raced madly over the manœuvring ground,
galloping in all directions, as indicated to him by his adjutant. This old enemy of Prussia, who had never got over
Königgrätz and the peace treaty of 1866, was received with
every possible mark of distinction by Emperor William.
The Archduke's keen intelligence told him that the past
was now definitely buried, and that under the new Kaiser
an entirely new era had begun. It was an era of much
splendour. The Archduke spoke of his impressions with
courtierly deference.

But perhaps the splendour of the new era was illusory
—for it was dimmed here and there by fleeting shadows,
first harbingers of evil.

CHAPTER IV

BISMARCK *FURIOSO*

JUST before Emperor William's tour of visits, Professor Geffcken, of Hamburg, a man closely associated with the diplomatic service of the Hansa Towns, and long in the confidence of Emperor and Empress Frederick, had published extracts from Emperor Frederick's war diary of 1870.

The Professor had undertaken the publication on his own responsibility. Emperor Frederick was capable at times, both in speaking and in writing, of attacking in unmeasured language. He had always been fond of chaffing, and often wounded; he might then himself take deep umbrage, and would note down his displeasure in sharp terms. The war diary, which had been passed to the Professor confidentially for inspection, recorded the friction and misunderstandings, the difficulties and personal antipathies without which the German Empire could no more be founded than any other. History had long passed them by. But the publication was bound or was at least likely to give deep offence. King Ludwig II was remembered by his people as a martyr. It was understandable that his proud insistence at all times on Bavaria's rights and claims, her significance and her services in connexion with the foundation of the Empire, should at times have irritated the Crown Prince Frederick. But Bavaria now had one more reason for honouring the memory of the unfortunate King and for giving plain expression to the old aversion to Prussia.

Emperor William himself realized that there were grounds
for that attitude; and during his visit to the Prince Regent
on his way to Vienna he had, by an adroit phrase pub-
licly dropped, softened the impression which Professor
Geffcken's action had begun to produce. There was much
in the book to create astonishment abroad.

Prince Bismarck was furious. He no longer needed to
consider the Dowager Empress Frederick. He suspected
that the Professor had acted with her knowledge, perhaps
even with her authority. It was a convenient way of once
more giving publicity to her own and her husband's line
of thought, and so showing all that the rule of her son—
which was also his, Bismarck's—was preventing. The Chancellor had no intention of allowing so wide a measure of
licence to the written word; it was quite enough in his view
that the newspapers were free from dictation in regard to
questions of the day. He advocated very severe punishment.
He himself drafted the "personal report" to the Kaiser.
He alleged that Geffcken had betrayed secrets of State and
falsified secret State documents. He represented the whole
affair as so dangerous, and so abominable, that the Kaiser
ordered a prosecution.

For the first time since he had been on the throne, he
discovered that he had shocked public opinion. Beyond
question the unfortunate Professor had acted from no dis-
honourable or self-seeking motives; yet he had been at once
arrested. What was going to be the end of it if anyone
whose writing gave offence, although he had written in the
interest of historic truth, was liable to find himself in prison?
Everyone knew that the Chancellor was at the back of the
Kaiser's command. Public opinion did not entirely support
the Chancellor's harshness; the judges were entirely against

it. The Supreme Court acquitted the Professor, on the ground that he had been innocent of any conscious or deliberate illegality. He was set free.

There was great excitement all over Germany and everywhere abroad. The Chancellor had brought an offender to justice without first ascertaining whether his offence, if any, was really punishable. The Chancellor had secured the Kaiser's assent to the prosecution without having first made sure that there was no risk of having to draw back. He had also misjudged the effect which the affair would have on the popularity of the Empress Frederick. Her popularity did not suffer: her friends noted that it increased.

But the Chancellor scarcely had time to take much notice of the three months of excitement over the Geffcken affair; the Professor was no sooner sent home than new trouble filled the newspapers: the Geffcken affair gave place to the Morier affair.

Prince Bismarck had an old account outstanding against Sir Robert Morier, the British Ambassador in St. Petersburg. During the Franco-German war Sir Robert had been Secretary of Legation at Darmstadt, and had been much in the entourage of Crown Princess Frederick. She had treated the English diplomat with marked attention—had not only honoured him with her confidence but brought him entirely into the circle of her friends. In the end he had moved among the Deputies and politicians who were associated with the Crown Princess almost as a fellow-countryman of theirs. He had shared their views, been acquainted with their plans, and originated many ideas in the liberal direction in which the whole group tended; on many of the occasions on which Bismarck had found cause for vexation with the "Englishwoman" he had suspected that the real trouble came from Sir Robert Morier. In the end the Chancellor had become immovably convinced that Sir Robert was making use of his friendship with the Crown Prince and Princess in open antagonism to him, both in Homburg and Berlin.

Now at last the Chancellor could settle his account. He had received from the German military attaché in Madrid a communication which contained a grave charge against the Ambassador. It alleged that during the Franco-German war Morier had betrayed to Marshal Bazaine information that he had gained in Homburg concerning intended movements of the Crown Prince's army. Incredible as the charge was, Bismarck seized on it. He hated the man; it was doubly troublesome to have him in the neighbourhood of the Tsar, who was so easily influenced; he was determined to disgrace him and get rid of him at any price. He would thus get in yet another blow against Empress Frederick. Once he had dismissed a Minister, von Puttkamer, to do a service to his present bitter opponent. He had known then that it was necessary to keep on the right side of the Kaiserin, and that the move would be bound to improve his relations with her. Now she was no longer in power. He now repeated, without regard for her, the treatment that he had once given the Minister in order to gain her favour. He did not suppose that the young Kaiser would be particularly upset if his mother's political prestige were once more to suffer. He sacrificed it in order to serve that of her son. He knew that the Kaiser could not have any excessive love for his mother.

From the first he had always had a real regard for Prince William. From across the great gulf set between them by the tremendous experiences of his long life, he had liked him in a slightly patronising, almost a grandfatherly way. So far as it had been possible to venture to do so in front of Emperor and Empress Frederick, he had taken some share in the Prince's education by talk and letter, through missions and tasks assigned. He had encouraged him to rely on himself and had always impressed on him his high mission and his power of Monarch. He had had hopes of the grandson of Emperor William I. He even still liked "the young master," in spite of his own lack of enthusiasm for the dynasty, avowed in confidence twenty years before. Since William II had ascended the throne there had been no disagreement between Kaiser and Chancellor, not the slightest difference of opinion in any direction. The Kaiser had discussed with him every step of importance. He had gone carefully into every question. At times he had failed to get a thorough grip of the material dealt with by his Ministers. "Send for the fellows, your Majesty," the Chancellor would say then; "have a talk with them." Prince Bismarck readily furthered every opportunity of giving the Kaiser the satisfaction of exercising his functions as Monarch. He himself suggested anything that he thought would be a satisfaction to the Kaiser. His conflict with Empress Frederick was in his eyes one of these services to his new master—quite apart from the old score against Morier.

Attacks on the Ambassador began to appear, grave imputations were spread abroad in full detail. Sir Robert indignantly rejected them; he turned to Marshal Bazaine, and the Marshal branded them as lies. He turned to Count Bismarck and demanded a public exoneration. The Secretary of State declined in a way that lent colour to the charges. The Ambassador then published his letters to the

Secretary and to Marshal Bazaine and the Marshal's reply. He was not recalled from Petersburg. He cleared himself completely abroad, in London, in the Tsar's eyes, and with German public opinion. The incident only strengthened his position in Petersburg and in London. The Dowager Empress also came through the affair unscathed. Her son had had no part whatever in the matter; and he wasted no words on it now it was over. Bismarck had failed utterly. The Morier affair had been another misfortune for the Chancellor.

One thing was evident: the Chancellor's luck was out at the moment. He hoped to avert any evil results of the Geffcken and Morier affairs by reversing his tactics and bringing a sacrifice to conciliate the very people against whom he had aimed in his attack on Empress Frederick and her friends. He would drive Stöcker, the anti-Semitic Court preacher, out of political life. If the Conservatives howled, let them. Stöcker had proposed to found a Berlin City Mission, and had interested Prince William in the project; but a year had now passed since he had had to bury his project in consequence of Bismarck's opposition. The Chancellor had demanded that no use should be made of the Prince's name, as he must not be used as a screen for party operations. Prince William had explained at length why he wanted to support Stöcker, but had accepted the Chancellor's view. After that less had been heard of this Court preacher for a while, but suddenly he began to be active again. He made aggressive speeches in political meetings in the capital. He went into Catholic South Germany, which showed no enthusiasm either for the tone or the contents of Stöcker's public speeches. He spoke in spite of the promise which he had given to the Kaiser.

If in striking at Stöcker he could annoy the Conservatives, that in itself would give the Chancellor pleasure; he had no love for them. But after all that had recently happened he was especially concerned not entirely to alienate the Liberals and the National Liberals. If Stöcker were punished they would regard it as a service to freedom of thought and to progress. Prince Bismarck could be progressive in season: Stöcker should be removed from his post at Court. The Kaiser, too, was plainly anxious to get rid of him. His appointment of Professor Harnack had shown that he preferred a more liberal attitude than that of this Court preacher. Stöcker should be made either to confine himself to preaching or to confine himself to public speaking for the future.

Stöcker made his choice. He decided for the future to eschew demagogy. With that, as a politician he had been put on the shelf for all to see. The Chancellor was content. and the National Liberals equally so.

But it was only a moment's respite of success for the Chancellor. A fresh incident had cropped up, in Switzerland. It threw a lurid light on Bismarck's struggle against the German Social Democrats, and still more on his methods.

An Alsatian police spy named Wohlgemuth had come to an arrangement on Swiss soil with one of his confidants in Switzerland, with whom he had for some time been in correspondence and to whom he had written the indiscreet phrase,

"Go right ahead with your agitation!"

The German Government was concerned not only to keep an eye on the German Socialist movement, but also to discover the sources in Switzerland from which the movement obtained its supplies of prohibited pamphlets, leaflets, and manifestos. But the way its police agent set to work not only went beyond all that is considered legitimate by watchful authorities in the ordinary, respectable police work of their own area; his activity on foreign soil was entirely unconstitutional and naturally aroused Swiss resentment. He had hardly crossed the frontier into Switzerland when his confidant denounced him to his group of Swiss Social Democrats. The spy was arrested and kept ten days in gaol; the Confederation took no notice either of his protests or of the fuss made by the Chancellor. Bismarck sent the Confederation a sharply worded note. Nothing had been done which called for an apology; yet he demanded not only apologies but undertakings that would make it impossible in future for German Social Democrats to receive assistance from Switzerland or to settle there. He required no less than that Switzerland, if she set store by friendly relations with her neighbour, should settle her account with her own Social Democrats.

The Confederation declined to do so. The Chancellor began to hurl threats. Small States whose neutrality was guaranteed had not only rights but duties which they owed it to their guarantors that they should fulfil. To those around him Bismarck declared that he would not shrink even from war with the Confederation. About the same time the Swiss authorities had arrested in Zurich a number of anarchists caught in the act of making bombs. They admitted that the bombs were intended for Russia. The Chancellor tried to persuade Russia to take action jointly with him against Switzerland, which had suddenly become so dangerous a country. But great as the fear of anarchists had at all times been at the Court of the Tsar, he had no

Adolf Stöcker
Court Chaplain

Emperor Francis Joseph of Austria
as Grandmaster of the Order of the Golden Fleece

desire for complications with Switzerland, of all States the one that mattered least to Russia; still less to engage in a campaign amid the glaciers. There would certainly have been an element of the ridiculous in the advance of the armies of two Great Powers against little Switzerland. But the Chancellor was not satisfied to let matters rest. He threatened to put difficulties in the way of passports for tourists. Customs restrictions would make the Swiss still more uncomfortable and hurt them in yet tenderer spots. Finally he denounced the immigration treaty between the Reich and the Confederation.

All the Chancellor's efforts did nothing to destroy either the Socialist idea or the Social Democratic movement. But even Germany's friends in Switzerland drew unfavourable comparisons between the autocratic methods which he wanted to apply at home and the milder methods of their other neighbour, France. The Chancellor's passport restrictions, his tariff obstacles, his interruption of traffic to and from Switzerland did not confine their effects to the seditious persons at whom they were aimed. The people of Baden and Württemberg began to complain. The Social Democrats might be a nuisance, but if the Chancellor knew of no better measures to take against them than to cripple business at the frontier and to inflict real injury on all the border territories, then the Social Democrats could be put up with for a while.

Gradually the whole affair began to take on the aspect of a fresh failure. For years the Chancellor had been in the habit of acting entirely on his own judgment and commanding in accordance with his own will, and he had dealt with this incident more roughly than its nature warranted. But he was shielded by the enormous prestige of his

great life's work; if now and then he went wrong in
trifles it had to be put up with. Almost every genius was
liable to be obstinate, but it must not be forgotten what the
Prince had founded. Above all it had to be remembered
how the Empire owed it to him that it had the peace that
enabled it to breathe and work, achieve and flourish in
Europe. It stood safe and inviolate in the sight of all, protected by manifold safeguards of its peaceful existence. All
of these were the work of Bismarck, his conception, carried
out and securely established by him. The testy old man
might make mistakes, but he was still the finest and most
accomplished of sorcerers. Volcanoes constantly smoke and
rarely erupt. The conflict with Switzerland was a grotesque
intermezzo. Like the Geffcken and Morier affairs, it
passed. Once his wrath had subsided, these trifles no longer
troubled his peace at Friedrichsruh.

All was well if only his alliances endured.

CHAPTER V

THE INCUBUS OF ALLIANCES

THE Empire's alliances were an involved complex, a many-meshed, not easily penetrable network. The Chancellor himself had devised it, and the Chancellor alone knew his way about it. Since his foundation of the Empire he had had the one purpose of maintaining it in peace. He had thrust Austria out of Germany, but in 1866 he had neither destroyed nor humiliated her. He had known or suspected that Königgrätz was not Prussia's final settlement. The enemy of yesterday might be valuable as a friend on the morrow. He had rendered her substantial services at the Berlin Congress, had shown her there a way in which she could find consolation and compensation for her lost influence in Germany and Italy. It had then been only natural that the Empires of the Hohenzollerns and Habsburgs should become reconciled and ally themselves together, and not only because they inherited a common history and kindred culture: after her recovery from defeat Austria-Hungary had still her enemies, while the brilliant victories of the German Empire had awakened jealousies and certain perils.

But the Dual Alliance with Austria-Hungary was not enough for the Chancellor. The German Empire would only be safe when a system and a situation had been created all over Europe which compelled all the Powers to keep the peace.

The Chancellor succeeded in his great work of reconciliation by bringing Italy into the Triple Alliance with Austria-Hungary and his own country. He had set up a great coalition which would stand solidly against Russia if she were to show her teeth, and would cool France's ardour if she were to be stirred by a lust for revenge. The only way to peace in Europe was, in Bismarck's view, to make aggression impossible, and alliances were only serviceable and justifiable if their purpose was defence. He intended to give no encouragement in any quarter for further adventure, to allow no one to disturb the existing order. There were still two Powers in Europe with incalculable aims, both independent of him and beyond his influence: Britain and Russia. He did not trust Britain—she was too democratic, too independent, too inaccessible to influence; Russia he feared as his nearest neighbour and a conceivably violent one. He suffered no sleepless nights on account of France; French passions and French longings for revenge left him cold, whether it were the hothead Boulanger or anyone else that stirred them up. If France wanted another war, so be it; but not a general war, in which every account would come up for settlement, tempting such mighty voices as those of Britain and Russia to intervene. There was no certainty that they would intervene on the side of Germany and her friends; Russia, at all events, would be more likely to do the opposite, for it was precisely against the Russian colossus that he had formed the Triple Alliance.

He had done his utmost not to irritate Russia in building up the Alliance. He had drawn up the terms of alliance with Austria in such a way that it would be difficult for the Dual Monarchy to envisage such complications with Russia as must require war for their unravelling. Bismarck knew that any armed conflict between Austria-Hungary and the Tsar must begin, if the Dual Monarchy was to have any prospect of success, with an Austrian attack. The Monarchy was incomparably the smaller and weaker Power, and if it waited for as much as half of the Tsar's armies to get on the move it would be crushed. Thus, in any war against Russia, Austria-Hungary must be the aggressor, whether she were so ill-advised as herself to work for war or were driven into it out of desperation. Consequently, as the Chancellor knew, he held in his hand the issue of war or peace between Russia and the Dual Monarchy. Under the terms of alliance he had to come to the aid of the Monarchy only in the event of aggression against it; and under no circumstances could there be Russian aggression against Austria. Bismarck hoped for the maintenance of peace on the Continent by all the Powers; from his ally he demanded and compelled it. Militarily Austria-Hungary was in any case in a precarious situation with regard to Russia; Bismarck made her yet more so.

He threw his whole weight into the support of the British Mediterranean agreement with Italy, under which the two Powers guaranteed the continuance of the *status quo* in the Near East. He continually urged Austria-Hungary to give her adhesion to the agreement, until in the end it was developed into a treaty between the three Powers. The Triple Alliance, and especially the alliance with Austria-Hungary, was then at last fulfilling a useful purpose. If Germany were attacked by Russia, Emperor Francis Joseph's army, which was not as negligible as some thought, must march to her aid. Against Russia the Dual Monarchy could embark on no enterprise on its own initiative. The Mediterranean agreement made it impossible for

Austria to lift a finger in the Balkans. Bismarck's ally was dependent on his fiat, and her whole function in Bismarck's policy was to serve as an instrument of war, to be a threat against Russia. In supporting the Mediterranean agreement his ideas followed the same line of policy; this agreement too was a threat against the Tsar. Wherever the Tsar might think of taking a stroll into the Near East, he would have to bear in mind that Britain, Austria-Hungary, and Italy might march simultaneously against him. And it would then depend entirely on Prince Bismarck whether or not he should join them. The moment might dictate that course even if Russia were the party attacked. Or he might find it advisable to make no move, on the ground that his ally had embarked on a war of aggression, the burden of which must be supported entirely by the signatories to the Mediterranean agreement. If he remained neutral he might stand to gain both ways. One factor remained common at all times to the Triple Alliance and the Mediterranean agreement—the threat they represented against the Tsar.

He feared Russia. He knew that the Berlin Congress, which he had summoned, had ended in a British-Austrian victory over the Tsar. But he also feared Russia's restless ambition, her unreliability, her policy guided entirely by the fiat of the Tsar, and the character of the men around him who actually dictated it. Russia was restless by virtue of the tradition, dating from Peter the Great, of a mission to break through to Constantinople, by virtue of the self-suggestion of her Orthodox "Popes," who minted policy out of religion, by virtue of the Pan-Slav movement with its claims to protect the Greek Catholic Bulgars. It might be impossible for Austria-Hungary to move out of the cage which Bismarck had nailed down around her; but Russia might move. If Russia were to make war against Germany, whether on account of Austria or on any other account, Germany would certainly have to reckon also with France. It was undoubtedly wise in any case to stand across the line of communication between France and Russia. The threats involved in the Triple Alliance and the Mediterranean agreement were useful. But they were not enough. A direct rapprochement with Russia, if attainable, would, the Chancellor considered, improve matters. The first suggestion of a friendly agreement between Germany and Russia was thrown out at a breakfast with Count Shuvalov, the Russian Ambassador in Berlin, in May, 1887. An agreement fully binding both parties was secretly concluded on June 18th; for Germany it was a sort of "reinsurance" treaty.

The Chancellor meant honourably to assist Russia in her aspirations. Russo-German relations were in future to be surrounded by a friendly and peaceful atmosphere. He had barricaded the way against any Austrian advance into the Balkans, but if Russia had really set her heart on penetrating to Constantinople he saw no reason why she should not be allowed to do so. In Bulgaria, too, if "legitimate" conditions were at last to be attained there, the Chancellor was prepared to give Russia all permissible assistance. As to the constantly menacing spectre of war, if any Power were to go to war with Russia the Chancellor promised that Germany should remain neutral. The Tsar entered into a similar undertaking towards Germany. There was one exception: Germany could not remain passive in the event of hostilities between Russia and Austria-Hungary, Russia being the aggressor.

The Chancellor felt that he had made a good step forward towards peace in Europe. France and her plans of revenge might almost be regarded as counting now for nothing. Russia had in some degree committed herself: she could no longer act in entire independence. She too was more or less tied.

Not everyone, even among the initiated, clearly understood what the Chancellor was up to. Count Hatzfeldt, the German Ambassador in London, a man of ripened experience and shrewd insight, more statesman than diplomat in the breadth of his ideas and his range of vision, was one of those who failed to comprehend Bismarck's intention. As he saw it the new secret agreement with Russia directly conflicted with the Triple Alliance. "Don't be alarmed," the Chancellor replied—"if I do not want to support Austria I can easily give matters such a turn that it will be the Austrians who are the aggressors; and then I do not come to their aid."

Thus, even Germany's shrewdest Ambassador confused treaties and morality. Bismarck did not. Naturally not everyone would be able to grasp these extreme subtleties of true statesmanship; it would, therefore, be much the best to keep the new agreement entirely secret—both in Berlin and in Petersburg. No more than three or four persons knew of its existence. With the whole weight of his responsibility the Chancellor had impressed on the old Kaiser that he must not speak a word about it to the Austrian Emperor when they met in Gastein. The old Emperor William I maintained a troubled and embarrassed silence on the subject in front of Francis Joseph. Frederick III died without ever learning of the existence of the treaty. The Tsar was told that Prince William knew of it. In reality Bismarck had told him nothing about it: the Chancellor regarded the manipulation and development of alliances as his own exclusive province.

He refused to follow either of the two broad paths which lay open before a State in Germany's situation in choosing its alliances. He just went ahead with the weaving of his network of treaties, which seemed to him of more importance than any outright decision. He might have united for better or worse with Russia as a Conservative well-inclined towards that country. He would then have been able to solve the great problem of the balance of power in Europe, and at the same time the permanently acute problem of the Balkans, by the partitioning of Austria-Hungary. He was not the man to be deterred from this by any sentimental considerations. This policy would have enabled him, instead of the semi-betrayal involved in the Reinsurance Treaty, to launch an open demand for the settlement of Europe's outstanding problems. But though he could see that the Dual Monarchy was doomed to dissolution, he shrank from the operation that would bring it about. Alternatively he could have pursued the opposite policy, of making Austria-Hungary—his ally—as strong as possible, of assuring her every opportunity of development and increase of strength as a Great Power, making her voice in the end a really powerful reinforcement of his own. He could have picked up the line which led to him from Britain through Austria-Hungary and Italy, and have worked the four States into a powerful coalition. Actually he wavered continually between East and West, between Britain and Russia. He eluded the big fundamental issue.

Austria he crippled. Russia, whom he had promised to support in the Balkans, he was opposing by his support of the parties to the Mediterranean agreement, who refused to countenance any change in the Balkans. If after all Russia were to produce complications in that quarter, if they brought war with Austria-Hungary, and if the guarantors of the Mediterranean treaty then came to her aid, Germany would be so placed through her alliances that she must both fight and remain neutral. She was committed to fighting for Austria-Hungary and Italy on the Russian front, but if British troops were also engaged she must pile her arms under the Reinsurance Treaty. The Chancellor did not believe that this imbroglio would ever come; none the less, his arrangements had made it possible. He regarded any radical solution of the problem as too dangerous, and prepared to avoid it by means of a bundle of agreements, all serving the one aim of the security of the German Empire—assuring it protectors and sympathizers if it were attacked by anyone, while it was free itself to remain neutral in whatever quarter war might break out, even if German's nearest ally, Austria-Hungary, had to embark on it. Everything in his system of interwoven treaties, separate or tripartite, could be so interpreted that Germany could never herself be called to arms by those whose protection and assistance she demanded. He imagined that he could wall out Russia with the Triple Alliance, set an attacking column on the march against the Tsar from Britain and Italy, and yet leave Austria to face Russia without his help; play off Britain against Russia in the Near East, and yet live in the midst of all this in peace, never himself in any danger. He imagined, in short, that he could continue indefinitely a policy of alliances in which Germany had only to receive and never to pay.

Recently, however, under the new Kaiser, there had been various incidents which had disturbed the Chancellor's composure. He was startled by a report from Prince Reuss, the German Ambassador in Vienna. He had sent the Prince to Count Kálnoky, with urgent advice, tendered by the Chancellor under Russian influence, that Austria-Hungary should desist from any sort of adventure in the Balkans. He had forgotten that he had himself given Emperor Francis Joseph his consent to the Austrian seizure of Salonica. Count Kálnoky sent the Chancellor the answer that he must have forgotten 1866. The Monarchy had lost its freedom of movement in Italy; it no longer had any say in Germany; it must be allowed some field of activity, and only the Balkans were left. If Bismarck had let the Russians have Bulgaria as a sphere of influence, that was his affair and Russia's; nothing could alter the fact that Bulgaria had no geographical connexion with Russia, that she was widely separated from Russia, but on the other hand lay actually along the Danube.

The whole complex of Near Eastern questions seemed to Bismarck, and to his immediate advisers, no longer so clear or so easy to settle one after another as he had formerly believed. In spite of the objections of the Austrian Emperor, and of his own promotion of the Mediterranean agreement, he had had no objection to Russia's claim on Constantinople. He had even seen an advantage in it—that the Russians would be more vulnerable in the event of a British attack than, for instance, in the Crimea. But to get to Constantinople the Russians must pass through Roumania, and Roumania could only be expected to allow the march through if she were allied with Russia. His hope, however, was that that Kingdom, which, of course, knew

Coburg.

Family group taken after the Engagement of the Zarowitsch Nicholas to Princess Alexandra of Hessen.

from right to left, & from below upwards:

Princess Feod Saxe-Meiningen. Princess Beatrice of S-Coburg-G: Empress Fredrick. H.M. the Queen. The German Emperor. Duchess of Coburg (Grand duchess of Russia). Grand duchess Wladimir. Princess Henry of Prussia (Princess Irene of Hessen) Princess V: Sister of Battenberg (Princess V. of Hessen). Princess

Alexandra of Hessen (the Bride). The Zarowitsch Nicholas (Bridegroom). Prince Alfred of S:-Coburg-G: behind him the Prince of Wales. Princess Beatrice of Battenberg (wife of Prince Henry of Battenberg). Princess Alexandra of S-Coburg-G: Princess Charlotte of S-Meiningen (H.J.M. sister) Duke of Connaught. Grand duke Wladimir of Russia. Grand duke Serge of Russia. Prince Ferdinand of Hohenzollern-Sigmaringen (late King of Roumania). Prince Henry of Battenberg. Duke of S-Coburg-G: (formerly Duke of Edinburgh). Grand duchess Serge (Princess Ella of Hessen). Count Mensdorff. Prince Philipp of S-Coburg. Prince Louis of Battenberg.

The Royal Castle (Schloss) on the Spree Berlin

nothing of the Reinsurance Treaty, would be gradually drawn into the Triple Alliance.

The disquietude which began to affect the Chancellor was not diminished when he considered the attitude of his new friend Russia. With the Reinsurance Treaty in his desk he had no need to take it too tragically, but it was disturbing to be continually warned by the Chief of Staff that Russia was preparing for war. Count Waldersee was able to make some impression on the Kaiser, who was inclined to caution in regard to all things Russian in spite of the cordiality with which he had been received in Petersburg after his ascent of the throne. So far Bismarck had been able to allay the Kaiser's apprehensions without having to show him the secret treaty. But beyond all doubt the Russians were busily arming in spite of the treaty. They were issuing a big loan, and it was no consolation to the Chancellor that they were issuing it in Germany. He had no means of preventing the banks from granting loans on Russian securities, but he had a public warning issued against the loan. He definitely forbade the Reichsbank to accept it as collateral. For all that, the Russians continued arming, and refused to be frightened out of their financial schemes.

The Chancellor was not at all times satisfied that his good relations with Russia could last, and at times his thought wandered to Britain. There had actually been an opportunity of coming to an understanding with Britain, perhaps even concluding an alliance. In connexion with the Mediterranean agreement Lord Salisbury had asked for a measure of "reassurance" for the future from the Chancellor. In conversations with the German Ambassador, Count Hatzfeldt, he had again and again raised the

question in the vague but pregnant outlines which had
always been the special forte of British statesmen. The
Chancellor had at once understood this covert speech.
Britain would be greatly "reassured" if Germany were to
promise her support should war come with Russia. If she
would do so, the outlines would become definite and Britain
would pay the full price. She would be ready steadily to
work towards an alliance with Germany; the great quad-
ruple coalition could be fashioned before which Russia—
Russia and France—and all the Continent would be
powerless.

But the Chancellor had concluded his Reinsurance
Treaty with Russia. His disingenuousness with Austria
was avenging itself. No agreement with Britain was possible without deceiving Russia. The idea was, therefore,
out of the question. Prince Bismarck answered Lord Salisbury in a note in which every sentence, every expression
bore the mark of Bismarck's own strong, clear phrasing.
Yet all that he could do was to make a virtue of necessity.
Germany, he said, could only go to war if her people willed
it on account of their own vital interests. The age of mer-
cenary wars was over. The truth still remained that the
Chancellor was unable to accept because of his Russian
commitment. He could not stir. He had set out to weld
his neighbour States all over Europe firmly to their places.
And he had welded himself fast.

Considering, however, that Lord Salisbury had put forward a proposal, on his own initiative and without any sort
of prompting, which he felt held out prospects of fruitful
cooperation between the two Powers, there might perhaps
be a possibility of at least some measure of rapprochement
with Britain, even if the great agreement was impractica-

ble. The network of German treaties still had one gap not entirely drawn to—the assurance against France. Bismarck was not afraid of France, especially after the secret treaty with Russia. But for the purpose of further discussion with Britain and of rounding off the whole system of alliances, since he had to abide by that system, the desire for assurance against France provided a welcome pretext. Shortly after the correspondence with Lord Salisbury he made Britain the offer of an agreement. It was just as possible that France might attack Britain as that out of lust for revenge she might fall upon Germany. Let each State undertake to come to the aid of the other if attacked.

But Britain declined. The Chancellor was not offering a fair deal. If France saw any opportunity of revenging herself on Germany, war was certain. That France could ever venture on war with Britain, break through the fleets summoned from every naval port and embark on the wild adventure of a landing in England, the Chancellor himself could not imagine. Yet he was trying to make Britain imagine it. He was asking everything from Lord Salisbury and offering nothing.

He had lost his opportunity of a radical solution of the problem of the safety of the Empire, of assuring it on both flanks, east and west. He was fixed like a spider at the centre of his system of alliances radiating in all directions; but he was unable to move without damaging it. He had played off his allies against one another, but in doing so he had hemmed himself in.

"Le Prince de Bismarck a le cauchemar des coalitions!" said Peter Count Shuvalov, the Russian Ambassador in London.

"Nécessairement!" replied the Chancellor when the phrase was repeated to him.

The Ambassador had heard of Bismarck's renewed effort in the direction of Britain. No doubt he knew from his brother of the Chancellor's Reinsurance Treaty, or at least had some inkling of it. There was also a Triple Alliance, another of Bismarck's creations. There was a Mediterranean agreement, over the conclusion of which no one had taken more pains than the Chancellor. . . .

The incubus of the treaties weighed more heavily on the Chancellor than the Ambassador dreamed. Prince Bismarck slept uneasily in those days. His nerves were affected. The alliances still stood, but not solidly.

CHAPTER VI

WORKERS AND SOCIAL DEMOCRATS

AT about the same time as the incident in Switzerland which so violently excited the Chancellor, a great coal strike broke out in the Rhenish and Westphalian mines, unexpectedly and with no prior public notification.

The movement was new to Germany in character and extent, and in its violence. During the period of the bubble companies, some fifteen years before, there had been sporadic attempts at wage conflicts on a smaller scale, but these had not seriously troubled industry or the State or caused appreciable injury to either. The disturbed state of public opinion which dated from those first strikes, the blow which they struck at the traditional ideas of public order, and the new attitude and language of the Social Democrats, never before ventured on in Germany, had been quite enough to move the Chancellor to introduce and pass a Socialist law through the Reichstag in the autumn of 1878. Its purpose was to protect the Monarchy and the possessing class "against the danger to the commonweal of the activities of the Social Democracy." This exceptional law was three times renewed. The strikes of the company-promoting boom had quickly flickered out, and the exceptional law was not intended to be administered with excessive tenderness, but steadily the Social Democracy grew. There were times when Germany's situation between dangerous and heavily armed neighbours gave the Chancellor sleepless nights; but every hour, every moment in which he gave a thought to the rise and the continual growth of this movement with its new conceptions of human relationships and of the State, and to the footing already gained by a growing body of its prophets and apostles in Parliament, filled him with exasperation. The problems of 1864, 1866, and 1870, settled with "blood and iron," had been simple in comparison with the problems which had been set him since the Berlin Congress by the developments within the borders of the Empire of his creation. He was accustomed to rule. He had dealt independently with the fabric of Germany's friendships and alliances, without much reference to colleagues and advisers; and he had been equally accustomed to exercise sole authority at home. The *"L'Etat, c'est moi!"* of Louis XIV became yet more emphatic in Bismarck's version—*"Moi, je suis l'Etat."*

In this new "Social Democracy," which was pushing to the front against his desire and even against his veto, he saw the arch-enemy. He saw in it, if it persisted, the end of the Monarchy, of all ownership, of any sort of social order and morality. He was determined, he staked his soul on its destruction. At the first signs of its power he brought all his strength to bear against it. He would not content himself with defeating it as a party; he would refuse it a place in the country's constitutional life. He was determined to strike it to the ground. If he failed in this he would declare actual war on it. Over the border lay Russia, a possible enemy; France, an undoubted one. But the arch-enemy, the mortal enemy were the Social Democrats. The first attempts of workers to resist the established order and combine to enforce their "demands" had been met by the Socialist law. Workers or Socialists (for all that they were not necessarily the same thing) were equally liable to imprisonment and exile from their homes under this law if their evil disposition were evidenced by action, speech or writing. The Socialist law placed heavy fetters on recalcitrant workers, on Socialists and revolutionaries; it was enacted against them and applicable to them at any moment; for in the Chancellor's eyes they were all equally enemies of the State, all moved alike by nothing but lust for intrigue and revolt. His relentlessness had brought him its reward: for a long time he had seen the Empire and the established order perfectly protected. But now new sparks had suddenly begun to fly up. The work of the German police on Swiss soil was laying bare underground activities. The Chancellor in his wrath ordered them not to be deterred by prohibitions of systematic search in their hunt for hiding places and dens of secret activity.

But there was more work for the police to do than carry on their war against sedition and Social Democracy adventurously on foreign soil; there were open fires nearer at hand. The sparks were very soon crackling and flying up not only in Rhineland and Westphalia but in every corner of Germany, wherever industry had gathered its workers together. Trammers and drivers had begun the strike in the first days of May, 1889, in the mining area of Gelsenkirchen. A few days later the whole of the Ruhr was involved; a hundred thousand miners were idle. The mines of Dortmund, Witten, Bochum were closed down. The movement spread to the district of Hamm. It leaped to Essen, and not a hammer moved in the Kingdom of Krupp. But the miners in the Rhenish coal basin and the Saar had no sooner dropped their picks than those of the Upper Silesian coal mines also struck. Coal extraction ceased in the Aachen area; in Saxony the mine workers demanded increased wages from the owners. Increased wages were demanded everywhere. No man was going to continue to be content with 24 marks a week and less to support his wife and children. The miners also stood out against a ten hour shift at the surface, and eight hours underground was enough for anyone. Everywhere the miners had been demanding this reduction of working hours and the granting of endurable conditions of existence. Finally they had refused to descend the shaft.

The mining areas lay in an unaccustomed silence. The workers, normally out of sight, stood about the pitheads. Then there began the incidents that come in all strikes. Strikebreakers came forward, indifferent to their comrades' cause. The strikers closed ranks against this betrayal. They were not to be defeated in that way. Mine managers and owners called for military protection. The authorities knew the views of the Chancellor's office: they sent Uhlans and infantry. Shots were fired—for the first time there were bayonet thrusts and volleys in time of peace. No one knew how the incidents had begun, but there were dead left lying at many points. In one place a sentry was attacked and bayoneted his aggressor. At more than one point officials were hustled and maltreated. Bitterness grew on all sides. Traffic on the roads stopped entirely; train services were interrupted. Police and military enforced martial law conditions, with curfew and passes. There could be no question that the police and military, led by officers thirsting for a fight, were doing their best to turn the disturbances into insurrection.

The Kaiser was displeased. He ordered the General Commanding in the disturbed area to give his personal

attention to the restoration of order and the cooling of the
soldiers' tempers. He called for a report on the actual
situation. Von Michaelis, Colonel of Hussars stationed in
the strike area, sent the laconic message:

"All quiet, except the authorities."

But the shooting ceased.

The Kaiser removed the responsible officials. The
incompetent he dismissed. But the movement went on
extending. It spread all over the Empire. In every possible
place mechanics and labourers were striking: in Leipzig
the smiths, in Bremerhaven the bricklayers, in Hamburg
the brewers, in Thuringia the tanners, in Langensalza the
joiners, in Bergedorf the glass makers. In the capital the
painters, the furriers, the cabinetmakers struck work. The
strike fever spread like a new epidemic; everyone was
seized with it as with a sudden religious mania, as though
it were a new gospel of salvation for the working world.
Finally the miners sent a deputation to the Kaiser. He
received them in the palace in Berlin, in the presence of
von Herrfurth, the Minister of the Interior.

The spokesman of the deputation brought the Kaiser
the "most loyal greeting of the miners." "We are demanding," he said, "only what we have inherited from our forefathers, namely the eight hour shift. We do not attach most
significance to an increase in wages. The employers must
negotiate with us; we are not deaf to all reason. If your
Majesty would speak just one word there would very soon
be a change, and many tears would be dried."

"Every subject," replied the Kaiser, "who has a request
or a petition to put forward, has the ear of his Emperor
as a matter of course. I have shown that in permitting the
deputation to come here and represent its case to me per-

sonally. But you have put yourselves in the wrong, for the movement is illegal, if for no other reason, for the simple reason that the fourteen days' notice, after which the workers would have been entitled by law to leave work, has not been observed. Consequently you have broken your contract. It is only natural that this breach of contract should have irritated the employers; it has also inflicted loss on them. Moreover, workers who did not want to strike have been prevented by force and by threats from continuing at work. In addition to that, certain workers have assaulted representatives of the authorities, have done damage to property, and have actually offered resistance in some instances to the military forces summoned for its protection. Finally, your idea is that normal working shall not be resumed unless all your demands are complied with in all the mines.

"So far as your demands are concerned, I shall have them carefully examined by My Government, and shall have the result of its enquiry transmitted to you by the proper authorities. But if there should be any disturbances of the public peace and order, if the movement should prove to be connected with Social Democratic elements, I should not be in a position to consider your desires with My royal favour. For every Social Democrat is in My eyes virtually an enemy of the State and his country. If, therefore, I should discover that Social Democratic elements are associated with the movement and are inciting it to illegal resistance, I should proceed with relentless severity and bring to bear all the power which I have at call, and it is a great power.

"Now go home, consider what I have said, and try to persuade your comrades to think twice over all this. But above all you must under no circumstances stand in the way of those of your comrades who may desire to return to work."

Immediately after the miners the Kaiser received a deputation of the mineowners.

"I have permitted you this audience," he said to them, "because it is the obvious duty of the Monarch to hear both parties. So far as the cause of the strike is concerned, and the means of settling it, I am waiting a full report from My authorities. My main concern is to make an end as soon as possible of this great strike in Westphalia. I wish to express to you My satisfaction at the accommodating spirit in which you have met the workers, with the result that the basis has been secured for an understanding. I shall rejoice if on this basis employers and workers come to an agreement. I should like to lay stress on another aspect of the matter, as I see it: if you gentlemen should be of the opinion that the deputies of the workers were not the responsible representatives of the districts in which the strikes have occurred, it does not matter. Even if they have only a section of the workers behind them, the moral influence of the effort at an understanding must always be of great value.

"I should like to take this opportunity urgently to recommend to all concerned that, in the future, the mining companies and their officials should always keep as closely as possible in touch with the workers, to avoid the recurrence of such movements as this. For it is impossible that the strike can have developed entirely without preparation. I should like to ask you to take care that the opportunity is given to the workers to formulate their desires, and, above all, always to keep in mind that those companies which give work to a great section of My subjects and take them into their employ, are also responsible to the State and the communities concerned to do their best to watch over the welfare of their workers, and above all else to prevent the population of a whole province from again being involved in such troubles. It is only human and natural that everyone should try to secure for himself the best attainable conditions of subsistence. The workers read the newspapers and know the relation of the wages paid to the profits of the companies. It is understandable that they should desire to have more or less share in them. Accordingly I should like to ask you gentlemen on every occasion to examine the state of affairs with the greatest care, and as far as possible, to try and prevent such things from happening in the future. I can only urge you to try to bring a satisfactory ending as soon as possible out of the first step which the chairman of your association successfully accomplished yesterday."

Neither of the delegations left the palace satisfied. To both Emperor William had expressed his desire for an understanding, his will to promote it, and the power that lay behind his will. But neither of the contending groups was able to maintain that the Kaiser had taken its side—which was what they had come to him for. He had demanded of the miners respect for the law and the observance of their legal obligations. He had reminded the owners of the unwritten law of humanity and fair dealing. The two sides had to return to their negotiations. At last an agreement was reached. The strike came to an end at the beginning of June, and everywhere the excitement subsided.

But the affair was not over for the Kaiser. He began to study the comprehensive reports on the movement for which he had called, from all the strike centres. This stoppage, which had brought the State an entirely new anxiety

and had aroused and startled the whole world, had laid
bare to him a whole problem. He began to discuss it with
the Chancellor.

To his surprise Prince Bismarck proved to have a totally
different view of the problem from his own. He knew that
the Chancellor saw in the Social Democracy a mortal enemy
of the State, that no harshness was too harsh in his view
in striking down its hated members. The Kaiser's views of
Social Democracy differed little from those of the Chancellor. But in spite of this there was a great divergence
between the points of view of the two; for in the Kaiser's
view the movement in the mining areas that had just been
stilled had had nothing to do with Social Democratic
designs or ideals. The Chancellor, however, could see no
difference between Social Democrats and workers. He was
quite prepared to admit that Socialist, Worker and Anarch-
ist were not always the same thing; but he saw them all as
rebels. The Kaiser, on the contrary, spoke only of workers
and saw only workers, entirely dissociated from politics,
which he believed had had no part in the stoppage. A mass
movement was only of political importance and a menace
if the masses were kept in a prolonged ferment, and if, in
the struggle for bread and advancement, new slogans and
new ambitions entirely foreign to them were introduced
from without. The Chancellor was instinctively on the side
of the mineowners and against all strikes and strikers; in
this he was merely continuing his old struggle against the
Social Democracy. The Kaiser maintained, however, that
the miners had not in the least gone over to the Social
Democrats; and it was precisely that that he wanted to
prevent. He did not want their demands for bread and for
the right to live, which he regarded as natural, to lead them
on into the broad current of political programmes and

activities. As yet the men on strike had been only loosely organized. They were not yet under the direction of associations or of trade union resolutions. As yet each man was guided by his actual personal needs. In his kingdom the Kaiser saw none but subjects and citizens with equal rights: such was the tradition, and even the advocates of a manly pride in front of the thrones of Kings had never made the slightest demur to it. For his subjects he was bound to take thought with just impartiality. He had to provide for all of them conditions of life which would attach them to their country. It was for that that he had been installed by God in his dominion, and for that that he was responsible as Monarch and servant to the State. The workers were suffering, suffering acutely. They were living in homes that were no homes. They worked in factories and workshops amid vapours and gases which gnawed at their flesh; they worked dangerously in the bowels of the earth, far from the light of day, with menaced lungs and hardly time enough to clear the coal dust out of them when they were allowed to see the sun again. All of them were doomed to a precarious old age if they attained it at all: when their strength gave out they were cast into the gutter. No one took thought of their future if they were victims of a mischance: they were sent packing to endure want and anxiety through the remainder of their life; their compensation scarcely sufficed for a crust of bread. When they thought of their conditions of life they would not blame only the mine-owners who extracted from their labour the profits that paid for splendid town and country houses; they would ultimately criticize a State which delivered over a great part of its population to such a fate as they endured.

The Kaiser thought of his old tutor Hinzpeter. He had

Professor
Georg Ernst Hinzpeter

H.I.M. reviewing Bavarian
troops near Nürnberg, to H.I.M.
right Prince Regent Luitpold of
Bavaria. H.I.M. is wearing the
the uniform of the Bavarian
Lancers of whom he is Colonel-
in-Chief

been a dry pedant. In his cast-iron pedagogy he had
stamped down and destroyed pretty well all of the qualities
that he should have trained and tended into healthy growth
and full fruition. His ideas of the duties of Monarchs to
humanity had merely been spun from his brain, instead of
his heart and his daily practice. He had instilled them with
the same ruthlessness with which he had had the young
Prince taught riding. For all that, it was plain now that
he must be credited with one good service: the Kaiser knew
his subject and could trace the process from cause to effect.
He saw once more in spirit the workers' dwellings, into the
gloom of which the tutor had made him penetrate in the
past. He saw their narrowness and wretchedness. There
rose before him the factories, and the tenements for the serfs
on the farms, through which he had wandered as a child.
There was no need for him to read propaganda pamphlets
in order to know perfectly well that the employers continually exploited the workers in every possible way, and
continued the process until the time came when they were
no longer serviceable and were cast out. He had seen all
that with his own eyes, had learnt while still a Prince how
callous injustice reigned supreme. If the mineowners and
industrialists took from the workers their strength and the
service of their whole lives, it was their bounden duty, as
the stronger, to provide for the workers the means of living,
protection from danger, compensation for accidents, and
health and joy in normal life. Such obvious truths had
nothing to do with politics. It was only the inhuman denial
of these things, robbing the workers of their heritage, that
drove them into radicalism and hostility to the State. He
wanted to see workers' settlements, workers' schools and hos-
pitals and holiday homes. He wanted to see workers develop

into citizens. Their children should know what laughter was, like other children—except young Princes like himself.

All this he put to the Chancellor. But to the Chancellor it was all *schwärmerei*—sentimental moonshine. The Chancellor had no room for humanity in his policy. He would not even admit morality. In a well-ordered State no one had any right to be dissatisfied, at any time, under any circumstances, even if he were a sufferer. Decisions in the State were always dependent on power alone, and those who were not prevented from trying to attain power would attain it in the end. He did not at all agree that the strike had been simply an outcome of hunger. During its course the Kaiser had sent Professor Hinzpeter into the strike area. The Professor had returned with the news that conditions were worse than they had ever been. The Chancellor listened to the Professor unmoved. The workers might be starving, but for the Chancellor the main point was that he believed they had been got at by agitators. The Kaiser was for saving the good seed; the Chancellor was for rooting up the whole. The Kaiser talked of workers; the Chancellor of defeating the Social Democrats. For that matter, the Chancellor had not been dismayed at the extent of the strike; he would much rather have had the whole country in the grip of an open Social Democratic rising. The Revolution of 1848 had been met with firing, but the firing had not been thorough enough. The Chancellor wanted to see a universal, open, mutinous rising of the Social Democrats. Then what had been omitted in 1848 would be made good in 1889, so thoroughly that thereafter shooting could be dispensed with for all time.

The Kaiser was horrified. "I am entering on my reign," he said, "after a long period of peace. There has been no trouble since 1848. All has been quiet, all has gone well and peacefully. Am I now to begin to have men shot down in the streets of Berlin? Do you realize, your Highness, what that means?"

The Chancellor was unaffected by the Kaiser's agitation. "I accept full responsibility," he said.

The Kaiser saw that he was face to face once more with the old generation—Bismarck still belonged to it. Emperor William had the urge of youth, of the thirties, to make the world a better place. The Chancellor had the contempt for humanity that comes with age.

But the Chancellor saw no great urgency in the question at the moment. The Socialist law expired in 1890 and would without doubt be re-enacted. Now that the country was quiet again, there was no pressing need for discussing with the young Kaiser problems which he saw mainly in a romantic light. The Chancellor went back to Friedrichsruh. He began to prepare for permanent residence there. State papers were sent there to him. In the capital he was represented by his son, the Secretary of State. The Kaiser continued his study of the reports on the strike. The country might be quiet again, but his own peace of mind was gone.

All the reports confirmed that the strike had had nothing to do with any political undercurrents. All the evidence and statistics they produced merely showed the exploitation of the workers by the industrialists. It was impossible to let the Chancellor go on ignoring it all at Friedrichsruh. Bismarck was so great, his intelligence so keen in face of all problems of actuality, that the Kaiser hoped to bring him round to his own view. On one occasion when he had been in the Chancellor's house, the Chancellor had him-

self introduced to him the Vice-President of the Prussian
Ministry of State, Bismarck's loyal colleague, von Bötticher.
He had described him to the Kaiser as his best representative, and later he had frequently and of set purpose invited
this trusted colleague when he was expecting the Kaiser to
dinner. The Chancellor had been anxious that the Kaiser
should not overlook or underrate the Vice-president. The
Monarch had frequently met von Bötticher on various subsequent occasions, even on hunting expeditions. He determined to send this closest colleague of the Chancellor's to
him to convey certain suggestions. He felt that the Chancellor must at all costs be won for a scheme of social reform,
that the condition of the workers in Germany had got to
be improved. He would get the Minister of State to use
his influence with Bismarck.

"After that the Prince must put proposals before me,"
declared the Kaiser. He was surprised at the Minister's
reply:

"Ach! He never does that! I have so often tried to
get him to, and in this case too I have told him something
must absolutely be done on these reports. But he rejects
every suggestion! 'Guns and rifles are enough.' I will
gladly take your Majesty's suggestions to Bismarck at
Friedrichsruh. But it won't be of the slightest use. He will
fly into a rage, call your Majesty a dreamer and me an
intriguer and fomenter of opposition—and will reject the
suggestion. Nothing will come of it. He simply will not
do anything, and no one can do anything with him!"

It was news to the Kaiser that Bismarck could "fly into
a rage." He had to admit that he had always been able to
discuss anything with the Chancellor in the friendliest possible way; the Chancellor had always done his best to settle

all questions in entire agreement with him. Considering that he had to all appearances taken pains to do this, it might perhaps be well if von Bötticher were to go definitely in his, the Kaiser's name. He asked him:

"But suppose the suggestion, or the invitation, comes definitely from me, the King, surely he must enter into it!"

He formally commanded the Minister to visit the Chancellor at Friedrichsruh. His envoy came back surprisingly soon. He had been received by the Chancellor exactly as he had expected and predicted. Prince Bismarck had no suggestions to put before the Kaiser.

The Chancellor only rarely referred to the subject in conversation, and then only in passing, when he was actually staying in the capital. The best solution he could offer was the introduction of twelve months' compulsory service in the mines. The Empire could only gain greatly by this— "An army corps of colliers."

An unbridgeable gulf divided the views of life of the Kaiser and the Chancellor. To each of them it was beyond all comprehension how the other could see the world as he did. The Chancellor blamed the new times for the Kaiser's ideas. The Kaiser was distressed at the old man's attitude. The Kaiser was concerned for the workers. The Chancellor was concerned with the Social Democrats.

CHAPTER VII

THE YOUNG MASTER

THE personality of Emperor William II was many-hued. No one could have recognized the Prince from the moment when he came to the helm. Until then he had usually been silent in the presence of parents and friends, Chancellor and courtiers; at times he would seem to be getting restive, even rebellious; then he would bury himself once more in his work and duties, fanatically engrossed in his soldier's life. As a Prince he had been restricted in his movements and shut out of life; he became life itself when he came to the throne. He was determined to make up for lost time, to conquer every field instantly in enhancement of his new-won glories. The seclusion of the Potsdam days gave place to bustling activity and excitement.

The new Kaiser entertained to the limit of his capacity, though he did not receive everyone whom he should have done; on one occasion when an Ambassador from a foreign Power was passing through Berlin the Kaiser, in defiance of all tradition, refused to see him, protesting that he was too much occupied elsewhere. Sometimes he would announce his intention to visit a subject whom he desired to honour, and then some military call would seem to him of more importance, and he would suddenly cancel the visit at the last moment, although his host had had his *schloss* entirely renovated in honour of the Monarch. His decisions seemed insufficiently considered; often he would give an order only to rescind it the next moment. In most cases his visits took his hosts by surprise, giving them insufficient time to get ready for him. Often he produced the very opposite impression to that which had been anticipated; those who approached him in fear went away surprised and captivated by his graciousness. The city fathers came from the capital to thank him for the gift of a fountain; he received them coldly, ungraciously, and with unconcealed displeasure, in resentment over things which had appeared in the radical papers of the city concerning the affairs of the Imperial Family, and for which he had mistakenly credited his visitors with responsibility. On the occasions when he appeared among his officers, they felt the honor of the supreme commander in their midst and stood stiffly at attention before the Kaiser. But he had come as a comrade and wanted to join even in their frivolities.

He was impetuous at all times, and loved to speak his mind unreservedly. In his intimate circle he trusted all and threw caution to the winds. On board his yacht *Hohenzollern* he liked to collect his guests round him in the evening and to talk freely to them on a hundred subjects. He liked jolliness, even noise. Then the Kaiser would seem to have forgotten his Kaiserdom. He was Monarch only when he was inspecting troops, when he was surrounded by business of state, by Ministers and Generals, when he had questions to settle and issues to decide. In the evening on board the *Hohenzollern,* or on similar occasions, he was a young man of thirty among comrades. He felt himself to be their host, and wanted to have them all around him; he told stories that lacked nothing in broadness. But he steadily avoided the erotic, and could not endure the slightest allusion in that direction. If anyone approached it he cut him short and himself began again to pass on to his guests everything he could think of. Yet, a little later, he would be surprised to find that his words had travelled. He assumed that everyone in his circle was reliable and all his Generals discreet. But even the Generals told what they had heard from the young Kaiser:

"Today the Kaiser said—"

"Yesterday the Kaiser said—"

These stray dicta, distorted and given an interpretation which had not been intended, did harm or at least caused unpleasantness. A shocked Catholic priest reported to a Bavarian General one of these carelessly dropped phrases— it showed the Kaiser's hostility to all Catholics:

"The Catholics are the purest pagans! They pray to their Saints!"

Things said in joke failed to be understood as jokes and were repeated in all seriousness. Even Generals Commanding infringed the rule of secrecy, which had not been definitely impressed on them but had been assumed by the Kaiser to need no impressing. Prince Luitpold of Bavaria enquired one day in amazement of his Berlin Legation how it was that confidential matters had become public property the day after they had been under discussion, and even before he himself had knowledge of them. The Kaiser had no idea that they were being retailed. He had merely had a free and easy evening.

"I have occasion every day," Dr. Leuthold, of the General Staff, physician in ordinary to the Monarch, said to Count Széchényi, the Austro-Hungarian Ambassador, "to talk to Emperor William II, and I have a high admiration for his qualities of mind and heart. But he was too long at Potsdam, and knows too little of the world, and he judges everything from the point of view of the ex-Colonel of Hussars. I am very much afraid that my most gracious master may have to endure many a disappointment and many a bitter experience before he attains an unwarped and a ripened judgment. In personal intercourse, too, the Kaiser has not yet got adjusted to his new position. On board, for instance, there would be any amount of freedom, especially in the evening, and next day it would be no end of a business to recover our bearings."

Next evening, however, the Kaiser would be talking away with the same lightheartedness. He was content if everyone around him was having a good time, if all were shaking with laughter, and if he could be the provider of real entertainment. Almost always he did all the talking. Gradually he noticed it less and less. No one ventured to interrupt him. When he was in high spirits the roars of laughter developed into a dutiful chorus. Rarely did some particularly courageous guest venture to begin a story himself. No one would ever start a subject whether Minister or General or young Lieutenant.

When he went out driving or riding, the population acclaimed him. Huzzas came from every street. There were always curious observers loitering about the palace. Even the old Kaiser had only occasionally been greeted aloud, only on quite special occasions, indeed, when he showed himself in the city streets. The Ambassadors from abroad, and all who saw importance or occasion for irritation in it, attributed the manifest popularity of William II to the appeal of his youth and liveliness. Anyone who had to do with him officially or in virtue of his social position would be utterly puzzled about the Kaiser. He would

often express his dissatisfaction like a scolding comman-
dant; yet he could be of consummate courtierliness. In the
middle of a word he could turn his back on the person
whom he was addressing, and yet he could smooth away
awkward incidents with a delicacy and good judgment
which no one expected from him in so high a degree and
many failed to understand. Ruthlessness would alternate
with the finest tact. The Kaiser was indeed a man of moods.
Among officials and statesmen he produced uneasiness. In
his determination to rejuvenate the corps of officers he was
often unjust. Sometimes he would deliberately do the opposite of what was expected of him merely because he saw
that it was expected, even though it might be justly due
from him. But amid all his moods, all his errors of exuberance and manifold weaknesses, he was at bottom unchang-
ingly filled with good will and the desire to be of service.

The notable thing about the Kaiser was that in spite of
all the misdeeds laid to his charge he charmed everyone who
really got to know him. Court society sighed over his tactlessness, and everyone complained of it—the way he would
carry his jokes to excess, would pat a fat General on the
belly, meaning no harm, would laugh at a nose of grotesque
length, would fire up and shout in the face of an alarmed
subject, would scold in unbridled language, his eyes blaz-
ing, and his clenched fist menacing his speechless victim;
and yet, in spite of these truly unpleasant manifestations,
he won over all who came into close contact with him and
had any serious conversation with him. It was entirely
owing to his personality that the slight clouding of the relations between England and Germany over the Empress
Frederick and subsequently over Bismarck's correspondence with Lord Salisbury gradually passed away after his

first visit to Osborne. His liveliness, his spirit and youthfulness captivated everyone when he chose that they should, as he did almost always. He won the affection of many besides old Queen Victoria. She found him sensible, pleasant, and ready to discuss anything. If she wanted his advice or opinion she would generally, after the days at Osborne, send privately to him little notes asking him to tell her what he thought. But he talked to many others besides the Queen, besides Emperors and Princes and Cardinals, and he impressed everyone; in all grades of society every individual he met, no matter how independent in spirit, felt his influence. Scholars and men of letters noted with the greatest respect his quick intelligence, his daring logic. His very glance was arresting. On Theodor Herzl, a keen spirit, trained in critical observation, he made in Constantinople a strong and vivid impression:

"When the Kaiser came in, he looked searchingly at me with his big sea-blue eyes. He has really an Emperor's eyes. I have never seen such eyes. In them there lies a notable, courageous, seeking soul."

But the Emperor William had more than a single soul. His was a character with many offshoots from its fundamentally complicated nature; and many currents played across it. Within him there lived not only the soul of a Kaiser but many others, with strong individualities of their own, that wrestled with their master.

The Kaiser's features were marked with mysticism and romanticism, but the realist in him kept pace with the idealist. He was keenly interested in the symbolism of prehistoric peoples, as yet only partially interpreted by science, and sought in it imagery representing birth and passing and rebirth through all eternity. The nature of freemasonry,

the mysterious, subterranean forces of its lodges, which in
his view were forces of destruction, gave him no peace.
He was fascinated by Richard Wagner's magic world of
the grail, which yielded him models of knights and heroes,
symbols of all the virtues. In this he was like most of his
contemporaries, who took all their ideas from Wagner,
loyalty as the heritage of the Nibelungen, retribution from
Hagen, and their whole ethical system from Valhalla. He
had caught the infection of the magnificent bombast of
Bayreuth. Like so many others, he too was affected and
influenced by Wagner's resplendent leit-motifs, his sense of
the decorative in exalted passions, more than life-size characters, supernatural powers, the atmosphere of incense hanging over every scene, Lohengrin's glistening armour and the
glory of Siegfried's sword; all these heightened the colours
of life for him, gratified the sense of romance and the desire
for the scenic and picturesque, so that he seemed himself
to be on the stage among the bright footlights. His ready
response to all mysticism naturally brought the mystics and
transcendentalists swarming round him. Count Philipp
Eulenburg, who quickly became intimate with the Kaiser,
told him of the many spiritualistic marvels and apparitions
that he had witnessed, hoping to secure him as a fellow-
esoteric. He had met him as Prince William in Reichen-
hall; the Count was then Secretary of Legation in Munich.
Every word and every gesture of the Count's betrayed
the *grand seigneur,* the Brandenburg notable. He became
a close intimate of the Kaiser's. Count Eulenburg wrote
verses and set them to music, and sang them with genuine
artistic feeling. He could convey the charm of old
ballads. He had stories to tell of far countries, and could
make the landscape stand out in vivid colours before his

Meet of the Royal Boar hounds, S.
Huberts day. Count Dohna-Schlobitten
the Master behind him H.I.M. on
the Emperor's right Count Wedel,
Master of the Horse;

H. F. M. and the Vize-Ober-Jägermeister
Baron von Heintze, Boar drive.

audience. He knew a good deal about the history of art. Of men and politics he spoke wittily and always in a mild spirit of compromise and toleration. Long as he had been in the circle of the Prince and Kaiser, he had never asked any favour. He was eloquently persuasive in all that he told the Kaiser, but he was careful never to go beyond the bounds of prudence. Hitherto Emperor William had been surrounded only by officers; his new companion was of a fundamentally different type. It might very well have been that the transcendentalism of the Count would infect the mystic in the Kaiser. But the Kaiser merely asked:

"Well, what have your mediums told you?"

Count Eulenburg wore a mysterious, almost unearthly smile when he spoke of his experiences.

"Amazing landscapes! Women in gorgeous raiment! Flowers, a wealth of flowers!"

Drily the Kaiser rejoined:

"All that we have on this earth! I don't need mediums and spiritualistic wrestlings for that. I can arrange all that myself. There's nothing supernatural in it."

He put no faith in the Count's marvels. He was a faithful adherent of Christianity, and the doctrines of the spiritualist Du Prel, then the height of fashion and in the Count's eyes a man inspired, failed to fit in with his faith. His mysticism and romanticism were often abruptly dissolved in the light of his realism, and not only in these talks with Count Eulenburg. No idealism, no mysticism could prevent him seeing the things of this world in their true light. He had been accustomed from his army days to root about among a hundred bales of leather and examine them, when new saddles had to be made. He was a keen disputant over leather prices and qualities with makers or dealers.

One had to talk with artisans and shopkeepers in their own language if one was to understand what they wanted or were concerned about.

He was always turning out different from what was expected of him. The supreme commander would unexpectedly give place to the business man. The Kaiser would suddenly become archæologist, or embark on the higher criticism, or begin to discuss torpedo making. He had worked on every subject at some time or other, and an unexampled memory would bring up, as though he had but to press a lever, something heard or read years before. Then it might happen that his knowledge suddenly reached its limit. He had wearied of the subject, or it had reminded him of the Hinzpeter days, or the very method of study imposed by the Professor had prevented him from pursuing it with thoroughness. Often he noticed the gaps in his knowledge himself. They brought him discomfort. He was King of Prussia and had to confess to himself that he knew nothing of the history of his house save a few stories told to him by his father or Hinzpeter; he had a fair knowledge of the history of Germany only as far as the Peace of Cambrai. He knew little of the Reformation period, or the Thirty Years' War; neither his tutor, Hinzpeter, nor the master at Cassel Gymnasium had ever spoken to him of these subjects. Now he began to browse in books. Adjutant General von Wittich, an authority on military history, was commissioned to tell him between audiences and the reception of Ministers the history of Napoleon's campaigns. The General entered upon his duties; he found an eager and earnest pupil.

The young Kaiser always seemed to have six or seven personalities within himself, and still more expertises. Each of the seven had its own separate existence. No one could say in advance which of them was going to emerge. When he spoke he carefully calculated the effect of what he meant to say, and with good judgment. In point of fact he was an orator of rare and perilous effectiveness. He was always in earnest about the orator's subject. He had an immediate command of eloquent language; he scarcely ever prepared a speech. Sentences which flew round the world, impressing or scandalizing, were born of the second and irrevocably fixed in it.

His whole manner was strongly tinged with the rhetorical. But for all his incontestable love of theatrical gestures, he was not merely playing a part with his various personalities: he actually lived them. Queen Victoria had made him an Admiral of the Fleet. He saw more than the uniform; his inborn imaginativeness invested it with a significance to which he desired to give practical effect. He felt himself brought closer to England. A few months after the visit to Osborne he went to Greece, and while there he paid a visit to the British Mediterranean Fleet anchored off Salamis. When the ship on which he was calling hoisted the Admiral's flag in his honour, he took it for something more than a mere courtesy on the part of the British Admiral. This foreign Senior Officer opened his heart to him. The Mediterranean Fleet, he said, was going to the bad. It would soon be no longer a match for the French fleet—simply through neglect. It was, of course, a strange thing for a commander to be enlisting the aid of a foreign ruler in this way, asking the Kaiser to speak for him in England. It was naturally a strange thing for the foreign ruler to do so. It was equally natural that Lord Salisbury should reply that Admirals are always anxious to get more ships. But in the whole incident the Kaiser's one feeling had been that he was an Admiral in the British navy. His honorary rank was a reality to him and he was keen to fulfil its duties; that was why he had put in a word for this foreign fleet.

There were many native characteristics, many instinctive ideals and aspirations at work in competition with one another in Emperor William. All of them bowed before one symbol—that of the Monarch. This subordination marked a fundamental duality in his personality.

He made a sharp distinction between the person and the mission. He subordinated himself to the Kaiser in him, who had received his powers and duties and responsibilities by the grace of God. He saw the Monarch that he was as a power isolated from his everyday existence, a second, disembodied ego, eminent, remote, exalted by the will of God. This power must, he felt, represent for himself the same grave symbol that it should for all others in the State and in history. He was a living, breathing human being like the rest; working in many moods and in many different fields. But his discussions and examinations of public business, his decisions and commands, he must carry through simply as Kaiser. The Monarch was inviolate, he stood above party, above his people; his interests were not earthly interests. If he signed a dispatch, if he summoned Ministers or assembled his Generals, if he visited foreign rulers, it was not a mother's son who performed these duties, not a son of earth moved by passions and desires like the rest— he signed as Kaiser, commanded and acted as God's Chancellor. He might have many desires, but the Kaiser must approve of them. The Monarch's veto was for him the supreme ruling, and frequently it was laid on himself—in spite of his suppressed youth, perhaps because of it, for he had never been allowed to show what he could do; his gifts

Ivory bust of H.M. Queen
Victoria
Confirmation gift to her grand-
son William September 1874

Kaiser-Manoeuvres in Bavaria,
next to H.I.M. aide-de-Camp
Col: von Lippe, Majors von Moltke
(later Chief of the Staff) & Count
Hülsen (later Chief of H.I.M.
military Office)

had not been cultivated to ripeness. But "The Kaiser" was for all that something more than a Prince of no matter how great ability or how attractive qualities, even a Prince of genius. He had to be regarded differently from other men, not for his own sake but because the Kaiser was the synthesis, the mouthpiece and the symbol of a great people, because tradition had imposed this high office on him as his destined, God-sent burden. The thing before which all men bowed was the exalted task to which he was called and the duties it laid on a single man chosen out of many millions. "His Majesty"—the mission conferred was implicit in the phrase. It was independent of personal, human considerations. Prince William's relations with Emperor Frederick III had not been very happy; he himself had been very unhappy. But this had had nothing to do with his reverence for the ruler. His father, he had told himself, was Kaiser. The Prince's duty had been to accept every injury and every humiliation. Before "His Majesty" he had bowed dumbly.

In his own private thoughts William II separated his individual existence from his mission even more stringently than in public. He spoke of himself in the third person, and in talking of his plans and decisions he achieved the feat of endowing the Kaiser with the quality of a personality supreme over and separated from all human beings, even himself. He spoke of himself as an officer speaks of the Commander in Chief, with the reverence with which the priests in the Vatican bow when His Holiness is carried past. If he dispatched a note, he wrote on its envelope "From His Majesty." If the knowledge of this mystic dualization reached those nearest to him, if it spread to the Court and to many outside, heads might be shaken over it. It was less easy for the Kaiser to explain this psychological

duality, which he felt with all the force of religious conviction, than for the observer to smile at it. The Kaiser's
intelligence was not so narrow that he could not realize
that he ran the risk of looking ridiculous. But in his concern with the ethical proposition which he wanted to define
and crystallize in this excarnation of the Monarch, this
raising of the Monarch's personality out of his own, he
inverted the common phrase and held that it is only a step
from the ridiculous to the sublime. Before every act of
state, every signature, his desire was to be reminded that in
his exercise of the Imperial office he was carrying out imper-
sonal functions. He told himself that as Kaiser he was
bearer of a high office to which he owed respect in every
moment of ruling. Intervals of failure did not upset the
principle for which he had to strive. He was not only
Kaiser: he was also human. Disobedience was rarely a serious matter, humanly speaking; but if a command of the
Kaiser's had not been complied with, His Majesty called
for an explanation and administered correction, or granted
pardon. It was almost as though when the Kaiser—he himself, that is—came into his presence he quite seriously made
invisible obeisance to him. He did so without irony; quite
coolly and as a matter of course; the German Kaiser was,
in point of fact, the divinely appointed protector of fifty
million Germans, the royal successor of a race of Kings,
and so truly a Majesty. Yet the deep conflict, carried on
through a thousand years of history and now repeated in
him, between the material and the religious call in one and
the same being brought him pain and unrest. What the
others laughed at was to him a duty before God. It was
nothing to him that, for that matter, other people laughed
at religion.

The religious element was not the only one in his atti-

tude toward this conception of Kaiserdom. The division
between Monarch and man gave room for an observer. He
listened to himself, kept watch on the Kaiser. He shoul-
dered the responsibility for the holder of that high office,
who himself bore the supreme responsibility before the final
Judge.

The world around him, however, saw in this Majesty
only the power which decided the affairs of the State. The
Kaiser raised men up and cast them down. Where he
entered, men were consumed with awe. The Empress spoke
of him and conversed with him in low, deadened tones.
She, too, unreservedly recognized this Majesty, regarding
any opposition to it, any criticism as indecent and unlawful.
The Generals and courtiers did not venture to open their
mouths to express an opinion to the Kaiser; or, if they did
find a word to say, it descended to unexampled flattery.
Often the Kaiser listened to the national hymn—not so
often as to render it meaningless to him. At times he turned
away with unconcealed disgust. Yet the world around him
took him for a lover of Byzantinism if he allowed a courtier
to kneel, a megalomaniac if he even kept him standing. In
his Court he sought for personalities; he found only servants, who gossiped when they left the presence. At his
festivities and banquets—arranged by Count Eulenburg as
Marshal with rare taste, a taste until then unknown at the
Prussian Court,—they sat dazzled. They were his guests,
they drank his champagne (which he himself took only
very moderately). But they were no sooner descending the
steps of his palace than they began to make mock of his
style and the well-spaced little tables, with their harmonious flickering lights. Wherever he went he saw nothing
but backs bent in obeisance. All the world bowed or curt-
seyed. He was bound soon to remark how all these people,

who had scarcely known him from Adam when he was
Prince William, began to stammer as soon as he spoke to
them as Kaiser; how envoys whom he received lost the
thread of their speeches and in their confusion called him
Excellency. It was indeed remarkable if in the end he did
not imagine himself a demigod.

Yet he of all men wanted to meet real human beings
and real intelligences; for with his own perpetual intellectual tenseness he needed unceasing stimulation. He listened to every objection and every criticism—provided that
it was made personally and in private to him, and with the
respect that was due to Majesty. Among men of intellectual
eminence he was still of significance. He travelled not only
for political purposes and for love of the picturesque and
exotic, but also because he wanted to meet men and minds,
for instance Gladstone (whom he met in Venice—he had
talked of Greece and Homer), or Disraeli or Crispi. At
home he met none, not even a Rampolla, at best an Eulenburg or a Waldersee.

His quick perceptions brought him with lightning rapidity to the heart of his subject. Whatever it was, he leaped
past the obvious, leaving his interlocutor behind. So in the
end he spoke out his thoughts alone, in a long monologue,
which his Generals and Chamberlains and even polished
diplomats, full of the dust of immemorial perruques that
filled their files of documents, failed to understand. They
did not realize that these were really big, intelligent, creative suggestions, and that this fact was in no way modified
by caprices and roughnesses born of the mood of the
moment. He had, indeed, much in him of the young Roi
Soleil, the love of magnificence, the sparkling, ready wit,
the will to power, the self-confidence and the tendency to

autocracy. But he had neither a Richelieu nor a Mazarin at his side. No one straightened himself, no one stood up to show the impetuous young man the way that might lead him to clear and ripened thinking and even perhaps greatness. Only one had the intelligence and the wide knowledge, the wisdom born of experience, the high qualities that might have been applied to forming the Kaiser's great gifts—the Chancellor, Prince Bismarck.

"One of the most noteworthy and interesting features which at the present time come to the notice of the observer is the great and far-seeing prudence of the Imperial Chancellor in his approach to the Emperor. As long ago as the month of December in the year that last elapsed I was able to realize how much Prince Bismarck had made it his duty to introduce a *great deal* of reserve into his relations with his Monarch, and to avoid everything that might be calculated to make perceptible to the Emperor the pressure of his individuality, grown over-powerful by virtue of his natural gifts, of a rare measure of good fortune, and of events that have made world history. In Bismarck's house the watchword was passed, 'The principal thing is that the young Emperor should learn to stand on his own feet, and to conduct his life as ruler independently and uninfluenced.' This formula, which was perhaps given expression in a rather demonstrative way, was at least to the extent of one-half nothing other than the euphemistic paraphrasing of another, which might run as follows: 'The new Emperor is so strong and self-confident an individuality that he would be unable to have patience with the uninterrupted exertion of pressure by anyone—and least of all by the Imperial Chancellor.' If this self-restraint of the most powerful of German statesmen became plainly apparent as early as the close of the past year, the history of the political development which has since set in shows with certainty that the Imperial Chancellor is not only carefully maintaining the restriction of his own initiative as a necessary element in any fruitful collaboration with his Imperial master, but is increasing and intensifying it."

So wrote Count Wolkenstein, the Austro-Hungarian Ambassador, to Count Kálnoky from Petersburg. Count Széchényi confirmed his view:

"People are saying that the Chancellor has no longer been his former self for some time past. He used to be hard, immovable, implacable: now he is mild, gentle, considerate. There is no making him out. Formerly anyone associated with him could see the 'Why' of anything, but today, it is said, everything here is obscure and inexplicable as things are at present."

The Chancellor passed by the young Kaiser on the other side. And since he was unable or unwilling to try to influence him and bring out his good qualities, and train or trim his asymmetries, no one else could attempt the task. The Kaiser remained alone with his ambitions and his capacities and his weaknesses, and with his monologues, to him conveying constructive thought but to others mere prattle. The Chancellor continued indulgent. He was ageing: Count Waldersee was not the only one who had been noticing it for some time. The Chancellor did nothing to liberate the "young master" from the dross of youthful crudity. All that Bismarck still saw was the danger which might rob him of power and the machinery which might enable him to retain it. He was not living with thought for the future of the young Kaiser, whose ordered progress and advance could only have increased, not reduced his own prestige. He lived now between the past and the Foreign Ministry. The Chancellor was not merely "ageing"—he had grown old.

CHAPTER VIII

THE FOREIGN MINISTRY

EVERYTHING in the Foreign Ministry in Berlin, in the Wilhelmstrasse, rested on the unquestioned fiat of Prince Bismarck; his will, his every decision was law. It was he who had built the Empire. The statesmen of Europe had once been assembled around him, at the Berlin Congress. Nothing like that had happened before in Prussia. Everyone could see how greatly his opinion counted in the counsellings of the Powers. Everyone knew that the old Kaiser, for all that he had a strong will of his own, had always recognized in the end the Chancellor's better judgment, and that Emperor Frederick had never opposed it. For twenty years everyone in the Foreign Ministry had been used to serving Prince Bismarck as its supreme and absolute ruler.

The discipline was stern; the whole Ministry functioned as a single unit, ceaselessly at work. Its hierarchy had no existence for the Chancellor. The whole staff, from the *Vortragender Rat* to the Secretary of Legation and from the attaché to the youngest messenger boy, had to be uninterruptedly at their duties, and every member of the staff at call every hour of the day and night. No one was permitted to go out without leaving word where he was going. Every *Referent* and senior official must be accessible for recall at a few minutes' notice from theatre or function or wherever he might be spending the evening. No one was allowed to plead the excuse that personal affairs had put him out of reach. The Chancellor inspired and maintained among the whole staff the feeling that they were "in the firing line at all hours." Urgent affairs that were not settled within twenty-four hours did not exist. Urgent papers—they were called "Cito" papers—were transmitted in red portfolios. But for years it had been customary for every question to be dealt with "Cito," whether in a red portfolio or between the less clamant grey covers. No one felt that he was performing the duties of a bureaucracy. Everyone in the office knew or believed or imagined that he was making world history.

The Chancellor himself was almost invisible. He had the whole set of levers of his machine at his side, but he rarely touched a lever or pressed a button. He used to dictate until evening to one of the latest of the officials attached to him personally—these were now Rottenburg, the head of the Chancellor's office, Count Rantzau, and Bauer. He did not himself go to the Ministry; everything was sent to the Chancellor's official residence. In the evening the red portfolios journeyed to him, and next morning they were back at the Foreign Ministry. He had no personal contact with the departments of the Ministry: the Secretary of State, Count Herbert Bismarck, was the connecting link with them, and in this way the Chancellor shut himself off from his officials. Occasionally he would work on a particularly troublesome draft, which had not in his opinion been adequately put into shape, with the officials responsible for the drafting. They would then stand for hours around his table. They knew that the draft could be passed on for copying if the Chancellor had put on the MS. his initial "B." It was

rare for the Prince subsequently to send instructions for
an initialed paper to be stopped. When that happened it
was put away again, marked "Cessat." The papers were in
perfect order; the Chancellor quickly lost patience if any
paper was not forthcoming as soon as sent for. Every document was registered in and out. Yet it occasionally happened that a draft of the Chancellor's bore his initial and
was then due for despatch, that there was no note from the
Chancellor recalling it, and that the document nevertheless
failed to reach the addressee, though the staff could give no
explanation of the failure. There could be no doubt that
the Prince had reasons of his own for dealing with the paper
in this way, that he had himself diverted it of set purpose,
dealing with it himself and admitting none to his confidence.

Important and secret matters of state he dealt with
entirely with his son. Ambassadors' reports from all the
capitals of the world he minuted, on his own authority and
as he thought fit:

"Not to be put before the Kaiser."

"Not for the Kaiser."

"Revise for the Kaiser."

The drafting officials, the clerks who made the fair
copies, the officials in charge of archives, who ultimately put
away the Ambassadors' reports, and through whose hands
all documents passed, learned from those four words
who was master in the office in which they served, who
it was that guided Germany's destiny, who alone had
knowledge of all that was going on in Europe; who, moreover, determined their own advance or their submergence
among those with no future. They knew from them who
decided what they might say and what they had to bury

in silence. They did not know that Prince Bismarck had absolutely forbidden the old Kaiser to speak a word to Emperor Francis Joseph about the Reinsurance Treaty with Russia, but they saw with their own eyes that Emperor William II had no authority whatever in the Foreign Ministry.

The Secretary of State received all official reports. Count Herbert had breakfast every day with the Chancellor, took to the official residence any questions for which even the red portfolios were too slow a method of settlement, and brought Bismarck's reply to the office at noon. The reply finally and definitely settled the question: under Prince Bismarck's régime no other will than the Chancellor's had any conceivable existence. There was perfect orderliness and clarity at all times in the high political affairs of the Foreign Ministry, except when the Prince himself had them surrounded with impenetrable obscurity and a barrier of the strictest secrecy. Yet he was disappointed with important elements in his machinery. There were undercurrents affecting it which he could not trace to their origin, or traced in the wrong direction. From the Secretary of State downwards he saw only confidential officers "with their coat-tails under their arms," dropping them when the Chancellor called. He knew that he was in exclusive control of the machine. He did not know that a *Vortragender Rat,* Fritz von Holstein, was beginning to get the control so firmly into his hands that at the critical moment it might even become doubtful whether it was not von Holstein instead of Prince Bismarck who was really exercising it.

Years before, the Chancellor had set Baron Holstein on his career, and had smoothed the way for him. He did not penetrate to the depths of the Baron's nature, but divined enough to call him, with a vague sense of it, "the man with the hyaena's eyes—"

"Extremely useful as second or third in command, but dangerous at the top."

Prince Bismarck forgot to add that he had himself had some share in Baron Holstein's spiritual development, and that he himself, in the moment of opening the way for him to a splendid future, had broken his career. He had taken Holstein, then a young Secretary of Legation, with him to Versailles. During the war he had already assigned him to the general administrative organization in France. Since the war he had drawn him more and more into his own circle of confidants and entrusted him with confidential tasks. In the middle of the 'seventies the Chancellor was considering the removal of Count Harry von Arnim, the first German Ambassador in France after the war—the Count had had the hardihood to work against Bismarck's French policy and Baron Holstein was entrusted with the special mission of preparing the way for this. Emperor William I had refused to recall the Ambassador: he was well-disposed towards many members of the Count's widely branched family, and remembered with gratitude various services which ancestors of the Count's had rendered in the past. He demanded incontrovertible written evidence of the truth of the charges against the Count—that he was favouring Monarchist elements in France against the Chancellor's instructions, that he was closely in touch with them, and that instead of consolidating the existence of the new Republic where he could, as the Chancellor desired, he was actively assisting to undermine it.

"Bring me evidence!"

Prince Bismarck sent for Holstein. He chose him for the task of providing evidence for the Emperor. As Secretary of Legation he was to be attached to the German Embassy in Paris, and was there to collect information as to Count von Arnim's associates and activities. Baron Holstein did not fail to appreciate the nature of his mission:

"Your Highness, it smells of espionage."

If the Secretary of Legation was in want of a phrase, that one might fit his delicate task. But Prince Bismarck overcame his hesitation. He pointed out that there were two sides to the question, as always. The Ambassador was supposed to be pursuing a policy of his own in defiance of instructions, but it might be untrue. Up to now the Prince had had only vague indications of it, the feeling of it rather than any certainty. Thus what was needed was to procure evidence to refute the rumours that had reached him. That would be doing the Ambassador a positive service.

The Baron was in the presence of the powerful Prince Bismarck, in whose hands his future lay. He was, no doubt, doing the Chancellor an important service. Moreover, the Prince himself had disposed of his objections. Baron Holstein set out for Paris.

Arrived at the Embassy, he was unable to escape from the uncomfortable feeling that, in spite of the Chancellor's version of his task, it had its objectionable side. He preferred never to be seen in the Ambassador's palace to which he was attached. He worked at home. He had the papers he wanted sent there. And he obtained evidence which confirmed Prince Bismarck's suspicion. He enclosed with his reports to the Chancellor in Berlin copies of papers which incriminated Count von Arnim—and betrayed him. The Ambassador was recalled and transferred to Constantinople. Baron Holstein returned to Berlin.

Emperor William the Great
in his 85th year

Count Harry von Arnim

The service he had rendered was recognized by the Chancellor. But from the day of his return every acquaintance at his club cut him. He was just a spy: no one would shake hands with him. He returned a third and a fourth time to the club: there was no change. The many Counts von Arnim, their cousins, their friends were stronger than even Bismarck's efforts for his protégé. The spy was not only ostracised, he was quietly driven out of the club. He knew that he would have to fight a duel if he demanded reparation for an insult, and not one only, or two, or three: the whole club had its pistols ready. The Baron could not be accused of cowardice. He had cheerfully fought a duel under difficult conditions in Washington over a lady. His inclination towards gallantry, some sudden attachment that paid no heed to obstacles or rivals, had been liable at any time to land him in dangerous situations, but he had not been deterred by that. Here, however, there was not only a whole club up in arms against a traitor: the whole of society threatened to follow suit, spreading the scandal and driving him beyond the pale. Suddenly the truth broke upon him: the path of advancement might lie open in the Foreign Ministry; all other paths were closed to him.

He was fond of women. He forgot the world around him and almost forgot the proprieties when he was under a woman's influence. He had become a ladies' man in the middle of the fifties, carefully groomed, his beard exquisitely trimmed, his top hat faultless. He had come into contact with all the distinguished personalities in Europe, he knew them all, their peculiarities, their weaknesses. He described them with a ready malice, and took pleasure in doing so. He was a fluent and effective story teller, and full of wit. He was used to luxuries of all sorts and was a connoisseur in the choice of occasion for them. He was fond of *primeurs,* the first strawberries in April or the first asparagus. By nature he was a seeker after the good things in life. But now life had thrown him out of her great reception room into the anteroom. He went no more to the club, no more into society at all. He would not even order an evening dress suit from his tailor. He withdrew entirely, took a simple lodging, received no one, had no valet. An old woman looked after the needs of this ex-cavalier and hedonist. Two consolations only still held him to life: Prince Bismarck and the work in the Foreign Ministry.

When he became *Vortragender Rat* he had long been a solitary. Formerly he had travelled all over the world; since his ostracism he had gone no further for his holidays than to the mountains. There the gentleman in the dark suit turned into a pilgrim. He wandered about the woods and mountain villages, a man already half out of this life. But in his room at the Foreign Ministry a new world rose before him. Every draft and every document passed through the hands of the *Vortragender Rat:* Ambassadors' papers, consular reports, staff changes, questions to Ministers. He arrived early, and himself opened, read, and prepared for transmission or for putting away in his private files all despatches that had arrived by post or courier. He was fully acquainted with all the material, with every question, by the time his colleagues arrived at the office, hours later than he had done. No one could compete with him in capacity for work. The rooms and corridors of the Ministry sank again into darkness and dead silence, but the Baron still sat on at his table. At last he too went, at all hours of the night, but never before eleven.

Gradually he grew into the habit of replying at once to communications which he did not consider worth submitting. Gradually his personal dealings by way of letters and telegrams and interviews grew in extent until they amounted to universal supervision. If the Chancellor would not allow anyone but the Secretary of State to receive ceremonial visits at the Ministry, Baron Holstein would not allow anyone to see the Secretary without first being brought in to him. He brought all his seemingly unstudied charm, all his wit and vivacity into his room at the Ministry, the only bit of the living world that remained to him. Here he was no pilgrim come down from the mountains: he was the man of the world that he had dreamed of remaining always.

Count Bismarck's house was the only one that remained open to him. After the Paris trouble the Chancellor made a closer friend of him, feeling, perhaps almost remorsefully, that he owed him the satisfaction of the freedom of his house. But this did not save the Baron from the consequences of the affair. In every commission he saw dangers, in every proposal a trap, all the world was against him; he was determined in the future to be on his guard against everyone. Society had ostracised him as guilty of incorrect behaviour, but he had belonged to it and knew—no one better—that there were few members of Society who could not equally be charged with some incorrectness or other. The only difference was that people took no notice of it. In his office, shut off from the world but connected with it by countless threads from all the world over, the Baron began to compile a register. He had long known something about everybody, and with time he could learn something more. In the end he had a register of the homosexual, of divorcées; of debtors, gamblers, drinkers, sadists, habitués of the insolvency court. He could strike down whom he would with a single unexpected blow. If anyone had offended him, he could slake his thirst for revenge, if anyone failed to carry out his wishes to the letter he could break him. As time went on, he banked on his register, and made masterly play with its contents.

Every day brought him its offence, and in the course of his official duties everyone gave him offence sooner or later.

If he did not take breakfast at the office or with his land-lady in his flat he took it always in the same restaurant, one well known in the city and frequented by the gourmets of the period. Here too he was to be found only in a room hermetically sealed off, alone or with some colleague who had come into favour with him. It was a precarious favour: a smile which the Baron had not expected at the moment, which perhaps he had mistakenly imagined to have come, a word or a gesture that displeased him, would make a sudden end of it. He changed his favourites at moments when they had still no inkling of any change in his feeling towards them.

All who had anything to do with the Baron had long been used to peculiarities. He knew that Prince Radolin, the Ambassador, possessed the confidence of the old Em-peror and of Emperor Frederick, and that the young Prince William frequently met him. Prince Radolin was a statesman of weight, with powerful connexions, and dangerous through his position at Court. Baron Holstein was glad to talk on many things with him. There was no need for anyone to learn that he was doing so. He agreed with the Ambassador to meet secretly at midnight in the Zietenplatz in Berlin.

He suffered from imaginary persecution; it may be that it was a mania. If it was a mania, it did not prevent him from preserving irreproachably correct demeanour; nothing more was observable than a faint, ghostly shadow. On an evening in Prince Bismarck's house he might pay court to a society woman so ardently as almost to compromise her, until the Princess smilingly intervened. Next morning he might meet the charmer with no memory left of his avowals, might keep his hat on his head and go past without a word.

Two attendants in evening dress stood before his room to deal with visitors. The Baron's favourite had *le droit de la porte,* as he called the right of coming in unannounced at any time. There were always three or four of his colleagues in the Foreign Ministry to whom he granted this distinction. He liked especially to bring out from their obscurity young and gifted diplomats and secretaries. He would do much for them. If they had no means he would secretly supply them. He was the son of an officer with a moderate estate, and so had a small independence. Gradually he gave it away in benefactions. He said nothing about it. From time to time, if his gifts brought serious confusion into his own finances, he tried to make them good by small speculations on the Stock Exchange. There was not much to be hoped for from these, for he never allowed his banker to commit him to more than ten shares.

Alongside his register of dark points in the humanity around him he had one for the specially gifted. It might be that he would telegraph to some completely unprepared and unexpectant young diplomat on leave, to ask whether he wanted to go as Minister to Copenhagen or the Hague. The astonished recipient would imagine that some friend was playing a trick. He might have no acquaintance with Baron Holstein, might never have spoken to him. The explanation would be that the *Vortragender Rat* had read at some time a report sent in by the diplomat, and something in it had struck him; he had noted his name, and the day had come when, with no preparation of any sort, he had sent for him. The young man would then become the Baron's latest confidant. Before he began his duties in the unexpected post, the Baron would instruct him in the "five golden rules" of diplomacy. He must, especially, never forget this chief one of all:

"If anything goes wrong, take the blame on yourself.

"If anything is well done and succeeds, give the credit to the Foreign Ministry."

The young man thus raised up in a night would scarcely be seated at his desk before Baron Holstein sent again for him. Evidently he could not do without him. Now they would work next door to one another. Naturally the new favourite had *le droit de la porte*. The Baron would reveal to him his most secret plans, his whole technique of diplomacy, and all his recipes for efficiency and success. He would pour out to him all his misfortune—Bismarck's pressure, the painful time with Count Arnim, the ostracism, the whole story.

Then one day the two swallow-tailed attendants at the Baron's door would step in front of the favourite.

"The Herr Baron is not receiving today!"

"Ach so!" the young favourite would reply, "probably he is dictating."

"Perhaps. Perhaps the Herr Baron is dictating," the attendants would echo.

Later the Baron's confidant would come back.

"The Herr Baron will not receive you. We were not to say so at once. The Herr Baron will not see you."

And he would never see him again. Perhaps the two had been working two years alongside one another, separated only by a thin partition. Yet, at a moment's notice, the favourite would be cast out, with no notion whatever as to the reason; not even allowed to discover indirectly that he had fallen out of favour, but suddenly sent packing by two attendants in evening dress at the Baron's door.

The Baron had perhaps learned that his favourite had lunched twice in one week with Count Herbert Bismarck. Day after day the Baron had taken him to the hermetically sealed-off room in the famous old city restaurant, had fed him on the choicest of *primeurs* and engaged in long talks with him. He had been allowed to pay for the delicacies himself, even if he secretly regretted the extravagance, for his circumstances were not so narrow that the Baron needed to give him charitable aid. But the distinction had been a great and rare one for the young diplomat. Then the Baron had been seized with mistrust. The persecution mania returned. The Baron might nod to the young man thereafter, but would never again speak a word. The young Count Pourtalès came one day in this way, totally unexpectedly, to the same *droit de la porte,* and later to the same cool dismissal through the two men in evening dress——

"The Herr Geheimrat is not to be disturbed."

The Baron did not even, afterwards, nod to the Count.

Baron Holstein seemed to be on good terms with the Chancellor's son. They met daily. The Baron saw Count Herbert Bismarck in the evening in his father's house. The two addressed one another by their Christian names. Yet when the Austro-Hungarian Ambassador had a particular request to make of the Kaiser, Baron von Holstein recommended him to apply to the Chamberlain, von Liebenau, rather than officially to the Secretary of State. And, knowing that the Chamberlain was supposed to be in the confidence of the Chancellor and his son, in spite of his service in the Kaiser's immediate entourage, he advised the Ambassador to keep the whole matter from the Secretary's knowledge. His best course would be to rely in future entirely on the Chamberlain.

The Baron was intriguing, spinning a threefold net. The Chamberlain was not entirely straightforward with the Emperor. He went with the things he knew, or the secrets which he claimed to know, to the Chancellor and Count Herbert. What he learned from them he told Holstein. The Baron knew of all three what they themselves did not know. He brought them all together when he wished to do so. He kept them apart when this seemed preferable. Invisibly and unnoticed, he played all against all. Meanwhile he was doubtless on the search for a dark point in Chamberlain von Liebenau.

Thus, in reality he was not on a good footing with Count Herbert Bismarck; nor was he with the Count's mother, the Princess, though she showed him marked friendliness; nor with the Chancellor, to whom he owed his position. It was not only that he could not forget the Count von Arnim incident; the feeling that he had had of a certain social compensation for it in the close association with Prince Bismarck was gradually spoilt for him by the Chancellor's sons, Herbert and Bill. While they were young boys the two sons had been hearty and jolly and full of friendship, but as they grew up the Baron grew to be more and more in their eyes a mere chamberlain, no longer indispensable, whom they began to order about. They let him realize his different origin and power and standing, and at last they dropped all reserve, threw away the last respect for his superiority in age, and teased and tormented him. They

Holstein

Herbert Bismarck

tortured his sensitiveness with innuendos. When he was at work in Bismarck's house they would rush shouting into his room in the midst of his work, and begin shooting at a target with toy pistols. For a while the Baron made the best of it; then he began to stop coming to Bismarck's house, the last house open to him. He could not go so far as to stop the ordinary civil intercourse with the Prince; nor could he venture to do so with the Secretary of State. But he began to exclude him. He worked secretly at the opening up of paths to the sources of power, without the knowledge of the Secretary or the holders of supreme power. He had his intermediaries always ready. The day was bound to come when he could dispatch the formal letter which would clearly and coolly announce the end of his friendship with the Count. He worked on the letter, carefully choosing its terms.

The Chancellor underestimated the significance of Baron von Holstein. He was not only "dangerous at the top": the *Vortragender Rat* was dangerous at all times, whether he was negotiating or silent, whether he smiled or seemed out of humour; whether he was dealing with unimportant staff questions, or giving instructions to Ambassadors of which the Chancellor and the Secretary of State knew nothing, or "bottling" reports because that suited him best. The time had not come when his power was as great as his ambition. His longing was not yet quite fulfilled to be the sole arbiter of the fate of the Empire, and of that of Europe if this depended on Germany. He still had to move warily; he still had above him hated men who were more powerful than he. One opponent in particular was still there, too powerful an intelligence to be played with like the others without peril.

Slowly he gained control of the Chancellor's machinery. He turned it to his own purpose, made of it his own instrument. Prince Bismarck's day was nearly over. If the end was too long in coming, it might be hastened. At the next safe opportunity the *Vortragender Rat* would denounce his allegiance to the Chancellor. Bismarck's power would be broken, and thereafter he himself would have unfettered control. In addition, an old score would have been paid off.

Baron Holstein determined at that early hour that he would shortly be the Kaiser's man.

CHAPTER IX

THE BISMARCKS

FOR a long time Prince Bismarck had been able only to see to the maintenance of the work he had done in consolidating and unifying the forces of the nation which he had brought into existence. As to the future of the Empire, he was convinced that it was beyond the power of any statesman to penetrate the opaque and formless veils which shrouded it. He did not believe that the fate of any Power on the Continent surrounded or flanked by other Powers could be foreseen, or predetermined with any confidence, for more than five or ten years ahead. Even the problems of the moment only forced themselves on the Prince's attention now when they had become patently urgent, had begun to threaten his achievement, so that he rose up to defend it in all his formidable power. His outlook no longer had the old creative splendour, cold, self-sufficing, unemotional, unresponsive to all outside influence. He still had the commanding presence of the powerful individuality that Bismarck always was, and the consciousness of his power, a power so enormous as had rarely been concentrated in the hands of a single man. His eyes still blazed with dæmonic fire in anger or scorn. He could still fight with hard and terrible weapons, which could strike a mortal blow if he wished. But he no longer brought them into play for a forward-storming idea, for the making of a State. The

State had been created. He was now fighting only for his own power, and here too only for its maintenance. He was fighting for his own dominance as Chancellor—for the ascendancy and the prestige of the *major domus,* the "mayor of the palace."

He withdrew from direct administration of the affairs of the Empire, although he himself decided, or at all events intended to decide, everything. By the end of the first year of the rule of William II he was rarely to be seen in the capital. He remained at his country house, "Friedrichs-ruh," in the seclusion of his Saxon forests. Everything that he wanted to know, all reports, came in writing from Berlin, and he dictated all instructions to his secretaries. Count Herbert Bismarck, the Secretary of State, travelled incessantly to and fro between the capital and the Chancellor's seat, to keep him in personal touch with affairs. At Fried-richsruh the Chancellor was surrounded by his family, who were accustomed to giving unquestioning service in their veneration of his genius. His days passed in almost undisturbed harmony.

When his son Herbert was twenty years of age, Bismarck had taken him straight from college into a full comradeship as between man and man. The Count had never had any serious difference with his father, still less offered any resistance to him. Now the Chancellor made his colleague and Secretary of State his entire representative in his absence, treating with Ministers and diplomats, and making to him proposals which Bismarck would accept or improve on, reject or modify. The Count's drafts—he had begun also to draft the Kaiser's writings and speeches—were subtly and cautiously written, with more reserve than he showed in conversation. The Chancellor hoped that Count Herbert, acquainted with every detail of his technique and the organization which he had built up, might one day succeed him as Chancellor. The Count was almost on terms of intimacy with the young Kaiser, to whom the Chancellor had attached him as "mentor" years before, to give the future ruler an insight into the business of the Foreign Ministry. His mother, Princess Johanna Bismarck, was even more anxious to make sure of his succession to the Chancellorship, and had always tried to bring him to the front, sometimes more than had quite pleased her husband. It was a natural and human ambition to see her son assured of succession to his father's post, but not a few scarcely well-advised suggestions were made by the mother for the conferment of important commissions on the Count; often the Chancellor used his influence in his son's favour with discomfort, not of his own will or with any conviction, but simply to please the Princess. Princess Johanna Bismarck never took any direct part in political affairs. This lively, dark-haired woman with the big grey eyes had always known that her strong point was her naturalness, her womanly charm and above all her splendid gift of humour, which kept the Prince in laughing mood. Instinctively she watched, as her one concern, for friendship or enmity towards her husband. She hated whomever he hated, and loathed all who opposed him. Then her words would come with a cutting edge, regardless of guests or servants, and not entirely without influence on the Prince. She was concerned only with persons, not policies. Her supreme interest was confined to one policy—a dynastic policy, and it was she who had aroused and kept strong in the Chancellor the hope of the ultimate succession of Count Herbert to the Chancellorship. If in the Chancellor's circle there was really something of the ambition for a

"Bismarck dynasty," it was not so much the Chancellor himself as Princess Johanna whose thoughts ran in that direction—associating the idea with the tradition of the Prince's
great ancestor. Bismarck himself had eyes only for his own
work, his own power. Work and power were all that he
asked for. His wife—whom he adored—was concerned
further to secure that the family should remain at its
exalted, unexampled eminence.

Prince Bismarck's enormous services in the unification
of Germany and the consolidation of her position in the
world were beyond all controversy. Each and all of his
compatriots bowed low before him. But this due honouring
of his genius had gradually been qualified by fear of the
power possessed and exercised by the Chancellor and his
house and his whole army of followers. No position of real
importance in the Kingdom of Prussia, perhaps none in the
whole Empire, was filled except on Prince Bismarck's decision. He summoned and he sent away. There was no matter
of real importance which was dealt with otherwise than as
the Prince determined. No one up to now had had the
hardihood, the madness to stand out against a decision of
the Chancellor's. Everyone felt the pressure of the great
figure, of more than life-size, of this man. For the time the
counter-pressure of those who wanted to make their way
upwards but did not venture to force it remained underground.

Anecdotes were told of the "dynasty," some entirely in-
vented, some merely highly coloured, and had their effect
on opinion concerning the Chancellor and his house.
Opinion was not made more friendly by the character of
Count Herbert Bismarck. He obeyed the Prince implicitly:
Bismarck never tolerated opposition to his authority, but

had never had need to exercise his authority in his relations with his son. Count Herbert regarded his father, the Chancellor, not as a man but a demi-god; or at the least a sort of Michelangelo. His homage to the Chancellor amounted to a cult, almost to divine worship.

There were many who underestimated Count Herbert Bismarck alongside his father. He worked with thoroughness, and enjoyed his work, in strong contrast to his brother Bill, who was regarded as the abler. The Secretary of State had a considerable stock of knowledge. He spoke more than one foreign language with fluency, though not with the mastery of his father, whose command of French, English, and Russian surprised all foreigners. He had something of his father's heroic stature and outward appearance, but in his nature he had more resemblance to his mother, Princess Johanna. He had her humour—his narrative, in his deep bass voice, bubbled over with wit. He was impulsive and always ready for complicated intrigues, full of life and inclined at all times to heighten the colour of everything through the play of his wit; yet he often looked at matters more soberly than his father. He was equal to the ordinary duties of his father's post, but without his father's great qualities. An unpleasant feature was his excessive consciousness of his origin and his immoderate use of his position in pushing in front of all around him. He showed at an early age that he knew who the Bismarcks were and expected it to be acknowledged. He would give uncalled-for provocation where full respect had been shown. His tone was then rough and his language overweening and unbridled; he always had a ready reply, but expressed it with poor taste. The unceremoniousness of this marchland junker, which often startled the guests in his father's house and brought

them discomfort, became yet rougher in all ordinary intercourse away from home, though in the home circle he was
the soul of consideration and tenderness. He threw about
strong language as Prince Bismarck threw cutlets over his
shoulder at table to his dogs. Yet this big, strong man had
sensitive nerves. Never averse to indulgence, he tried them
severely. He was liable to lose his temper over trifles. He
was very dependent on the weather. He preferred genial
acquaintanceship to friendship, but he remained loyal to
friends who really gained his intimacy. Frequently he
offended even his friends. In intercourse with foreign diplomats, if he had had precise instructions from his father or
was concerned for an individual or a situation, he could
make himself easy and friendly and conciliatory in tone.
But even with diplomats his colleagues generally found him
too forceful, too brusque in his consciousness of his power.
With the Kaiser he was supple and full of bright ideas.
Even here, however, his autocratic nature sometimes showed
itself, as on one occasion when he was sailing to Constantinople, in the Kaiser's train, on board the Lloyd steamer
Danzig. He caught up and passed the Monarch's flagship,
on his own responsibility and against all the orders of the
Admiral in command of the squadron. The astonished Admiral asked what this meant. The Captain of the *Danzig*
reported that Count Bismarck wanted to reach Constantinople in advance of the Monarch, to discuss certain matters
before his arrival. The Kaiser ordered the ship to take up
its proper station again.

The Secretary of State liked to take rapid decisions on
his own responsibility, even over the head of the Sovereign.
If they were then frustrated, or if at any time he felt that
his eminence had not obtained due recognition, he carried

his personal feeling of injury into the current correspondence and reports. He regarded the whole Turkish journey as a failure. There had been the incident in the Dardanelles; and he did not receive from the Sultan the order which he had hoped for. After his return he painted to the Chancellor a dark picture of the whole situation in Turkey.

In everything that did not directly affect him personally or touch his vanity, the Secretary was thoroughly competent, though without has father's genius. He constantly took refuge behind his father as the final and supreme authority. He did many things not because he regarded them as important in his capacity of Secretary of State, but because he considered that Prince Bismarck's son was entitled to do them. If he found that he was arousing astonishment, he simply gave that explanation, as the most natural of things. He was a conscientious assistant to his father, but he did little to strengthen his father's position. He shared his mother's sense of what was due to the members of the "Dynasty." The great Chancellor was hemmed in by envy and malice and hatred. This dynastic policy did nothing to soften them; it accentuated them.

Prince Bismarck was now fighting with less steady nerves for his position and power as *major domus*. This man of gigantic stature had never had complete command of his nerves among his intimate associates, save when some question of peace or war or some other crucial step was at issue. For years past his lachrymal gland had been brought into play by any strong excitement, so that he had frequently burst into tears in the presence of the old Kaiser, though not actually weeping. In outbursts of wrath he was terrible to all who saw him so, no longer master of himself,

his whole body trembling violently. Yet, like almost all
men and women with the sensitive nerves that respond at
once to every sort of excitement, he could suddenly, at
moments of the utmost tension, take a firm hold of himself,
recover entire self-command, and become incredibly calm,
not permitting a muscle of his face to move, and sur-
rounding himself with an unapproachability which left
everyone wondering where he stood or what was to come
next.

The giant had one aspect when he was talking to the
old Kaiser or the difficult Crown Prince Frederick: it often
seemed then as though he had the bad nerves of an operatic
star. He had a different aspect in the Cabinet, where he
knew how to break down all opposition with his unbending
insistence, and a very different one when he was receiving
subordinates.

He was born to dominate, and it was always the question of power that determined his attitude. Perhaps there
had been only one occasion since he held his position of
power on which he had failed to impose his will—in 1871,
in the days of Versailles, when he found himself at logger-
heads with Field Marshal von Moltke. Crown Prince
Albert of Saxony had come from the front to the army
headquarters at Versailles, and had been walking up and
down in front of the house in which the supreme army commanders were sitting in council, when Moltke suddenly
came out through the porch. The Commander in Chief
was in an extraordinary condition, his face flaming red, his
helmet askew. He went striding past the Crown Prince
without greeting or seeing him, until the astonished Prince
saluted him with an audible, emphatic clinking of the heels.
The Field Marshal looked up:

"You here, your Royal Highness? What's the news from your army?"

The Crown Prince only answered with a question:

"For God's sake, your Excellency, what's up in there? I've never seen you like this before."

"Your Royal Highness," Moltke burst out, "I wish you had been there! Bismarck now wants to have the General Staff of the army under his command! I have sent in my resignation."

Nowhere on German soil, nowhere within Germany's borders were there any limits of power which the Chancellor would have foreborne to overstep. All that stood on German soil was flesh of his own flesh: his creation and his own person were indistinguishable to him. Opposition to him was sedition. Since Providence had assigned him so tremendous a rôle, he believed in it with a mystical devotion, as he believed in the divine right of his Kings, being himself a Prussian of the most pronounced and exalted type. The divinity that surrounded the thrones of Monarchs connoted restrictions which might even be applied to him; but he was accustomed to regard himself as entitled, as a mighty paladin, to overstep them; and to being allowed to do so by Kings themselves; even to their becoming accustomed to his doing so. His nerves gave way at once when the lords installed by the Almighty remembered for once their own divine right. That was a thing which he could not break, could not forcibly suppress; he was no condottiere, and not a Wallenstein. Here, therefore, he met with limits to his power, shackles on it; and the colossus would then have a nerve storm. He would burst into tears. He often did so in front of the old Kaiser. He did so in front of the Crown Prince in 1866 when King William refused to abandon the march on Vienna. This too was in keeping with the *format* of Prince Bismarck; he wept only in the presence of Kings.

At the end of the 'eighties his nerves were troubling him severely. They tortured him with incessant pain, often entirely exhausted him. He suffered from facial neuralgia, and Schweninger, his own medical attendant, was unable to tell whether it was due to teeth or some other cause. The Prince had a splendid set of teeth, entirely perfect in spite of his great age. Schweninger declared that it would mean breaking the Chancellor's jaw to try to extract a single tooth, so firmly were all his great teeth still set in it. The Prince cut down his indulgences; his doctor forbade all wines. Sometimes he would break bounds and send for a bottle, but Schweninger would stand up from the table and declare categorically:

"I cannot permit the Prince to drink wine."

Then Bismarck would give way. It was high time that he did, for his nerve troubles and his sleeplessness were reaching a stage at which it was becoming impossible for days at a time for him to do any sort of work. Schweninger admitted to the Kaiser that at such times, when the pain got beyond endurance, he gave the Chancellor small quantities of morphia. He did his best to save Bismarck all needless exertion and all excitement. He advocated his remaining permanently amid the peace of Friedrichsruh.

"Send for the people, your Highness, let them come here!"

But the Prince now had the feeling at times that he would be unwise to tie himself entirely to Friedrichsruh, that the conversations with his son and the written reports sent him were not enough for adequate supervision. Count

Waldersee came to see him in Friedrichsruh, and the Chancellor gave unreserved expression to his doubts whether it was right to remain in retirement there. Only a faint echo, or none at all, came from Berlin of stories and rumours in circulation; moreover, the Secretary had not the gift of smoothing away the resentments and the tension produced by his own angularities during the Chancellor's long absence. The Chancellor's cares were not confined to his nerve troubles. He was still more disturbed by fears as to the situation of the Empire.

In regard to home affairs he knew, or believed, that he had all the strings in his hand. He had the Ministers under his control. Each one of them he had himself tested, approved and chosen. General von Schweinitz, the German Ambassador at the Russian Court, wrote that "for more than twenty years past there has been no Minister appointed in Prussia except on Prince Bismarck's nomination. The Ministers with whom the Chancellor had surrounded himself in this long period (and who certainly include some men of quite exceptional gifts and capacity) had, by the very fact of nomination in this way, the character rather of clerks than of Ministers." Prince Bismarck could count on his will being the sole determinant of everything and on everything being done as he desired it to be done by these men of his own choosing. He was assured of their loyalty by his power over them, and compelled them to do his bidding by his dominant intellect. He encroached on their private affairs in order completely to shackle them to his service. He paid their debts. He not only extricated von Bötticher, Vice-President of the Ministry of State, from pressing material embarrassments, but rescued his relations from social ruin. In politics, and not only in politics, the

Chancellor was a master of the difficult and valuable art of using everyone as a figurehead in face of everyone else, and then playing off one dummy against another, remaining himself in the background. Not only this, but he understood as very few others how to keep everyone entirely dependent on him and to get rid of everyone who was not prepared to accept dependence. In his practice of high politics he was entirely unmoral. When he thought of Germany, his one concern in life and his last love, he was a fit subject of the phrase which his entourage often heard fall from his lips:

"My conscience is pointed at me like a cocked pistol."

But when he was considering the means of serving Germany—and Germany meant himself and his power,—then all means were justified if only they could be applied with success. His first method of approach to a problem was the broad way of conscious power. But there were byways by which important ends could be attained, if power alone was insufficient or was impossible to apply.

"I do not like telling lies," he would say. "But if an indiscreet Ambassador drives me to telling one, it is for him to answer for it."

In dealing with Ambassadors and Ministers he similarly recognized only expedience and not morality. In the days of the Zollverein he had sent a hundred thousand thalers to the Elector of Hesse to put him into an accommodating frame of mind. The Elector had accepted the thalers and had been accommodating. The Chancellor knew the exact value of money, as power and as property.

"Why, you have pigs yourself," he said to Prince Hatzfeldt, who had called on him about preventing prices from going up—"it is not to your interest to have them as cheap as possible!"

With his Ministers he was an autocrat. He did not offer advice, but announced his will. They were subdued either by his genius or by fear of losing their posts; or else he had secured unconditional subservience by a money payment. Save for the Social Democrats there was no internal problem of any sort to trouble about. There was only one power.

But that power extended no farther than Germany's borders. It was Germany's situation among the Powers, the problem of her vulnerability, that oppressed him. He was no longer quite so sure of the value of his many alliances and agreements as at the time when he had concluded his Reinsurance Treaty with Russia. There had been other things to disturb him besides the answer which Count Kálnoky had given to the German Ambassador in Vienna, Prince von Reuss. Count Waldersee daily cried "Wolf!" to the Kaiser with regard to Russian war perils, daily recounted to him the tale of Russian armaments. Prince Bismarck was openly and bitterly hostile to Count Waldersee; all the world knew it, and the Count was keen, even when he came to Friedrichsruh on a visit, to do his crafty best to deepen the gulf. The Chancellor set all his newspapers to work against the Chief of Staff, openly denouncing him as a war-maker and fomenter of trouble. But the truth remained that the Russian troops were continually on the move, and that the Russians had no sooner floated one loan than they were at work trying to raise further large sums, to get money at any price, which could only increase their adventurousness. On top of this there was

the Chancellor's undeniable failure with Lord Salisbury.
It had been natural that he should tell his lordship, in
effect, that Germany could not undertake to supply mer-
cenaries for England. But if he were sincere with himself
he had to confess that the real obstacle to a rapprochement
with England was the very treaty with Russia, the Reinsurance Treaty, as to the value of which he was beginning to
be apprehensive.

His cares and doubts pressed so heavily on him that
when the Tsar came in October, 1889, on a visit to Emperor
William, he completely forgot his neuralgia and his racked
nerves, and persuaded himself that he had suddenly recovered his old elasticity, and all the dæmonic fighting powers
with which he could capture minds and souls. He abandoned the peace of Friedrichsruh for a few days, had long
talks with the Tsar, and exerted himself to the utmost to
dissipate the Russian Emperor's apprehensions, awakened
by Germany's attitude and her attentions to England, of
a change in her feelings towards his country. The Chancellor was doing battle for the Reinsurance Treaty and the
policy which it embodied. He wanted it to be a living
reality. He hoped to renew it in the following year. It
lifted from him the incubus of Germany's long unprotected
frontiers. The Tsar seemed to accept and put faith in the
Chancellor's assurances; at all events, Prince Bismarck had
that feeling. The conversation became more cordial than
Bismarck had expected. He returned once more to the
Bulgarian falsifications, the alleged correspondence between
Prince Ferdinand of Coburg and the Countess of Flanders
and other letters which purported to show that Bismarck
was assisting the Prince. Here he was tackling the subject
which had confirmed the Tsar's mistrust of Chancellor and

Tsar Alexander III

BRITISH REPRESENTATIVES AT LABOUR CONFERENCE

WILLIAM H. HOULDSWORTH, BART., DAVID DALE, ESQ., CHARLES S. SCOTT, C.B., J. BURNETT, F. H. WHYMPER, ESQ., SIR JOHN GORST, J. BIRTWISTLE

Reich. The Chancellor believed that this time he had definitely convinced the Tsar that he had had nothing to do with the affair. The whole correspondence was in fact a forgery.[1] He had the impression that the Tsar had abandoned all suspicions and had now been entirely won over. Bismarck's anxieties passed away; he felt carefree as he had not since the days of the Berlin Congress.

After the Tsar's departure the Chancellor drove back from the station with the young Kaiser. Emperor William spoke of a possible early return visit to the Tsar. Prince Bismarck advised against it. Everything was already in order. It was not a good thing for Sovereigns themselves to have political discussions with one another. Nor did the Prince believe that the Tsar was genuinely in sympathy with the Kaiser. He remembered Count Hatzfeldt's report from London on his visit to Peterhof. The report still lay in his drawer. Meanwhile no one had upset it. Emperor William's suggested new visit was entirely superfluous.

The Reinsurance Treaty had thus been saved. Now at last it became really effective for good. The reverse from England now mattered less. He returned to the Chancellor's official residence rid of his cares and in almost youthful high spirits and confidence. In the end the Kaiser had dropped into silence. He had driven the Chancellor home and gone on to the palace. Prince Bismarck burst into the breakfast room.

[1] Tsar Ferdinand of Bulgaria wrote to the author on September 18, 1929, as follows: "I hereby declare that I had *no* correspondence *at any time* with the Countess of Flanders. Anyone who has any knowledge whatever of my line of political thought will recognize at once that this whole correspondence is a crude falsification. Those who in Berlin in the autumn of 1887 believed in the genuineness of the letters are to be pitied.—FERDINAND."

"Well, what shall we drink?" he cried to his guests. Schweninger was not there, only Princess Johanna. Boisterously he gave his order:

"A red Assmannshäuser!"

The servant hurried off, but came back at once. There was no red Assmannshäuser to be had. For two years past the Prince had made no request for this particular wine.

"The very reason why you should have made sure that there was some!"

But there was not the storm that so frequently came if the Prince was at table and the dishes disappointed him. When the issue was not one of dynastic policy, in which she was courageous and persistent, or one in which she could make the Prince laugh by her jokes and witticisms, Princess Johanna was terribly afraid of him. This time, however, although the roast hare and sausage had not come specially from Varzin, but had been hurriedly bought in town, the Prince took no notice of the fact.

The Chancellor returned to Friedrichsruh in the best of spirits. He had paid no attention to the young Kaiser's ill-humour, he had not even noticed it. The days went on as in all the months that had gone by. Once more the secretaries stood and Bismarck dictated in his study, which with evidently deliberate design he had had fitted up like the office of an ordinary official, with pictures of the Kaiser in wooden frames, and a plain writing table with paper weights and scissors and a couple of pencils. But Count Rantzau, the *Vortragender Rat,* no longer needed to be so alert in keeping up with the flow of words as on the occasion when the Prince had dictated to him in a single night the text of the Triple Alliance treaty. And gradually the work had to be put off as the nerves began again to suffer. Meanwhile reports that grew more frequent and more persistent, reports of trouble in Berlin, penetrated to Friedrichsruh. But the Chancellor paid no attention to them; he buried himself deeper in his solitude, far from the day's alarms. The Secretary of State, too, stayed away for quite a considerable period. Count Herbert had been in the Kaiser's train to Constantinople. When he returned to Friedrichsruh he had much to tell his father of changing opinion in the capital. Count Waldersee, the Chief of Staff, was working against the Chancellor more actively than ever. There was open discussion everywhere as to who would gradually take the place of the old Prince in the Chancellorship. The young Kaiser, alone in the capital, was doing much that was not on the lines that Bismarck would approve. He was giving evidence of the influence of the ideas of a new age, even more plainly than in the weeks of the coal strike. All who knew the Chancellor were bound to see that he could not possibly share the Kaiser's views and ideals. The Secretary of State faced the fact of the incompatibility which was already showing itself, though not yet openly declared. Perhaps, he suggested, the moment had come when they should leave the young Kaiser to work out his own ideas, and should think about retiring.

At that the Chancellor "sat up." It was in December, 1889; a new strike movement had recently flamed up in Germany. But the Social Democracy was a problem which Prince Bismarck intended at all costs to master, to dispose of for good and all. The Kaiser might have his views, but they did not settle the matter. As for ill-favour and friction, he was used to them.

"I am not going to go," the Chancellor replied, "merely on account of trifles of that sort."

Bismarck thought of Germany's treaties, of the difficult art of maintaining them and putting them to use. Above all he thought of Russia. He had recovered the Tsar's trust. That meant peace and security. All else was relatively of slight significance.

The Chancellor remained at Friedrichsruh over Christmas, and over the first day of the new year. Then, on January 23, 1890, he was suddenly informed that Emperor William had appointed the next day for a Crown Council. The Kaiser took it, the message continued, that the Chancellor could arrange to arrive by midday.

More curious than disturbed,—curious and a little irritated at his presence being commanded at the very beginning of the Crown Council; it would only have been reasonable that some consideration should have been shown for him: his illness had been reported by the Chancellery,— the old Chancellor now set out for Berlin.

CHAPTER X

SOCIAL REFORMS

THE Kaiser had considered the questions of the strike and of labour legislation, and had arrived at a definite decision. He had thoroughly discussed the reports from the *Oberpräsident* of the Rhineland, von Berlepsch, with Hinzpeter and with his mineowner friend Count Douglas; and he had gone on to the consideration of statistics obtained from all the coal mining areas. The result had been to convince him of the necessity of improving the conditions of life among the workers, as a simple matter of justice and humanity; and, moreover, of practical politics: the tendency to unrest among the workers would be bound to die away if their anxieties as to their subsistence were removed. They, too, must be enabled to feel that the fatherland into the defence of which they would hurl themselves in the event of need was a land fit to live in. Three times in the course of the autumn the Kaiser had had Prince Bismarck informed that he wanted an Amending Bill for Labour Protection submitted to him, with accompanying Regulations, with the publication of which the great work of reform was to begin. First he had asked, then "requested," and finally had his "desire" conveyed to the Prince. Bismarck had first made no answer at all, and then curtly declined to comply. But the Kaiser was not prepared to give up his plans on that account. He commanded that a Crown Council should be convened.

"For God's sake, your Majesty," cried von Bötticher, Minister of State, in alarm, when the Kaiser informed him of his decision, "do not do that! The Prince will not listen to the idea of meddling with the labour question!"

The Kaiser had prepared a memorandum for the Crown Council. He had plainly been fired with enthusiasm for the reform. He sent for von Helldorf, the leader of the Conservatives. That party had expressed a desire that the Kaiser should hear its delegate before a definite decision was made on the following day as to the Socialist Bill and, in consequence, as to the composition of the Cartel on which the Government relied for its majority. Von Helldorf represented to the Kaiser that it would be impossible for his party to vote for the bill if the Government insisted on maintaining Article 24, relating to deportation. That Article would enable the municipal authorities to expel all the Social Democratic demagogues and agitators from the towns, and so to drive them into the country districts. The Conservatives were in fear of the deportees from the towns rousing the villagers against them.

"I can do nothing here alone," the Kaiser replied, "but I will look into the matter. You authorize me, then, to tell the Prince that your party offers to guarantee to him the passage of the Bill if that provision is deleted; and that otherwise you must refuse to follow him."

Von Helldorf agreed and took his leave.

At noon Prince Bismarck arrived from Friedrichsruh. He had learnt vaguely from an exchange of telegrams with the Secretary of State that labour questions stood on the agenda of the Crown Council. Before he left Friedrichsruh he had summoned a Cabinet Council for three in the afternoon, in order to settle the attitude of the Cabinet in face of coming events. He told the Ministers that he did not know what was going to be discussed in that day's Crown Council, he had had no further preparation for it than a message by an aide-de-camp that His Majesty intended to hold a Council. He had no knowledge of the subject to be discussed, but suspected that it concerned questions of labour protection. In his view the Ministry of State should not enter into any such discussion without preparation, and should neither assent nor dissent but ask for time for the consideration of suitable proposals.

The Prince went on to give the Ministers instructions as to their attitude: "Should the Socialist Bill come up for discussion, there should be no declaration of readiness to accept it without Article 24, dealing with deportations. Nothing should be said in the Reichstag to facilitate the acceptance of the Bill without that Article. We have shown too much conciliatoriness in the past in order to secure other Bills a safe passage. If nothing is carried, the voters, who want protection from anarchy and revolution, will soon find it out; all the opposition to the article is coming from the party leaders."

The Chancellor had made sure of his Ministers and provided against the danger of rushed decisions in the Crown Council. He went on to the Kaiser, who wanted to receive him before the meeting, in order to let him know of the objection raised by the Conservatives. The Monarch described the whole position to the Prince. The Socialist Bill could be saved if the Chancellor would declare that the Government was "considering" the omission of the offending Article. The Conservatives would then vote for the Bill; they would vote against it if the Chancellor did not make the declaration. The Kaiser was in favour of the milder terms; he saw the risk of the collapse of the Cartel. It seemed to him of more importance that the Cartel parties should hold together and that the Government should have their support than that the deportation Article should be carried at all costs.

Prince Bismarck differed. He was unconcerned about the risk of the Government Cartel falling to pieces, and was unconcerned even as to the advantage if any, of sacrificing the Article to preserve the Bill. All he was concerned with was the fact that he was being resisted. Once more the resistance came from the very party which should have been the first to stand unreservedly at his side—the Conservatives. His indignation was boundless. He banged his fist on the table:

"These fellows are always offering opposition! They did it in 1864 and 1866, and they are still doing it!"

Nothing would calm the Prince. He would make no concession.

Meanwhile the Ministers went in to the Crown Council. The Kaiser took the chair.

He began with a reference to the "unsound development of German industry in comparison with that of England." Broadly speaking the German industrialists took no interest whatever in their workers. Hitherto they had "had them squeezed like lemons and then left to decay on the rubbish heap." He referred to his reports and his conversations on the subject with Hinzpeter and von Berlepsch and others:

"Just as a Company goes to pieces if its Captain does not himself watch everything, but leaves everything to the sergeants and N.C.O.'s, so it is with the workers in industry."

Revolutions resulted from neglected reforms. He was determined "to be *le roi des gueux,* the king of the beggars; the workers shall learn that I care for their welfare. My policy in these matters has got to be one of preventive war, and the best way I see of declaring this is in the form of a solemn manifesto."

The Ministers listened with growing astonishment, asking themselves who could have put such advice before the Kaiser, such ideas into his head. Soon, however, he handed his memorandum—that his views might be made clear in every detail—to von Bötticher, Minister of State, to read. The Minister read it so fluently and so plainly, emphasizing and bringing out the essentials, that the Chancellor inferred that he had long had the text in his keeping.

The Kaiser wanted to introduce Sunday rest, to restrict the working hours of women and children, to exempt women from work for a period during pregnancy and confinement. Workers' committees were to be called into existence and themselves to be responsible for watching over the welfare of their brethren. He proposed to entrust a State Council with the working out of these burning questions, which over-topped all others in importance. He proposed to invite all States, both Great Powers and the smaller Powers, to an international conference in his capital, Berlin, so that the whole world should collaborate in the creation of a code of labour legislation. The relations between employers and workers in all countries must be regulated with such uniformity that no one should be at a disadvantage in any country in comparison with others.

The Kaiser's whole thesis was fired by sincere enthusiasm, which lit up his imagination and gave warmth to his exposition. But the Chancellor poured no encouraging oil

on the fire. He saw in it only youthful exuberance. He
resolved to extinguish it.

The Kaiser waited to hear the views of the Ministers.
They shifted in their seats and got ready to speak. But
each time one of them had made up his mind to begin, the
Chancellor turned and looked him full in the face, with
a menacing glare. That silenced him. Prince Bismarck
opened the discussion himself. It would be impossible, he
said, for the Ministry of State to give its opinion in regard
to labour questions until it had had an opportunity of thoroughly considering them. He was against issuing manifestos. He could not alter his well-known objection to trying to effect reforms in the way suggested. However, "the
necessary steps shall be taken for the preparation of Bills in
the sense desired." Which, in the Chancellor's view, ended
the matter for the present.

Von Bötticher, Minister of State, made an effort to
produce a more hopeful atmosphere. He asked whether the
Kaiser intended to dissolve Parliament in person. But this
only made matters worse. Both the Chancellor and the
Secretary of State, Count Herbert Bismarck, were against
the Kaiser's doing this.

"Yes," the Monarch replied, "this Reichstag has, after
all, done very well, and I will close its session myself."

It was gradually becoming difficult for him to maintain
self-control. He had hoped that the contents of his message
would appeal to the Chancellor's humanity, even if he had
political qualms, and that in the end he would be able to
convince him. He had also expected at least one or another
of the Ministers, if encouraged to speak, to pluck up sufficient courage to put in a word. But the Chancellor's frown
intimidated every one of them. The Chancellor addressed

the Kaiser himself with ill-concealed animosity. He did not look him in the face. He did not attempt to suppress his prejudice. His replies were curt, gruff, and deliberately short of deference, in front of the whole assembly. The Kaiser was presiding over the Crown Council, and apart from that he was the Kaiser, but Prince Bismarck hinted pretty directly at his youth and immaturity. It was plain to everyone that the Kaiser was pale with excitement. But in spite of it he kept cool. He prepared to cut the sitting short:

"I hope that the Socialist Bill will pass, and that the deportation Article will be allowed to drop, as it is of less importance than the continuance of the Cartel, which would be endangered if the session were to close with disagreement in this connexion."

Even here there was nothing but opposition. It became evident that the Chancellor was now anxious to see the Socialist Bill defeated:

"I cannot prove that His Majesty's complaisance will have grave consequences, but that is my belief, based on long experience. If His Majesty differs on so important a question, it is beginning to be time that I gave up my post. If the Bill fails to pass, it will be necessary to do the best possible without it, and the waves must continue to mount; the result may be a collision."

Bismarck was once more working towards his favourite solution for Germany's internal political troubles—to foment disorder and excitement among the Social Democrats; and then to use the resources of the State for their taming. Until that point was reached he did not want to influence the course of events. He was back again where he had stood in the days of the May disturbances. His opposition to the Kaiser's purposes was evident at every moment during the Crown Council. If the Kaiser had other views, the Chancellor had plainly enough suggested that he wanted to retire. But Emperor William insisted that he wanted "to avoid civil disorder and bloodshed save in the last extremity; I do not want to stain my first years of rule with my subjects' lifeblood."

He had had enough of his first Crown Council, of which he had had such high hopes. The Prince sat facing him, without for a moment concealing his rage and exasperation. The whole atmosphere was heavy with hostility and menace. He dismissed the Chancellor and the Ministers. He took pains to express his appreciation, but there was no hiding his deep agitation. The Chancellor made a slight bow, and went away without a word. In the anteroom the aide-de-camp in attendance came up to him. The Prince stopped and let him too have a taste of his irritation:

"The Emperor forgot his scabbard," he cried in his high-pitched voice, rising now to a scream. "He no longer realizes that he is an officer."

He passed on, growling like a tempest. He saw no more of the Ministers that evening. Baron Lucius von Ballhausen, Minister of State, noted in his diary: "The crisis has begun with today's sitting, and will certainly become a grave one."

In the palace the Emperor William sat alone with von Lucanus, the Head of the Civil Cabinet. He sat in silent depression. He had the Chancellor against him. The Crown Council had shown, moreover, that the Ministers of State were not the King's helpers and advisers but the servants of Bismarck. But he would not admit defeat. He would not abandon his ideas. Only the realization that he stood alone, that he had no one on his side, gripped him at the throat.

Next morning in the Reichstag the Socialist Bill was thrown out by a large majority. The Chancellor had stood by his determination not to support the Bill in its weakened form. The Conservatives had accordingly refrained from voting for the motion for its modification. The Cartel fell to pieces.

A few hours later, when the Kaiser dissolved the Reichstag in the White Hall in the palace, the divergence of views between Kaiser and Chancellor stood revealed; for the Speech from the Throne made not the slightest reference to the Socialist Bill recommended by the Chancellor. It was no longer any secret to the Deputies that Emperor William had himself favoured the omission from the Bill of any excessively harsh penalties.

Later, when the Chancellor had had leisure to think over his attitude in the Crown Council, he had the feeling that he had, after all, exceeded the bounds of a wise moderation. In confidential conversation with his Ministers two days after the Crown Council he assured them that he loved the Kaiser "as the scion of his forefathers and as Sovereign; I regret that recently, in the excitement of my journey and the proceedings, I went, perhaps, farther than was necessary." Immediately before the Crown Council, during the meeting with the Ministers of State, he had shown considerable temperamental instability—dejected at one moment, flying out at the next. He had talked to them of his inclination to give up every office with the exception of foreign affairs. All that still needed his attention was the care of Germany's relations with foreign States, which for twenty years past had placed their trust in him personally.

Now that his exasperation had passed, he saw the situation more coolly. If the Kaiser had called for and listened to the advice of *Oberpräsident* von Berlepsch, without first discussing the matter with the responsible Minister of Commerce—that is, himself, Bismarck—then in future the *Oberpräsident* should at least give his advice with full responsibility. The Chancellor proposed to the Kaiser that he should retire from the office of Minister of Commerce and the *Oberpräsident* be appointed in his place. The new Minister of Commerce was appointed accordingly. Meanwhile the Chancellor worked on the two manifestos for which the Kaiser had called. In the presence of his Ministers he continued to oppose the manifestos. He recalled what he had said fifteen years before on similar proposals put forward by Deputies; his words sounded now like *lèse-majesté*. He also expressed his dislike of the whole business to Professor Hinzpeter. He had asked him to come, had listened to a long and thorough discussion of labour questions from him, and had not at any point disputed the justice of Hinzpeter's demands for social reforms; but he had so hotly opposed all the Kaiser's views that Hinzpeter cried out:

"Why, you are throwing contempt on my young Emperor!"

Prince Bismarck concealed his views from no one. He knew from the Kaiser that the support of the King of Saxony had been secured for motions on similar lines to the Kaiser's plans, and that the King wanted them put forward in the Bundesrat. Yet Bismarck announced to Count Hohenthal, the Saxon Minister, that "If the King of Saxony brings in a motion for labour legislation, I shall demand permission to retire."

He had no choice but to submit the two draft manifestos. But he introduced various alterations and additions into the Kaiser's first drafts, making them more non-committal. Finally he brought the manifestos for signature. Once more he tried to persuade the Monarch to abandon his purpose. He saw nothing that could come from it but trouble. The Social Democrats would make no legitimate use of the sense of justice and humanity that emanated from the manifestos; they would merely exploit them for purposes of agitation. The coming General Election, on February 20, would furnish evidence of this. He predicted that there would be an increase in the Social Democratic vote. In the Kaiser's view the danger in the election would not come from his manifestos but from the strikes of the past year and the unendurable conditions of existence among the workers. Finally the Chancellor recommended him to "throw these drafts into the fire—it is quite a good one." But the Kaiser took the documents and signed them. The first manifesto ran as follows:

"I am resolved to lend a hand towards the improvement of the condition of the German workpeople, so far as is permitted by the limits which are set to my endeavours by the necessity of maintaining the capacity of German industry to compete in the world market, and so to assure its existence and that of the workpeople. A falling-off in our industries through the loss of their market abroad would rob not only the employers but their workpeople of their bread. The difficulties in the way of the improvement of the situation of our workers which are due to international competition can only be overcome, or at least reduced, by an international agreement between the countries which participate in the domination of the world market. I am convinced that other Governments are similarly desirous of submitting to joint examination the aims concerning which the workers of these countries are already consulting one another internationally, and I desire, as a first step, to have enquiries made in France, England, Belgium and Switzerland, by my representatives in those countries, whether their Governments are inclined to enter into negotiation with us with a view to an international agreement concerning the possibility of meeting those needs and desires of the workers which have been brought to the fore in the strikes of recent years and otherwise. So soon as assent has been obtained in principle to my suggestion, I charge you to invite the Cabinets of all Governments which are similarly interested in the labour question to a conference for the discussion of the questions involved.

"WILHELM I. R.

"To the Imperial Chancellor."

The second proclamation was as follows:

"On my accession I announced my resolve to promote the further development of our legislation in the same direction in which my grandfather, now resting in God, interested himself in the welfare of the economically weaker section of the population, in the spirit of Christian ethics. Valuable and effective as the measures already adopted through legislation and administration for the improvement of the situation of the working class have been, they do not as yet discharge the whole of my task. In addition to the further extension of the industrial insurance legislation, the existing provisions of the regulations concerning the conditions of factory workers require examination, and the complaints and desires voiced in this field, so far as they are well-founded, require to be met. This examination should proceed from the principle that it is one of the duties of the State so to regulate the time, the duration and the nature of employment that the maintenance of the health of the workers, the injunctions of morality, and the economic needs of the workers and their claim to equality before the law are safeguarded. For the preservation of peace between employers and workpeople, legislative provisions must be contemplated concerning the formulæ under which the workers may be associated, through representatives who possess their confidence, in the regulation of matters of joint concern, and empowered to watch over their interests in negotiations with the employers and the departments of my Government. Through this organisation the workers must be enabled freely and peacefully to give expression to their desires and complaints, and the opportunity must be provided for the authorities of the State to keep informed at all times as to the conditions of the workers and to maintain contact with them.

"I desire to see the State mines developed into model institutions in regard to the provision for the welfare of their workmen, and my endeavour is to secure for the private mining industry the institution of organic relations between my mining officials and the managements, with a view to setting up a system of supervision corresponding to the inspection of factories which has been in existence since 1869. For the consideration of these questions I desire that a Council of State shall be assembled under my presidency, such expert persons being added to it as I shall summon. I shall myself determine the choice of these latter persons. Among the difficulties which stand in the way of the determination of the conditions of labour on the lines which I envisage, a prominent place is taken by those which arise from the necessity of not overburdening the country's industries in their competition with foreign countries. I have therefore commanded the Imperial Chancellor to propose to the Governments of those States whose industry together with our own, dominates the world market, that a conference should be summoned in order to endeavour to arrange for the uniform international regulation of the limits of the demands which may be made on the industry of the workers. The Imperial Chancellor will communicate to them a copy of my proclamation addressed to him.

"WILHELM R.

"To the Minister of Public Works
  and for Trade and Industry."

The Chancellor took away the proclamations. He published them in the *Reichs- und Staatsanzeiger* of February 4, 1890. He did not countersign the documents. He thus disclaimed all responsibility for them. The Kaiser really was a visionary.

CHAPTER XI

BISMARCK AS *MAJOR DOMUS*

EMPEROR WILLIAM and Prince Bismarck were almost at daggers drawn. They had begun, without yet having entirely made up their minds about it, to feel that they would be best apart.

The Kaiser was unable to tell whether he was more upset at the Chancellor's attitude or at the fact that, in a matter in which he had incontestably been in the right, not a single Minister had ventured to take his side. It no longer troubled the Kaiser that Prince Bismarck had plainly and bluntly proposed to resign. Right up to the day of the Crown Council the Chancellor had been for him the ancient paladin of superhuman stature whose words he had no desire to criticize, or even, as a rule, his actions. He did not take the offered resignation seriously, and had no thought of permitting it. But the conduct of the Ministers was another matter. To all appearance they had no opinions unless and until Bismarck indicated them, and in their relations with the Monarch they had no sense of a duty or a responsibility to him. They seemed to belong body and soul to the Chancellor. The Kaiser recalled how, not long before, Bismarck had come one day to him and declared that he wanted to dismiss one of his Ministers.

"What has he been up to?" the Kaiser asked.

"He does not suit me any longer," was all the reply the Chancellor offered.

The Kaiser had been startled at the idea that a Minister should be dismissed for no particular reason, for no apparent fault, simply because he no longer suited the Chancellor. He had expressed his astonishment to the Chancellor, but Bismarck had added, dismissing the man with a grimace of contempt:

"Ah, he is a bad character! He has taken money from me. I gave him thirty thousand marks."

The Kaiser's astonishment was boundless. But it was evident that the Chancellor had no desire to make any secret of his methods. Even outsiders knew that Prince Bismarck had paid the Vice-Chancellor's debts. He would have done as much for von Lucanus when he became Head of the Civil Cabinet, but the matter did not proceed as the Chancellor had expected. When Lucanus called on him on appointment to his new post, the Chancellor gave him a warm welcome.

"Congratulations on your new office, Lucanus. But of course you will have expenses in settling in; allow me to put the needful at your disposal!"

There was a big bag of money on the table. The Prince had had it ready, and took it up now as though it were a purse of sequins, holding it out to the utterly astonished and dismayed Lucanus.

"Your Serene Highness will excuse me—I have no need of money."

It was quite true, apart from the implication of the offer, that the Head of the Civil Cabinet had no need of a subsidy. He had an independent income and his affairs were in good order. But the Chancellor was unwilling to drop the subject.

"Why, my dear friend," he continued benevolently, "there is nothing in that."

The Head of the Civil Cabinet insisted:

"Your Highness, I do not want any money and I shall not take any."

The Prince burst out, in sincere surprise——

"You are the first man who has said that to me, and the first who has taken nothing. All my Ministers have accepted!"

The new Head of the Civil Cabinet had bowed and departed. The Chancellor's real object had been to buy his goodwill and support. From that day he was the embodiment of caution when he talked to Lucanus.

The Kaiser did not know everything; but he learned a good deal, and suspected more, and some things Prince Bismarck himself had recounted to him in open triumph. Now the Kaiser began to feel doubts. The Prince had free disposal of large sums of money. He had been entrusted with the administration of the Guelph funds which were confiscated in 1866. He could dispose of the money entirely as he thought fit. He was expressly authorized to do so, without any sort of check or any liability to render an account of his expenditure. Political purposes were an elastic term. In any case, the Chancellor had created conditions of dependence which were new in Prussia. At the thought of these Ministers and their debts and their presents of money, there flashed across the Kaiser's mind all the traditions on which he had built up his conception of the machinery of the Prussian State. So far as the officials were concerned, he was still where his forefather Frederick William I had stood. His own duties towards the State he intended to measure by the standards of Frederick the Great. The Prince seemed to preserve, or to have created, other traditions. He had more in him of a Grand Vizier than a Prussian Minister. The Kaiser regarded the Ministers as free from blame. But he suddenly found something sinister and gruesome in the principle on which the Chancellor dominated them all, the principle of unbounded power that shrinks from no means of exacting unqualified submission. He had now made the discomforting and embittering discovery that he stood entirely alone with his plans, that he could count on none but himself, and, further, that the immediate future would be absorbed for him by one problem—the struggle for power.

He still hoped to be able to have the Chancellor at his side, if not permanently, at least in the immediate future. He still hoped that the Ministers whom he, as their King, had appointed, would gradually get used to regarding themselves as not exclusively Bismarck's servants. This aspect of the difference with the Prince lent it added importance.

Emperor William resolved to put the issue of his power to the test.

Meanwhile the Chancellor was tempted to give way. He was very undecided what to do. He knew that the friction between himself and the Kaiser was being openly discussed by all who were in close association with either. Count Waldersee's phrase had been revived—it had long before been applied to the young Kaiser:

"If Frederick the Great had had this sort of Chancellor, he would not have been the Great."

The General's dictum had never been retailed to the Kaiser. The Chief of Staff had coined it in his own study, and when it got round to him again he did nothing to put it out of currency. Since the scene with the Count the Kaiser had determined at all times with careful precision how much he would tell him, and the Count knew even more exactly what he could venture on and what he could not. That dictum of Waldersee's was bound to disturb Bismarck, but so far it had not reached the Monarch's ears.

The General felt, however, that the time had arrived when the mantle of the old Chancellor might after all fall on him. The Kaiser still refused to entertain the idea of separation from Bismarck. But von Stosch, a former Secretary of State for the Admiralty, who had been a candidate for the Chancellorship under Emperor Frederick, was discussing, both in conversation and in writing, with the Deputy von Miquel, and both of them with Count Waldersee, whether the latter should be made Chancellor. At one time von Stosch had had doubts whether Waldersee was the right man to succeed Bismarck. But he had come back, with von Miquel, to the support of the General, who was as entirely in agreement with the idea of his nomination as Imperial Chancellor as the two others plainly were in their self-appointed mission to dispose of that high office. With the modesty and piety natural to him the Count had entered these prudent reflections in his diary:

"For the present, however, I am doing nothing at all, and would not for all the world create the impression that I have any further ambitions."

It was, in any case, a sign of a lapse in his usually fairly sound judgment that the Chief of Staff still entertained hopes of the Chancellorship. He ought to have known that he was the last man that the Kaiser would ever make Chancellor. All, therefore, that he achieved was to deepen the atmosphere of intrigue around Prince Bismarck by his energetic underground work in promotion of his candidature. For nothing happened in any camp, or was supposed to be happening, but all the camps knew of it.

Bismarck was overcome with weariness; he suffered from sleepless nights of pain, and from wounding experiences entirely new to him in the resistance put up by the Kaiser. A few days after the signing of the two proclamations he proposed to the Kaiser that he should also retire from the office of Prime Minister of Prussia, now that *Oberpräsident* von Berlepsch had replaced him as Minister of Trade and Industry. He would just wait until the elections were over, so as not to confuse the issues by any big change. Then he might resign every one of his offices. His health also, he said, made his resignation advisable, and ultimately his complete withdrawal from active public life. He did not want to continue the work of his various offices beyond June at the latest.

This was on February 8. Emperor William said nothing, merely nodding. Almost every meeting between Kaiser and Chancellor had been like this for some time past, the Prince talking and the Emperor remaining silent. The two had become strangers. The Chancellor was careful to maintain the cold, distant tone of a formal audience. Since the incidents in the Crown Council the Kaiser had similarly set himself to maintain the formal attitude of a Monarch receiving his Chancellor like anyone else who might have sought an audience. The end of the audience would find both of the two oppressed and out of humour.

But each time the Chancellor seemed to have settled matters to his satisfaction everything would unexpectedly be opened up once more. He had only just announced to the Kaiser his desire to retire from the Prussian Premiership, and also to begin to prepare for final retirement from public life. Two days later he had another audience with the Kaiser and retracted his decision. He had communi-

cated with the Ministry of State his intention to resign from
the Premiership. Not a single Minister had tried to dissuade him: on the contrary, the Chancellor had noticed that
when he told the Cabinet of his decision all the Ministers
"looked pleased." Consequently he had then determined to
retain all his offices, "just to rile the Ministers."

He could see that the Kaiser was astonished. It had
not occurred to him that any change in his decision would
depend not only on him but also conceivably on the Monarch. He simply communicated the fact that he had
changed his mind. The Kaiser replied that he accepted
this fresh decision of the Prince's and would be glad if
they could continue to work together. The Chancellor then
proceeded to attack the whole of his Ministers, one by one.
Emperor William had the impression that the Prince was
trying to make sure that he would not consider any one
of them a fit candidate for the Chancellorship. Then the
Prince cut short the conversation and took a chilly farewell.

The Council of State for which the Kaiser had called
was assembled, employers sitting alongside workmen. Emperor William opened the assembly himself. The preliminary ceremonial was short, and the Kaiser desired that the
business meetings should begin in the same month. Prince
Bismarck continued to show pessimism as to the prospects
of the Council of State, and as to all the Kaiser's purposes
and plans. He expressed his views with increasing openness in his intimate circle, and the response to him grew
correspondingly more plain-spoken. Sides began to be taken
for the Chancellor and for the Kaiser. An A.D.C. at Court,
von Bülow, took the Chancellor's side. He urged that big
allowances should be made for him in view of his services
to the country. General von Kessel, a cousin of the Chan-

cellor, also did his utmost to smooth away the many unpleasantnesses that now cropped up every day. He had been a
peacemaker between Monarch and Chancellor in the days
of Emperor Frederick. Bismarck was glad to have the
General as his guest for the sake of his ready wit and his
independence of mind, and had always given him a warm
welcome. Von Kessel tried now to influence him:

"Your Serene Highness should not forget—I can con-
firm it from personal observation—how much His Majesty
the Kaiser had to suffer in his parents' home for your sake,
when he had to work as a young Prince under you at the
Foreign Ministry. He suffered this, like all the other troubles that he had to endure in his parents' house, in silence.
Your Highness will be sure to remember now in His
Majesty's favour the attitude he took up when a Prince."

Bismarck became thoughtful and silent. He made no
reply. But his attitude and tone towards the Kaiser became
milder up to the moment when the spokesmen of the other
group were once more pressing their views on him. At a
soirée he complained to the Bavarian Minister, Count Lerchenfeld, of his troubles with the Kaiser.

"But," cried the Count, "you should keep the young
master on a tight rein!"

The Count was very proud of his freedom of language
about the Kaiser. He completed the sentence:

"Il n'est pas un monsieur."

Both phrases travelled round every group. Bismarck
had listened to them without protest, and for the time he
became curt once more with the Kaiser. He was not going
to be charged with weakness. The Kaiser became still more
reserved and formal. He would try to keep the Chancellor
so long as it was in any way possible. Bismarck's knowledge

was virtually irreplaceable. But in their human relations
a barrier was growing up between Emperor William and
the Prince. For some time past the Chancellor had made
life bitter for him, had destroyed all his pleasure in work
and rule; he had had to be continually on the defensive,
unable to undertake anything except against the perpetual
opposition of the hero of the people. Things were quite bad
enough without Count Lerchenfeld's two phrases, which
had both got round to him.

The Prince's prophecies were justified in the issue of the
elections, at all events so far as concerned the strength of the
various parties in the new Parliament. The Social Democrats secured considerably more votes than before. The
Chancellor felt all the more confirmed in his views. Against
the sedition and revolution for which Social Democracy
stood in his eyes, he saw only one remedy—"blood and
iron." He openly declared that he had no belief in labour
legislation schemes at all, or in Council of State or International Conference. He was determined to make quite different proposals to the Kaiser—it was high time for them. He
asked for an audience on February 24.

Just before the audience he was shown by Count Herbert
Bismarck a strange document. The dynasty of Count
Schwarzburg-Sondershausen was dying out. When the last
Prince, Karl Günther, died and his brother, of about the
same age, followed him—they were both without issue—
the succession to the throne would fall to the reigning house
of the Prince of Schwarzburg-Rudolstadt. Small as the
event was in itself, the question suddenly acquired importance in the Chancellor's eyes, as he went into it, whether
or not the house of Schwarzburg-Rudolstadt inherited with
the little realm the vote which the extinct principality had

in the Bundesrat. There had been a similar case twenty
years before, and he had then held the view that it was the
States of the Empire and not their Princes that exercised
their voting power through their delegates to the Bundesrat. This time he was inclined to the opposite view, that it
was not the States but the Princes of the Empire who held
the vote. It was a matter of complete indifference to the
Chancellor whether the principality of Schwarzburg-
Rudolstadt had, as hitherto, only one vote or acquired a
second one by inheritance. All that he attached importance
to in the matter was to establish the principle that it was the
Princes who held the votes and made the decisions in the
Bundesrat; for this principle opened up quite unexpected
prospects.

The Bundesrat had enacted the Constitution of the German Empire. Its resolution to give the Empire its existing
form and Constitution was, accordingly, an agreement between the Princes of the Empire. Pursuing this line of argument further, it was undeniable, or at least it was arguable,
that parties to an agreement could rescind their agreement
at will at any time. All that was required was for them to
agree to do so. If they cancelled and destroyed the old
agreement they could then, if they so chose, make a fresh
one. Suddenly the Chancellor conceived the whole Empire
as the exclusive creation of the will of the Princes, as no
more than an undertaking entered into between them. It
was open to them now to find that the conditions in the Empire had become intolerable. They could for that reason
annul the old Constitution, by simply withdrawing from
their agreement. The Reichstag would then no longer exist.
If this was the legal position, there were all sorts of ways of
entirely getting rid of the Reichstag, now that it had become

troublesome, or of gradually crippling it. The King of Prussia could refuse in future to appoint Prussian plenipotentiaries to the Bundesrat. They would then also be missing from the Reichstag, and it would become unable to function. For if the Reichstag rose in opposition it would be rising against someone whose presence it needed for legislative activity but who was never there, since the Bundesrat could adjourn *sine die*. The Reichstag would then have either to go home or to resolve on proceedings which it would be possible to prevent.

The fact that the Princes of the Empire controlled the Constitution, and that it followed from that principle that they alone represented the German Reich, provided a still speedier method of getting rid of the Reichstag. The Kaiser could give up the Imperial crown. The German Empire would at once cease to exist. There would, it is true, no longer be an Imperial Chancellor, but there would still remain the Prime Minister of Prussia. In 1865 Count von der Goltz, then Ambassador in Paris, had noted down these words of Bismarck's:

"The attempt to rule with the present system of Chambers must be regarded as having entirely failed. Constitutionalism for Prussia is an absurdity; we can only manage with one form of government, that of an absolute governing authority, whether exercised by a Monarchy or a republican dictatorship. When I first became a Minister, I was a radical constitutionalist in comparison with my attitude nowadays. I believe now only in absolutism for Prussia."

In a conversation with the Empress Eugénie, at about the same time, concerning the dissolution of the Prussian Chambers, Bismarck had expressed the conviction that "constitutionalism is entirely unsuited to Continental countries." In 1890 he still thought as in 1865. If the Kaiser would give up the Imperial crown and so create an entirely new situation, he, Bismarck, would be able to do as he chose in the administration of Prussia, without troubling further about the Reichstag, which would have been dispensed with for good. Not only that, but he would be able to come to an agreement with the federal Princes, who would have recovered their freedom of decision, as to fresh conditions for the restoration of a better Reich and the re-enthrone-ment of the Kaiser. It was impossible to know beforehand whether Emperor William would give his assent to an enter-prise which would in reality be a *coup d'état* of the first importance. Possibly, even probably, the Monarch might soon entirely fail in his schemes for labour legislation. Or the Reichstag, with its strengthened Social Democratic ele-ment, might give provocation which would quickly develop into disorder, necessitating resort to strong measures in place of any labour legislation. If that were the final outcome, the Kaiser would be entirely defeated and there could scarcely be any alternative for him save to give way. The power would then be in the Chancellor's hands. He, work-ing alone and with stark force, would restore order where the reforming ruler had failed and only produced confu-sion. The Chancellor had succeeded once in creating a Ger-man Empire, and it would be a slight to his powers to doubt for a moment his ability to repeat that gigantic achieve-ment. Then, however, it would be another sort of Empire. It would also be another Emperor, with other powers, and those harnessed, that he would reinstate. The Kaiser would have become entirely dependent—on the Chancellor.

Ideas of such pregnancy as this, and of such far-reach-ing scope, were born of the *aide-mémoire* which von Bötticher, Minister of State, had elaborated in the middle of February, and submitted to the Secretary of State at the Foreign Ministry by way of investigation into the anxious question of the succession to the throne of Schwarzburg-Sondershausen.

The Minister had shown that under the sixth Article of the Imperial Constitution "not the Sovereigns but the States are members of the Confederation." The Chancellor added a minute:

"Where is that said? The Bundesrat (Article 6 of the Constitution) consists of representatives of the members of the Confederation. The members, according to the opening passage of the Constitution are the Sovereigns."

On the margin of the memorandum he wrote: "Is that certain? According to the preamble the Confederation was concluded by the Sovereigns."

The matter was not yet ended in his view.

The time for his audiences with the Kaiser at Potsdam was now usually fixed at 9 A.M. He sometimes suffered the further annoyance of being kept waiting in the anteroom. There had been times when he visited the old Kaiser even at 2 A.M. without being kept waiting a moment. The young Kaiser had begun for some time past to keep the Chancellor at arm's length; evidently he wanted to make it plain that he was, after all, the Kaiser. It was hard for Bismarck to get used to this. But the proposals which he had to make were too important to be interfered with by questions of pride. He presented himself before the Kaiser.

A hot discussion arose at once over the labour legislation plans. The Chancellor referred to the election, almost in triumph. Then he became reproachful. There was only one way to work for order—with force; every other method was illusory. It was better to clear up chaos with sharp measures than to show a long-suffering tolerance that would still end in chaos. The Kaiser, however, refused to see any sign whatever of unrest. In spite of the election results the workers could not fail to see that work was in progress for their benefit. The Council of State was to begin its deliberations on the morrow. The time for the International Conference was approaching; there was no question that it would meet. No workman was insane enough to be lured into indiscretions under such circumstances.

"Your Majesty," the Chancellor exclaimed, "give me twenty-four hours, and I will arrange for you in Berlin a rising which will settle everything in a moment! You can give the people a smart dose of grape-shot!"

The Kaiser shook his head in emphatic disapproval. All his ideas on the labour question proceeded from the view that the workers were German subjects equally with any other class of the people. He was bound to do everything possible to use legislative methods in working for an ordered society. If he were to assent to the Prince's proposal and bloodshed were to result, he would be regarded by the people as the cause of it. No one would believe that the proposal had come from the Chancellor and not from him. Even if the truth were known and accepted as the truth, the Kaiser alone would be popularly held responsible. "When all other means have been exhausted," he concluded, "I will appeal to arms. If it must be so, I will wipe out a whole quarter. But I must be able to answer for it before my conscience."

The Chancellor dropped the subject, and went on to that of the new Reichstag. It was to be expected that it would prove restive. There would probably be no choice but to dissolve it and send it home. He proposed to lay before the House a new and decidedly more stringent Socialist Bill. The Reichstag would reject it. The new and considerably increased military estimates, providing 130,000,000 marks for armament, were a further means of provoking the Reichstag into opposition, which would again mean its dismissal. Again and again, if the need arose, the Reichstag could be dissolved over such proposals, until it showed a better spirit.

The Kaiser listened in great agitation. He neither accepted nor rejected the Chancellor's proposals; the time for their discussion was not yet. The labour legislation was in process of drafting, and it was bound to have salutary effects; the Chancellor's plans would then be robbed of their pretext. In any case, the Chancellor could not carry them out without his definite fiat. The time had not yet come for that. But he could not get away from the thought of the street fighting which the Chancellor had wanted. A suspicion arose in his mind. He had not yet been two years on the throne; and the character of his rule would be impressed on it for all time if now he waded through blood. He began to sense a trap. Whatever happened would be ascribed entirely to him. He returned to the subject. If weapons were forced into his hand as the only remaining argument, he said, he would not shrink from using them; but he would never permit carnage except in the case of the gravest necessity. He knew what it meant to give the order for soldiers to fire on the populace.

But the Chancellor cut him short in sudden anger.

"Sooner or later it must come to firing," he said, "and the sooner the better! If your Majesty is unprepared for this I hereby tender my resignation."

The audience, he considered, was over. He took up his portfolio and went. He had now announced his resignation to the Kaiser three times. He assured the Ministry of State that the Kaiser would change his mind in regard to gentle measures. He was prepared to "fight" him; the watchword must be "no surrender!"

Though Prince Bismarck had talked of Emperor William as to some extent sharing his views, his own hostility to those of the Kaiser only grew more active. On the day of the first meeting of the Council of State, twenty-four hours after his audience with the Kaiser, he attended the discussions for a short time. He made a bitter speech, pouring criticism on the Kaiser's plans of reform—the Kaiser himself being in the chair. His language strained the limits of courtesy. He had scarcely finished speaking when he rose and left the meeting, without waiting to hear a reply from any side.

The Ministers and others present sat silent and embarrassed. The Kaiser affected to have noticed nothing. Later the Ministers sought out von Lucanus, the Head of the Civil Cabinet, and asked him to express to the Kaiser their regrets at having offered no remarks with regard to his statement, and their thanks to him for not letting a further scene arise. The most dismayed among them was von Bötticher. For weeks he had felt that he was being made the scapegoat in all the dissension between Kaiser and Chancellor. The Prince had overwhelmed him with reproaches. He had let him see that he regarded him as a traitor. He had stormed at the young man and reminded him that he had been appointed to the Ministry of State only to represent the Chancellor and his policy. Bismarck had forgotten that he himself had brought von Bötticher into contact with the

Kaiser, and had himself wanted him to discuss everything with the Monarch. The Chancellor was the Minister's chief. Often in representing him in the Kaiser's presence von Bötticher had realized the usefulness of ideas and plans put forward by the Kaiser, but had been forced to reply:

"Your Majesty, I wish I could go ahead! But I must not!"

He could not deny that even though he himself was directly under the Chancellor, the Kaiser was still the Kaiser. He was deeply depressed. He found himself driven from pillar to post. Every fresh incident made his position more difficult.

Bismarck had his standpoint in regard to the significance of the Princes' votes in the Bundesrat defined in a communication to the Secretaries of State for the Interior and for Justice. He insisted that it was the Princes who made up the Bundesrat, and not their States. He placed the communication before Emperor William on March 1. He submitted the document as a simple definition of constitutional law. What was happening today in the case of the Prince of Schwarzburg-Sondershausen might happen tomorrow in some other Federal State. The question needed to be decided on general principles. The Kaiser noted the decision, without making any further remark. The Prince entered into no discussion and made no hint of the possible further consequences arising out of his case. The document was sent to the Secretaries of State—with a request that they "should be guided by this principle in any case that may arise, quite apart from the question of the succession to Schwarzburg."

On March 2 the Chancellor spoke in plainer language to the Ministers. He read to them the communication to the

Secretaries of State, said that the Kaiser agreed with it, and added:

"For the rest, in order to counter the continued opposition of a Reichstag in which the opposition elements have the majority, it will be possible to resort to other expedients. The King of Prussia has the power to lay down the office of German Emperor. Without applying this extreme remedy, he can diminish the taste of the Reichstag for opposition in other ways, for instance by delegating no Prussian Ministers or officials of the Reich to the Bundesrat; the party leaders will get tired in the end of making their speeches in opposition to nameless majorities in the Bundesrat. Even the Chancellor need not be a member of the Bundesrat, but only its president."

The Ministers were nonplussed. What the Prince was suggesting was—so much they realized—on the road to a pure *coup d'état* and breach of the Constitution. Germany was still living amid peace and order, and Bismarck could only be indulging in theoretical speculations, evidently spun from a special case by his always active mind. Since the Prince's return from Friedrichsruh to the capital, it had been impossible to tell where he would next fly off at a tangent, and equally impossible to tell how he would treat his Ministers. As a rule he had been treating them badly. He had been letting them feel that he distrusted them. This was the only possible reason for his dwelling more than ever before on his power. At the very outset of the Cabinet meeting he had read to them an "All-highest Order" of September 8, 1852, under which the gentlemen in charge of departments were to submit their reports in audience with the Sovereign "after prior discussion with the Prime Minister." He had added:

"This Order still remains in force, so long as it is not rescinded, and it is necessary that the Prime Minister should be informed beforehand of reports in audience affecting his general responsibility for the whole policy of the Ministry."

This Cabinet meeting had no lack of diversity. Those present were baffled and perplexed amid its clouded, oppressive atmosphere. On the distant horizon there appeared possibilities of a breach of the Constitution and of the public order. There had been talk of circumstances under which the Emperor might lay down his crown. In future the Monarch was only to speak to Ministers if the Prince agreed. No one but the Imperial Chancellor could have any clear realization of what all this meant. He had stressed his agreement with the Kaiser. He had explained to the Ministers that the time might come when the Reich would suffer dissolution, to be born again in a better shape. He had not spoken a word of this to the Kaiser. Now he was cutting him off from the Ministers. However matters developed, the Prince himself could count on remaining master of the situation—whether he was in earnest or was merely giving rein to his fancy. Fancy or serious purpose, the spectacle was in any case dæmonic, threatening to burst into flames reminiscent of a Nero. His underlings the Ministers had to assist in it without raising objections, without opening their mouths. He was giving orders after agreement with his master. He had reduced the Ministers to absolute submission. The Kaiser he had isolated.

The whole horizon was menacing if the Chancellor could see no other way out. But it was Prince Bismarck's greatness that in every affair he always saw two ways out.

CHAPTER XII

THE FALL OF THE FIRST CHANCELLOR

BY reviving the Cabinet Order of 1852 Prince Bismarck had forbidden Ministers to have direct communication with Emperor William. This almost entirely shut out the Monarch from the affairs of state; the Chancellor could now determine much on his own authority and without "All-highest" intervention. He alone was *au fait* with everything, and he alone decided what should be submitted to the Monarch. A further important advantage which he hoped to gain was that the Kaiser's self-confidence and faith in his abilities would suffer a blow, and the disillusionment would make him more manageable. The Kaiser was consistently refusing to entertain Bismarck's plans for resort to force.

Early in March the Chancellor submitted to him the "menu" for the new Reichstag, including the more stringent Socialist Bill and the increased military estimates. Troublesome agitators, instead of merely being deported from the towns, were to be banished from the Empire. A hundred and thirty million marks was demanded for armament. Both proposals would have an explosive effect in the Reichstag. Once more, however, the Kaiser refused to sanction the introduction of a severer Socialist Bill. He was ready to agree to the military estimates, but reserved the question of their amount for further consideration. It surprised him to find the Chancellor making provision for so long a time

188

ahead. It was only a short time since Prince Bismarck had proposed to resign all his offices. Now, however, the Prince had entirely forgotten all that. He was only interested in the future. He was full of life and activity.

Once more he declared to his Ministers that the Kaiser was in agreement with him. This news was promptly followed, however, by an express command from the Kaiser that the new Socialist Bill should not be proceeded with. The Chancellor offered no explanation of this exposure. He only sought the more eagerly for some means of destroying the Kaiser's inconvenient self-assurance. He hit upon the idea of upsetting the International Conference which the Monarch had summoned. He had represented its summoning to Ministers as the result of his own suggestion. Actually he regarded it as useless and harmful, and as he was unable to persuade the Kaiser that it was so he began to call to his aid the foreign Ambassadors and Ministers.

He suggested that they should make representations to their Governments, and that the foreign Powers should refrain from appointing delegates to the conference. Before the Emperor William's intention had become known the Swiss Government had been planning a conference of its own. It was not so long since the Chancellor had been showing uncommon incivility to Switzerland, but there was no reason why that should prevent him from now asking a favour of her. He suggested that she should proceed with her own conference plans and decline to take part in those of the Kaiser. Probably none of the other Powers would then send delegates to Berlin. Roth, the Swiss Minister, received a request from the Kaiser for his support for the Berlin conference—and one from Prince Bismarck that he should wreck it.

"I'll show Bismarck," the Minister assured the Kaiser, "how to give the Monarch the help that is his due," adding that he would request his immediate recall by his Government if it rejected Emperor William's request. The Swiss Bundesrat supported its Minister; it abandoned its own plans in favour of the Kaiser's, and the International Conference in Berlin was able to be fixed for the middle of March.

The Chancellor had suffered his first defeat. The reply made by Switzerland and by her Minister could not but give him to think. He evidently changed his course in considering his next move. He had just had evidence of the extent of the Emperor's prestige and influence; it might also be able to counter plans for a *coup d'état*. He had hoped to get the Kaiser regularly hemmed in, by denying Ministerial access to him and by enlisting support from foreign Powers. The encirclement had half failed. The possibilities of a *coup d'état* were still being revolved in his mind. But prudence suggested looking round first for other means of retaining his hold of power. He returned to the technique which he had pursued so long and with such mastery in foreign politics: he looked round for methods of reinsurance.

Perhaps there might be some way of taming the intractable Reichstag without resorting to a *coup d'état*, of winning it over by perfectly constitutional methods. The guns would go off even better against the Social Democrats, and with even less objection raised, if the Reichstag gave its assent; or at least said nothing and agreed to being dismissed for the period of the shooting. The Cartel had ceased to exist, but at this moment the Chancellor unexpectedly found a prospect of securing a majority after all in the new Reichstag. Bismarck's banker, Bleichröder, brought him into touch with the leader of the Centre party, Ludwig Windthorst. If the Centre would join the Conservatives in supporting the Government, all would be well. The only question was what conditions the Centre party leader made. The price was hinted at—the readmission of the Jesuits into Prussia and the granting to Catholics of influence over the Prussian schools. The Prince decided to hear what Windthorst had to say, and sent for him. In doing so he certainly brought to a head the crisis of which he was the centre, and which in spite of all changes of course and all the Kaiser's forbearance was still unresolved.

The Deputy's visit to the Chancellor's residence did not escape observation. The Prince himself spoke of it at table. It was an event for the Chancellor to receive any Centre party leader, and the newspapers published the fact. There was great astonishment, and great excitement among the very Conservatives whom the Chancellor wanted to associate with the Centre in a Government coalition. The Conservative leader von Helldorf asked for an audience with the Kaiser. He spoke of the danger which the Chancellor's new policy involved of a change in the attitude to the Crown of the group which was the most loyal of all to the King of Prussia. The Kaiser saw the whole significance of the incident. He made up his mind to use every means of preventing the Chancellor from alienating from him his most trusted party. Prince Bismarck could receive representatives of any other party entirely as he thought fit, without consulting him. But the Prince could not fail to be aware that the very sight of the Centre leader on his doorstep would be bound to produce storms, that the very fact of a meeting would have immediate consequences which would influence the whole political situation, and would mount even to the throne. If, on the other hand, he deliberately made out of a visit a political event of importance, it was the Chancellor's duty, the Sovereign considered, first to consult him. The Kaiser went on to the mention of Bismarck's plans against the Social Democrats, discussing them now for the first time with any politician. The Conservative Deputy was horrified; he described the plans as "diabolical." Such ideas emanated "no longer from the great statesman Bismarck but from an evil, disgruntled, aged man." The Kaiser calmed the Deputy; it would not come to shooting—he intended to talk to the Chancellor again about the matter; there was a great deal to talk about.

The Kaiser was thinking above all of the "All-highest Cabinet Order" of September 8, 1852. Whenever, just lately, he had asked for the attendance of any Minister, or had asked for information, he had in every single case met with objections based on this strange document, of the existence of which he had had no notion until now. The Chancellor could not seriously be proposing to prevent him from summoning his own Ministers. Bismarck himself had continually advised him "also to consult the leading officials and negotiate with them." Sometimes the Chancellor was crotchety. At present he was irritated, out of humour; obviously he wanted to show that there were regulations of which he could take advantage if in his resentment he wanted to make the Kaiser's life a burden. The Monarch went in search of the Chancellor. It was the day of the assembling of the International Conference, March 15, 1890. The Kaiser had no reason to carry on the conversation with the Chancellor in any but a friendly spirit. He came to him full of breezy good humour.

He saw at once, however, that he had run into a storm. Count Herbert Bismarck, who had been reporting to his father as Secretary of State, left the room. The Kaiser asked for information about Windthorst's visit. In view, he said, of the political tension at the moment and of the interpretation which would be bound to be put on the appearance of this of all men at Bismarck's house, the Chancellor should have discussed the matter first with him.

There was a crash, and the Chancellor sprang up from the table, drawing himself up to his full height. The Kaiser remembered a phrase which Count Széchényi, the Austrian Ambassador, had used a few days before about the Prince—

"Il a perdu la boussole."

The Chancellor had banged with his fist on the table. For twenty years, he said, he had been receiving Deputies and politicians entirely as he thought fit. He refused to allow his domestic concerns to be interfered with.

The Kaiser pointed out the special consequences of Windthorst's visit. Prince Bismarck replied that it was entirely his own affair who might visit him and who might not.

The Kaiser changed the subject. He turned to the affair of the Cabinet Order. He could not, he said, allow himself to be cut off from his Ministers. The Order might have had some justification forty years before; now it was obsolete. He requested that a new Order should be submitted to him, rescinding this out-of-date one.

Once more, however, the Chancellor strongly objected. The Order he insisted, still served a useful purpose. He would not depart from the constitutional procedure laid down. Altogether the Kaiser was troubling himself about matters which did not concern him at all.

Since William II had ascended the throne, Bismarck had tried to show in all his dealings with the "young master" what he had conceived to be indulgence and consideration and benevolence. He had gone so far that foreign Ambassadors and the whole Imperial Court had begun to wonder at the change in the Chancellor. It seemed to him now that he had sacrificed his personal dignity for nothing, swallowed for nothing slights and injuries which no one had dared to inflict on him until the "young master" came. The source of them all was simply the different political objective and the different view of life held by the Kaiser, and no personal feeling; but Prince Bismarck had never before yielded to any other man's will or policy, had never before had to get used to opposition. He had forced himself for months past to make every possible concession to Emperor William. Gradually, he had hoped, they would establish the right compromise—to the Kaiser the honour due to the Monarch, to himself, as of old, the power. But it had all been in vain. For months he had been unable to work with the Kaiser. Secretly he had begun to take steps to counter the presumption of the "young master," and meanwhile his tone towards the Kaiser had begun to change.

Now, however, he was completely indifferent to the tone he adopted. Indeed, since all his efforts to come to an agreement had been in vain he would, this once at least, tell the Kaiser the truth, as he saw it, without mincing words. Feelings that had long passed away or been overcome through his rise to power and his historic triumph suddenly returned. "I serve the King because I am devoted to him personally," he had said at Biarritz in 1865 to Count von der Goltz. "I should never agree to serve the Crown Prince, and have often told him so. He and the dynasty are of no interest to me." Von der Goltz had noted these and many similar phrases, in distorted form, in his secret report to the Minister in attendance on the royal house, Baron von Schleinitz.

All the conciliatoriness that the Prince had ever shown turned now to its opposite in his exasperation. He had had enough, he said, of being continually upset by the Kaiser. The Kaiser muddled everything. He hindered him in his work. He could no longer get any real work done. The Ministers were now all at sixes and sevens. He demanded to be dismissed. It was entirely impossible to go on as things were.

Beside himself with excitement, he threw his big leather case on the table in front of the Kaiser. Then he said no more. Tears came to his eyes. He waited.

The Kaiser sought for a fresh subject, and found it, but once more he was unfortunate. He touched on Russia and his intention of returning the visit of Tsar Alexander. The Chancellor had pulled himself together. The conversation once more had a connected thread, and Bismarck was calmer; but he felt that he must once more point out the objections to the Kaiser's proposals. The Monarch, he said, was under a misapprehension, as to the real feelings of Tsar Alexander III. The Tsar did not talk of his German cousin in the way Emperor William imagined; his actual views were revealed in a report which Count Hatzfeldt had sent him months before—and the Prince pulled the report out of his pocket. It had lain six months in his desk. Perhaps it really was only by chance that he now had it with him. Even if it were supposed that the document had been tampered with, it undoubtedly gave, he said, an accurate account of the feeling at the Court of St. Petersburg.

The Kaiser demanded to see the document. The Chancellor tried to escape from handing it to him. The document contained statements which, he said, he could not submit textually. The Kaiser insisted, and Prince Bismarck handed it over. In it was the phrase which the Tsar was alleged to have used of his host: *"un garçon mal élevé."*

The Kaiser got up. He did not believe that it was a mere chance that the Prince had in his pocket an old document that was bound to give him offence. He broke off the conversation. In his right hand he held his helmet by its spike, caught carelessly between two fingers. He held out that hand coolly and casually to the Prince. He said once more than he would expect a draft Order rescinding the old Cabinet Order. Then he went silently down the stairs. The Chancellor had accompanied him to the outer door. When he was on the point of getting into his carriage he suddenly turned back, hurried up the stairs, two or three at a time, and returned to the Prince. He grasped his hand and shook it, without a word. Prince Bismarck smiled. He had seen the storm and its ending from the outset. So, after all, all was now in order.

But he had misunderstood. This was the Kaiser's silent farewell from the man who had founded the Empire. At the outset of their meeting the Kaiser had had no thought of breaking with the Chancellor.

Throughout the period of tension, up to the days only just past, Count Eulenburg had again and again urged conciliation. The Grand Duke of Baden, who in all the differences with the Chancellor, had been a prudent supporter of the Kaiser's attitude, had urged that the Chancellor should be retained. But, after all, all was now at an end.

The Kaiser drove home. He knew that the Prince

Royal shooting-box "Hubertusstock"
in the Schorfheide near Berlin.
Emperor William the Great stand-
ing behind the carriage, next to the
door H. J. M. Oberjägermeister (Grand
Veneur) Prince Pless. In the carriage
on the side next to the Emperor,
King Albert of Saxony, on his left
Prince Albert of Prussia (later
Regent of Brunswick) Behind the
Emperor his faithful old page &
his trusted loaders (Jägers).

GROUP OF DELEGATES AT LABOUR CONFERENCE

JULES SIMON, DR. HAUCHECORNE, FREIHERR v. BERLEPSCH, MAGDEBURG,
FURSTBISCHOF DR. KOPP

would not rescind the Cabinet Order. Prince Bismarck's closest associates had once heard him say:

"I am not set on commanding. But I cannot obey."

So the fatal parting had irrevocably come.

The Kaiser saw quite clearly how great the gulf had been between himself and the Chancellor since the turn of the year. The alienation had begun with the impossibility of agreement on the question of labour protection. The gulf had been widened by the Prince's persistent advocacy of a sharp lesson for the Social Democrats. The time had been when he had done his utmost to develop Prince William's self-reliance. During that period he had regarded Prince William's very monarchical way of thinking as the most right and natural thing possible; and he had valued any co-operation in opposition to the Empress Frederick and her views for the help it gave him at Court. But since the Prince had become Emperor he had made a point of re-minding him at every step that he was only the "young master." In Emperor Frederick's time a visitor had once asked the Chancellor what sort of a person the new Crown Prince was.

"The young master," Bismarck had replied, "will one day be his own Chancellor."

But true wisdom and the right to rule had, in spite of all this, been claimed by Prince Bismarck for himself alone. The Monarch had found himself treated by the Chancellor on every occasion with much less than Imperial honours. He had resented the brusque and wounding tone which Bismarck had for some time past adopted towards him, even in front of strangers.

Quite apart from social questions, Emperor William viewed the practical problems of foreign policy differently from the Chancellor. They were in disagreement over Russia. They could find no common basis of agreement on colonial questions. The Kaiser spoke of the successful progress of German traders in overseas countries. Their trade must flourish in German ports and centres of their own even on distant shores. He spoke of the importance and necessity of a great merchant marine, as the only means of giving the German trader a really secure position in the world, and the merchant marine was not the only thing which would make questions of sea power before very long of importance to Germany. The Kaiser wanted to offer Zanzibar in exchange for Heligoland. He had carefully studied the map and had found that three good ports on the mainland of Africa would make Zanzibar virtually valueless, while in any war with England the possession of an effectively developed Heligoland would make it impossible for the enemy ships to appear off the Hansa towns. The Chancellor, it is true, had sent his son to visit all the statesmen of the British capital in an attempt of his own to put through the exchange. After he had failed, Queen Victoria had given her grandson at Osborne a promise that the exchange should be effected. But that was not the only element in Germany's colonial policy that had helped to cloud the relations between Bismarck and the Kaiser. The Chancellor was only interested in colonial policy in so far as it enabled Germany to hold and play off apples of discord against England. Whichever way the Kaiser turned in considering his relations with Bismarck, he saw nothing but strong and virtually irreconcilable disagreement. Ultimately he confessed to himself that the difficulty perhaps lay not in the actual subjects at issue, not even in personal incompatibilities; there rose before him once more the figure of the skipped

generation. Even a genius, a colossus like Bismarck could
not endure the grafting of the new into his own generation,
its invasion of his allotted sphere and career. It would
probably have been more than Emperor William himself
could endure. Once more the past age had risen in obstinate
resistance to the age of the heirs. The Kaiser, however,
was insisting on his right to live and work. Here lay the
primary source of all the collisions and conflicts. The difference was lasting and incurable. The Kaiser accordingly
resolved to part from the Chancellor.

There was further trouble only three days after the
meeting between the two, but it no longer mattered in the
light of the Monarch's resolve to make an end of the crisis.
At one moment he believed that important consular reports
concerning movements of Russian troops against Austria-
Hungary had been withheld from him. He imagined it
had been done of set purpose. He felt that the Chancellor
had informed him much too late of Russia's real attitude,
of the danger to his ally and the necessity of warning her.
Bismarck denied that he had at any time preserved silence
in regard to reports of importance. He declared firmly that
all military reports had been passed on by him to the General Staff. The General Staff might have passed them on
to the Kaiser either direct or through the Minister of War.
But the Kaiser no longer believed Bismarck. Long before
this, *Vortragender Rat* von Holstein had told von Lucanus,
the Head of the Civil Cabinet, that the Chancellor was
withholding various papers from the Monarch. But this
too was no longer more than a detail, no longer of critical
importance.

Out of all the differences of opinion there had gradually
emerged one question of primary importance for the Kaiser

—whether the Chancellor was prepared to recognize his rights as Monarch and accept subordination to him, or meant to continue to demand that the Kaiser should obey the Chancellor. No compromise was possible unless Prince Bismarck would henceforth admit the validity of his rights as Emperor. And the test and proof of this was the question of the rescinding of the Cabinet Order.

The Chancellor, however, gave no sign of compliance. The day after the encounter General von Hahnke, Head of the Military Cabinet, called on him by the Kaiser's command. He asked for the draft cancellation of the Order. Bismarck refused to submit it and added that he was sending in his resignation. The day passed and still the Chancellor made no move. Next morning the Head of the Military Cabinet returned, with the message that the Kaiser was still awaiting the cancellation—or the Prince's resignation.

The Chancellor then informed the Cabinet of his retirement. Professor Schweninger had reported to the Kaiser that Prince Bismarck's health was severely affected by the agitation from which he was suffering, and that if he was not soon restored to calmness he feared that he would have a stroke. The Chancellor had himself frequently spoken of his need for rest and his desire for relief from the burden of his public duties in view of his state of health. At the Cabinet meeting, however, he spoke of his good health at the moment; he added that he would find it difficult to accustom himself to a life with no active duties to perform. It was, of course, impossible for him to continue to bear the responsibility of his Chancellorship without the confidence of the Kaiser. It was also impossible because his views were no longer in harmony with the Kaiser's aims. In

H. J. M. and Admiral von der Goltz
on board H. J. M. Y. "Hohenzollern

General von Caprivi (Chancellor)
& General Count Wartensleben
as spectators at the Kaiser-
Manœuvres.

drawing up his resignation the Chancellor wrote of his reluctance to cut himself off from the service of the royal house. He left open the possibility of a return. He went on to emphasise the importance of a new occurrence: Count Shuvalov, the Russian Ambassador, had arrived from Petersburg with important news from the Tsar.

Emperor William was determined, however, to dismiss Bismarck. He summoned General von Caprivi to the palace, and introduced him to the Generals Commanding as the new Chancellor. Bismarck had recommended him as Prussian Prime Minister on the day on which he had expressed his desire to resign from the Premiership. The Kaiser had sent for Caprivi in order that he might make him acquainted with his political views. The future Chancellor was able at once to give the Monarch news of the meaning of Count Shuvalov's arrival, at which Bismarck had only vaguely hinted. The Ambassador brought with him the Tsar's proposal to renew the Reinsurance Treaty between the German Empire and Russia, which had been concluded in 1887 for three years.

The Kaiser was thoroughly astonished at the General's news. At first he had no idea whatever what Caprivi was referring to. He had never heard a word of the existence of a secret treaty with Russia. The news was of such enormous import that at first he did not believe it: the agreement was an obvious betrayal of the Triple Alliance. He demanded proof of it, and General Caprivi submitted the text of the secret treaty. At the Foreign Ministry Baron Holstein had decided that the moment had come when he must no longer be on Bismarck's side, but on the Kaiser's. Behind Prince Bismarck's back he had secretly passed to the General this highly confidential document.

Twenty-four hours later the Secretary of State, Count Herbert Bismarck, confirmed the information given by General von Caprivi. He wrote that Count Shuvalov was ready to sign a renewal of the treaty with Russia, but that the Ambassador had been directed to negotiate with the Chancellor and the Secretary and expressly required by the Tsar to secure their signatures. The Secretary, however, begged permission to retire. He declined to remain in office without the Prince.

The Kaiser had intended to dismiss the Chancellor but retain the Secretary of State. The Prince of Wales had arrived in Berlin. The Kaiser knew that his uncle was on friendly terms with Count Herbert Bismarck. The simultaneous retirement of Chancellor and Secretary might create an unfortunate impression abroad, the inference being drawn that Germany's foreign policy was changing, and the Kaiser was anxious to prevent this. But in spite of Prince Edward's efforts the Secretary of State refused to remain in office. The Kaiser tried once more to dissuade Count Bismarck from resigning, sending Count Wedel to him in his name. But his envoy only brought back the message from the Count that "I cannot appear with my papers under my arm before anyone but my father!"

The Kaiser now made the best of the retirement of father and son. So far as the Secretary of State was concerned, he was making a really unexampled sacrifice for his father's sake. Few would have expected it of him. Count Herbert Bismarck preferred to renounce his career and his life's work, and his chief interest in life, rather than remain and let his father go.

Beyond a doubt the reference to Count Shuvalov's mission had been deliberately made in order to put a certain pressure on the Kaiser. If the secret treaty could only be renewed through the Chancellor, the Chancellor must remain. But the Kaiser did not let the unexpected news from Russia deter him from dismissing the Prince. The issue was clear. If Prince Bismarck remained he would not rescind the Cabinet Order; the Monarch would remain dependent on him; and the new agreement with Russia would be signed—an agreement which he could not reconcile with his conscience. If the Kaiser dismissed the Prince, the Tsar would abandon the treaty, and Russian friendship, which he had worked to maintain in accordance with his grandfather's injunction, would turn to open enmity. Prince Bismarck had already announced the result—a Russia leaning in future on France.

The Kaiser sent for Count Shuvalov and told him that he would have to consider the treaty, which Prince Bismarck had kept from his knowledge. If the Tsar were disturbed at the dismissal of the Chancellor and, after the Chancellor had gone, himself expressed the desire for the Kaiser's signature, in place of the Chancellor's, as a visible guarantee of his personal friendship, he would be ready to give the signature.

Prince Bismarck now gave the Kaiser all the information he desired about the Reinsurance Treaty. He informed him of the Tsar's absolute insistence that the fact of the existence of the treaty should never be published. In his embarrassment the Kaiser saw only one remedy—to play for time; the opportunity for this was provided by his proposal to Count Shuvalov and by the difficulty that would arise later from his insistence on the publication of the treaty as an obviously indispensable condition of his signature.

The Ambassador could discuss the matter with Count Herbert Bismarck, who had not yet left his post.

But there was no renewal of the treaty. Count Shuvalov declared that his instructions were to deal with the Prince and his son, not even with the son alone; and, apart from that, the Kaiser was determined not to sign. The secret treaty remained in his eyes a betrayal.

The Prince made his round of calls on resignation. He did not regard his dismissal as final. He had scarcely ever called on foreign Ambassadors; they had always come to him. Now, however, he visited every one of them. From each one he took his leave with the phrase:

"Le roi me reverra."

His departure was made a state occasion, and was accompanied by all the honours due to his rank and his life's work. Troops presented arms; the whole diplomatic corps was present; the population of the capital filled the streets in order to see him once more. The Titan drove home to his Saxon forests. In view of the magnitude of the event the reserve shown by public opinion was remarkable. At his last audience the embittered old man had said to the Kaiser that he found himself being dismissed with ignominy. The Kaiser had made no reply, and while the Prince was driving to the station the Emperor rode in the Tiergarten.

It was less than two years since Emperor William II had ascended the throne, and the first big event of his period of rule had come—the parting from Prince Bismarck. He had not wanted it, or at least had done nothing to bring it about. He had looked forward to a parting long-deferred and a parting in friendship and peace. Nevertheless, he accepted the parting as the gift at last of freedom for himself and his plans. The first thing which he would do to avert the worst consequences, as he saw them, of Bismarck's heritage, would be to make the candid admission to Emperor Francis Joseph that his friendship with his ally had been suffering from the menace of a secret treaty with Russia. The Kaiser hastened to make his visit to Vienna. Francis Joseph learned the whole story, with horror, and with gratitude for the openness shown.

"Prince Bismarck and Metternich," said the Austrian Emperor thoughtfully to his ally, "both had the misfortune to be unable to find the exit from the stage, and to remain too long."

Emperor William had a long talk with Tsar Alexander at the Narva manœuvres. It was not the Kaiser but the Chancellor who had been under a misapprehension about the Tsar. Alexander returned to the subject of his conversation with Bismarck in Berlin:

"Je n'ai pas cru un mot de ce que le Prince de Bismarck me disait, parceque j'étais convaincu qu'il me trichait."

He added, when the Kaiser had related to him the whole course of the conflict and its stormy ending:

"Tu avais absolument raison! Le Prince, après tout, quoique Prince, n'était que Ton Ministre, Ton employé. Comme tel, son devoir était, avant tout, de T'obéir. La désobéissance à son Empereur a amené sa chute. A Ta place j'aurais agi de la même façon. Sa démission ne fera point du mal à nos relations personnelles, car j'ai confiance absolue en Ta loyauté envers moi et mon Pays."

("You were entirely right! The Prince, though a prince, was after all only your Minister, your employee. As such, his first duty was to obey you. His disobedience to his Emperor brought his fall. In your place I should have done just the same. His dismissal will do no injury to our per-

sonal relations, for I have absolute confidence in your loyalty to me and to my country.")

This scarcely expected announcement of trust in him
was the first important one which Emperor William II had
heard; the first word of encouragement, and one uttered by
lips which had not spoken so to him before. It is true that
the Kaiser had not finally thrown off the burden of the tremendous heritage of Bismarck; he was only now really
entering into that heritage. It was a heritage encumbered
with an internal policy of the order of experimentation with
guns and street fighting; with an extraordinarily involved
foreign policy, and, in the Foreign Ministry created by the
Prince, an instrument of state in which every thread was
controlled by the sinister Baron von Holstein; encumbered
also with the disfavour of almost every political party, and
especially of the Conservatives, because he had dismissed
a Bismarck—for all that they had often been at issue with
the Prince. Such was Emperor William's position at the
outset of his rule.

No one knew the whole story; no one had the curios-
ity to ask for it.

Prince Bismarck was gone. Great was now the responsibility of the Kaiser and his people. It was for William
II now to show the stuff he was made of. It was for the
people to show whether they had the strength and the
capacity to bear their share of the creative work of the
future.

APPENDIX

AUTHORITIES

I

Communications, written and verbal, and diaries of Emperor William II.

Written commentary of Emperor William II on the third volume of Prince Bismarck's "Gedanken und Erinnerungen."

Communications from Tsar Ferdinand of Bulgaria and his Adjutant-General, General Gantchev.

* * *

Communications from:

Prince Max Egon Fürstenberg.

Prince Hatzfeldt, Duke of Trachenberg.

Count Mont, former Ambassador.

Baron Gelbsattel, General of Cavalry.

Herr Raschdau, former Minister of Legation.

Herr von Treutler, former Minister of Legation.

* * *

Communications from the immediate circle of Prince Bismarck.

Communications from Baron Holstein's immediate circle concerning the Baron.

All other newly published details in the book, including those concerning Empress Frederick and the "ninety-nine days," have been obtained from persons closely connected with the events or from those associated with such persons.

* * *

Communications from and information furnished by Dr. Friedrich Thimme, editor of the series of documents published by the German Foreign Ministry under the title "Die Grosse Politik der Europäischen Kabinette, 1871-1914."

II

The whole of the documents covering the period of Emperor William II's rule between June 15, 1888, and April, 1890, in the secret State archives of Vienna, copied under the supervision of General Count Beck.

Relevant documents from the archives of the house of Hohenzollern in Charlottenburg.

Relevant documents from the Imperial archives at Doorn and other archives.

III

In addition to the general literature dealing with the subject, and to the documents in "Die Grosse Politik der Europäischen Kabinette, 1871-1914," the following have been drawn upon:

Emperor William II, "Ereignisse und Gestalten."

Emperor William II, "Aus meinem Leben, 1859-1888."

* * *

Sir Frederick Ponsonby, "Letters of the Empress Frederick."

Freiherr Lucius von Ballhausen, "Bismarck-Erinnerungen."

Prince Bismarck, "Gedanken und Erinnerungen."

Philipp zu Eulenburg-Hertefeld, "Aus 50 Jahren. Erinnerungen, Tagebücher and Briefe aus dem Nachlass des Fürsten," edited by Dr. Johannes Haller.

Ernst Gagliardi, "Bismarcks Entlassung," Vol. I, "Die Innenpolitik."

Justizrat Ferdinand Philipp, "Bismarcks vertrauliche Gespräche u. a. über Wilhelm den Zweiten."

General von Schweinitz, "Briefwechsel des Botschafters."

Alfred Graf Waldersee, "Denkwürdigkeiten."

Egmont Zechlin, "Staatsstreichpläne Bismarcks und Wilhelms II, 1890-1894."

* * *

Baron Lucius von Ballhausen's Notes on the dismissal of Prince Bismarck (printed for private circulation).

IV

The German and Foreign Press of the period.

AMBASSADORS' REPORTS

AMBASSADOR VON SCHWEINITZ TO COUNT HERBERT BISMARCK, SECRETARY OF STATE FOR FOREIGN AFFAIRS.

Private and Confidential. (Letter written in the Ambassador's own hand.)

ST. PETERSBURG, *May* 23, 1888.

I have the honour most respectfully to report the following, in completion of my report of today, no. 133, on the conference held on the 19th instant at Gatchina.

The Minister of War pressed M. de Giers closely, and was able, in view of the Central European Alliances and the important credits approved in Berlin and Vienna and anticipated in Budapest and London, to bring strong arguments to the support of his demands. M. de Giers had only one means of rebutting these arguments, and could not employ this in the discussion; he brought it to bear, however, on the Tsar, and with entire success—the fact of our treaty, which has still two years to run.

"It greatly depresses my master," the Minister said, "to be unable to mention the treaty to Emperor Frederick, whom He so honours; He sees, however, that this is impossible, and that we may place implicit trust in Prince Bismarck; moreover, your Crown Prince knows of the matter." [1] Tsar Alexander continues to attach the utmost importance to the strictest maintenance of secrecy.

The "implicit trust" of the Tsar and His Minister "in Prince Bismarck" refers, he added, not to the possibility of a German attack, in which there is less belief than last autumn, but to the prospect of His Serene Highness the Imperial Chancellor rendering harmless the Hungarian inclinations towards war.

VON SCHWEINITZ.

EMBASSY COUNSELLOR VON AEHRENTHAL TO COUNT KÁLNOKY, MINISTER OF THE INTERIOR, VIENNA.

No. 36 B.

AUSTRO-HUNGARIAN EMBASSY,
ST. PETERSBURG,
June 22, 1888.

DEAR COUNT,

The news of the passing away of Emperor Frederick created a deep impression in all quarters in Russia. Apart from human commiseration for the noble sufferer on the Emperor's throne, Russian opinion had set sanguine hopes on this Monarch's régime. It was argued here that under Frederick III the stiff Prussian element would no longer hold a dominating position; Prince Bismarck, the fountainhead of all that is evil, would finally retire, weary of the struggle, and a new Germany would arise in Europe, weaker politically and militarily, and one with whom, in consequence, her neighbours would be able to live more comfortably. This hope had so taken root that there was reluctance to credit the stories of the Kaiser's grave condition, and the bad reports were attributed to tendencious misrepresentations on the part of certain groups in Berlin. The news of the Emperor's death was thus bound to have a correspondingly depressing effect. At first the dominant note

[1] This statement by de Giers does not correspond with the facts.—
AUTHOR.

in the Russian Press comments on the event was one of disappointment. Emperor William II was given a very cold welcome, and the re-emergence of Bismarck's star was noted with unconcealed chagrin. This tone, however, was not maintained long. A hint from the Press administration was sufficient to turn the unfriendliness with which the new German Emperor was being received into its opposite. The *Journal de St. Petersbourg* led the way by recalling that the memorable words of the dying Emperor William were a sacred charge to his exalted grandson and would supply the guiding considerations in regard to the relations between Russia and Germany. The remainder of the Press readily followed this lead, and one now has the strange spectacle of the Russian papers beginning a sort of mutual outbidding for Germany's friendship. The proclamation to the army brought a revival of mistrust; but the young Kaiser's later pronouncements met with a very sympathetic reception. No time is being lost in giving some sort of hint to Emperor William and his Chancellor as to the conditions on which Russia's friendship is to be had. Thus, for instance, the *Novoye Vremya* hopes that Emperor William II will only concern himself with the Near Eastern question in so far as it directly involves German interests. Between Russia and Germany, it continues, there are no differences. It is for the new holder of power to show that he is able to appreciate Russia's love of peace. This same paper makes no bones about turning right round from its former attitude towards Prince Bismarck and now eulogizing him in the warmest terms. It hopes that in his rare wisdom he will also carry to completion the exalted mission which has fallen to him of the smoothing away of differences and the reconciliation of nations. This *volte-face* is primarily attributable to an instruction from the Press administration. I should like to mention another consideration which has probably played its part. Russian opinion had got thoroughly habituated to the expectation of a weaker Germany, without her Iron Chancellor. The latter's position now seems stronger than

ever. No one here, after past experience, has any eagerness
to start a quarrel with this powerful individuality, and consequently it is preferred *de faire bonne mine à mauvais jeu.*

The abrupt change in the line taken by the papers on
the questions of the day was bound to produce a reaction in
another direction. They were not permitted further to sow
mistrust of the new era in Germany. The inexhaustible
store here of poisonous ill-will had to find an outlet, and the
stream discharged itself against Austria-Hungary. The
Press here has, indeed, in the last few days done wonders in
its abuse of the Monarchy. This racket against us is likely
to continue until the Press politicians here, disappointed by
their campaign for Germany's friendship, turn their pens
once more to the onslaught on Berlin's supremacy.

Your Excellency's most humble obedient servant,

AEHRENTHAL.

EMBASSY COUNSELLOR VON AEHRENTHAL TO THE FOREIGN
MINISTER, COUNT KÁLNOKY, VIENNA.

No. 42B.

ST. PETERSBURG, *July* 27/15, 1888.

DEAR COUNT,

As I was able to report in my most respectful telegram
no. 95 of the 21st instant, I called on Count Herbert Bismarck in Petersburg on the afternoon of July 20; he had
just returned from his first conversation with M. de Giers.
Count Bismarck made me the following communication
concerning this conversation, requesting me to bring it to
your Excellency's knowledge in strict confidence:

The first meeting between the two Ministers had had
more or less of a personal character. Count Bismarck began
by explaining that Emperor William's visit had no other
object than formally to announce his resolve to live at peace
with Russia and to renew the ties of family and friendship
which had existed for a century past between the two ruling
houses. The Secretary of State stressed the need of main-

taining touch to some extent with the autocratic ruler of Russia, in order to assure by the cultivation of the personal element the possibility of bringing influence in case of need on this determining factor in Russian policy. Emperor William, who, he said, was a very able man, thoroughly appreciated the importance of these relations.

Count Bismarck was determined to leave it to M. de Giers to take the initiative in the discussion of concrete questions. After a little delay the latter found himself compelled to do this, and opened the conversation with the remark that, now that the German and Russian Foreign Ministers were together, it would be well to touch on questions of policy.

The Russian Foreign Minister began by mentioning that in regard to the further treatment of the Bulgarian question the Petersburg Cabinet had no definite programme, though it held to its well-known standpoint that it was unable to recognize the *faits accomplis,* or, accordingly, the Coburg régime. Russia would continue in this attitude of reserve, even if there should be a danger of the provisional régime in Bulgaria being continued for years. In the event of Prince Ferdinand withdrawing, Russia would accept any other candidature, simply in order not to have to hear any more of the troublesome Bulgarian question. Austria-Hungary, however, was not observing the same moderation; her representatives were showing great activity everywhere in the Balkans, and especially in Bulgaria. In Sofia Herr von Burian was the most influential personality, and his advice carried the day. M. de Giers would not consider it fair if the diplomatic representatives of a Monarch who is on terms of friendship with Tsar Alexander were to continue to make capital out of Russia's present disadvantageous situation in the Balkans. Count Bismarck asked whether there was any positive basis for these views; M. de Giers replied evasively, saying that concrete facts could not be produced, but all the news from that quarter was uniformly of this character. M. de Giers regretted the situation so produced, as Bulgaria was the thorn in Russia's foot, with the natural result of great sensitiveness in official opinion here. The activity of the Austrian diplomats was bound especially to annoy Tsar Alexander, who scarcely concerned himself with the Bulgarian question at all, but showed great sensitiveness to anything that reminded him of the failures of Russian policy in that country; this question was, after all, something of a hobby of his (*C'est son dada* were the Minister's words).

M. de Giers had brought forward no new suggestions for the settlement of the Bulgarian matter, but merely awaited the views of the German Secretary of State. Count Bismarck met this first thrust by pointing out that German policy in general and in the Bulgarian question in particular was a very clear and very well-known one. It was a matter of indifference to Germany what happened to Bulgaria and who reigned there.

German policy had always had only the one aim of producing an agreement between Russia and Austria in the Balkan questions, and to this end the idea of a division of spheres of influence had repeatedly been put forward in St. Petersburg and Vienna—an idea which, however, had found no favour in either capital. The same view was still held, that it would be a great calamity if two monarchical and conservative Powers were to shed their life blood over a wretched bit of land like Bulgaria. His Majesty Emperor Francis Joseph and your Excellency were both perfectly aware of this view of the German Government's and had shown agreement with it in principle, but so far the soil had been very unsuited to the practical application of the principle.

Bismarck found it entirely intelligible that the Russian Government should be unable to recognize the *faits accomplis,* but another remedy was conceivable, and this consisted in getting rid of the illegal rule of the Coburgers. M. de Giers showed himself very disconcerted at this suggestion, protested against any such far-reaching step, and declared that Russia was not pursuing any policy of expansion in the Balkans; Russia was big enough and needed no fresh conquests. On this Count Bismarck had developed the view that, if the idea of intervention was regarded with horror, Russia had a large number of experienced statesmen who could have no difficulty in working out a programme accordingly. This very winter Germany had shown that she was doing her best in support of every Russian proposal. More than that she could not do, for it was not for her to work out programmes for Russia for the solution of the Bulgarian question. If Germany were to come into conflict with some small State, such as Switzerland or Belgium, she would certainly not ask a third State for a project for the settlement of the conflict. The German Government would first itself make up its mind as to the methods of settlement, and only then would it approach the Governments affected with request for support. So far as specially concerned Bulgaria, it seemed to Count Bismarck that a direct agreement with the Great Powers mainly concerned would be a possible way of attaining the end in view.

M. de Giers then turned the conversation to the situation in Serbia, in regard to which he also expressed great alarm. In this country too Austria-Hungary was exercising a dominant influence; the conditions, however, were such that a collapse was one of the possibilities of the immediate future. In this event M. de Giers anticipated that there would be Austrian intervention; this would evoke a storm of indignation in Russia which the Russian Government would scarcely have the necessary strength to control. Count Bismarck did his best to allay these apprehensions. So far as the German Government was informed of the plans of the Vienna Cabinet, the latter had had no occasion for occupying itself with the idea of intervention in the internal affairs of Serbia. Nor were the internal conditions in the country such as to justify M. de Giers' apprehensions. According to the reports of the German Minister in Belgrade, all was completely quiet there, and even the conflict between the King and Queen had so far produced no alarming symptoms. Even assuming a case in which Austria-Hungary found herself compelled after all by the course of developments to intervene in Serbia, this need be no reason why Russia should come into conflict with the Monarchy. Russia could reply to an Austrian invasion of Serbia by an occupation to Bulgaria. M. de Giers energetically discountenanced the idea of any such policy, and once more declared that Russia was not pursuing egoistic plans of any sort in the Balkan peninsula.

According to what Count Bismarck told me, M. de Giers did not say a word about the intervention of the German authorities in the conflict between King Milan and Queen Natalie. Had he done so, the Secretary of State would not have failed to give his Russian colleague a clear and intelligible account of the standpoint of the German Government.

On taking his leave Count Bismarck was informed by M. de Giers that Tsar Alexander would receive him on Sunday afternoon. On that occasion the relations with Austria and the Balkan questions would without doubt come up for discussion. Tsar Alexander, said M. de Giers, entertains feelings of the profoundest friendship for the person of our all-gracious master, and places entire trust in him, but Count Bismarck would be able to convince himself that whenever Austrian policy is mentioned His Majesty *always* becomes more or less agitated.

Both from the tone in which Count Bismarck told me of this conversation and from his express remarks I was able to see that he regards the impotence of present Russian policy only with a smile of satisfaction.

I have the honour, etc.

AEHRENTHAL.

Note on this document by Emperor Francis Joseph:

"The standpoint of German policy is the old and familiar one, neither correct nor in harmony with the Treaty of Berlin.

"F.J."

FROM A REPORT FROM THE AUSTRO-HUNGARIAN AMBASSA-
DOR, COUNT SZÉCHÉNYI, TO THE FOREIGN MINISTER,
COUNT KÁLNOKY, VIENNA.

BERLIN, *January* 9, 1889.

If the youthful Emperor William II holds his head
rather higher than he should in view of his years and his
natural lack of any sort of effective activity in the past, this
is certainly not to be wondered at when the manner and the
circumstances of his coming to power are borne in mind,
and the personal satisfactions which have fallen to his lot
in so short a period.

The young ruler has ascended the throne almost with no
transition stage, when scarcely six months before his prospect of doing so seemed, by all human calculations, far
distant.

At this celebration he wants all the sovereigns of the
German Empire to assemble round him; they come, and the
spectacle has all the appearance of a regular acknowledg-
ment of fealty.

At the new year thanksgiving he wants the commanders
of all the German Army corps to be present, a thing that
was never demanded by Emperor William I; they come one
and all, and among them are two royal princes: Prince
George of Saxony and Prince Leopold of Bavaria. . . .

If it is borne in mind that the entourage of the young
ruler not only owe their present position to the favour of
their imperial master but also rest their hope of the future
on him, it is entirely comprehensible that they should take
care to avoid expressing any views that diverge from his
Majesty's intentions, representing such views only when
they are actually demanded, so that the youthful and hasty
initiative of the sovereign frequently lacks the desirable
counterpoise.

However, those in the immediate entourage of the
Monarch still have an adequate opportunity for exerting not
inconsiderable influence, at all events in the cases in which

their opinion is asked, and it is by no means to be assumed that the best use is always being made of this.

Thus, as Emperor William I was sometimes taken advantage of during the last years of his rule owing to his great age, and Emperor Frederick was taken advantage of owing to his hopeless physical suffering, it looks as though William II is now being taken advantage of owing to his youth. . . .

Yet there is no denying that in spite of everything Emperor William II is much more popular, especially among the general public and among the masses, than might be imagined in the circumstances or inferred from current gossip.

FROM A PRIVATE LETTER FROM COUNT WOLKENSTEIN, AUSTRO-HUNGARIAN AMBASSADOR, TO COUNT KÁLNOKY, VIENNA.

ST. PETERSBURG, *June 9/May* 28, 1889.

In the present phase of the development of the German Empire, His Majesty the German Emperor is naturally the most influential element. The Emperor's individuality is now revealing itself in more and more definite outlines. In this process of completion of the picture a few dark points at once make their appearance, but the general impression is decidedly favourable, and the outlook into the future is full of promise. The Emperor has beyond doubt a seriousness and an ethical sense that seek and find almost entirely in themselves the elements that inspire his thought and will and action. Thus there seems little likelihood of the Emperor falling under external influence.

This formation of his essential character—united with conspicuous will power, keen and alert intelligence intensively applied, and a highly developed physical and mental vitality—is bound to have its other side, especially when one considers how very young the Emperor is. This shows itself at the present moment in a certain impatience, sometimes joined to great ruthlessness, a notable lack of moderation and steadiness, an over-hastiness in decisions and in action, and finally a strongly developed self-confidence, resting on an undervaluation of other people's opinions.

Upon the one hand the Emperor, as already remarked, brings into play a high earnestness in his conception of his duties as a ruler, and an effort, resting mainly on ethical bases, to do justice to his tasks as ruler; upon the other hand, the undesirable consequences of those qualities of the Emperor which I have been at pains to describe above as the other sides of his essential character, cannot fail to appear. Certainly the Emperor often allows himself to be carried away in decisions, even in actions, which are regrettable and which would be avoidable without difficulty with riper reflection and with an appropriate introduction into consideration of competent views of third parties.

The Emperor's defects, although they must be construed as a *direct* efflux of his type of character, appear nevertheless not to be of an importance which need necessarily arouse apprehensions of a serious nature for the future. In any case the balance *even today* turns on the side of good and, in part, admirable qualities. It may, however, further be hoped that, with the probable early appearance of greater ripeness and intellectual clarification in the young Monarch, he will probably in a not too distant future attain the physical and moral balance which may allow him to bring more and more into play his superior qualities and good natural characteristics, which, moreover, are already present in predominant measure.

I have already remarked that, by virtue of his most intimate nature, the Emperor is little adapted to be influenced by third parties. . . . So far as the Imperial Chancellor is concerned, it cannot be denied that in important matters—in questions of the first order—the Chancellor still exercises a great and often decisive influence over the Emperor. . . .

It is a matter of constant surprise that in Berlin in society, and probably also among the masses of the people, there is infinitely little talk of the Empress Augusta, of Emperor Frederick, even of Emperor William I. This apparent or actual forgetfulness may have its cause in those questions of interest at the moment which claim the public attention in a high degree, or in the force, depth, and breadth of the impression which the weighty personality of Emperor William II already creates, or, finally, in both elements at once. Be it as it may, this far-reaching forgetfulness, in some ways striking, remains, nevertheless, a fact.

One of the most noteworthy and interesting features which at the present time come to the notice of the observer is the great and far-seeing prudence of the Imperial Chancellor in his approach to the Emperor. As long ago as the month of December in the year that last elapsed I was able to realize how much Prince Bismarck had made it his duty to introduce a *great deal* of reserve into his relations with his Monarch and to avoid everything that might be calculated to make perceptible to the Emperor the pressure of his individuality, grown over-powerful by virtue of his natural gifts, of a rare measure of good fortune, and of events that have made world history. In Bismarck's house the watchword was passed, "The principal thing is that the young Emperor should learn to stand on his own feet, and to conduct his life as ruler independently and uninfluenced." This formula, which was perhaps given expression in a rather demonstrative way, was at least to the extent of one-half nothing other than the euphemistic paraphrasing of another, which might run as follows: "The new Emperor is so strong and self-confident an individuality that he would be unable to have patience with the uninterrupted exertion of pressure by anyone—and least of all by the Imperial Chancellor."—If this self-restraint of the most powerful of German statesmen became plainly apparent as early as the close of the past year, the history of the political development which has since set in shows with certainty that the Imperial Chancellor is not only carefully maintaining the restriction of his own initiative as a necessary element in any fruitful collaboration with his Imperial master, but is increasing and intensifying it. In this wise self-limitation there lies for me a fresh proof of the great political wisdom of the Imperial Chancellor. If he were not to impose upon himself a far-reaching reserve of this nature, there might come only too easily, if not, perhaps, a complete breach of his intercourse with the German Emperor, certainly a decided clouding of the relations between Emperor and Imperial Chancellor. This disturbance might ultimately proceed so far that a grave endangering of the interests of the State might seem by no means out of the question. The Imperial Chancellor appears—as has already been remarked above—to preserve his influence and when necessary his right of intervention in questions of primary importance in two ways: he remains passive in regard to questions of lesser concern, but on the other hand, and this probably as the first and main consideration, he carefully avoids exercising on the ruler a permanent pressure—which would have not so much the nature of a series of separate acts as that of a condition, and which might only too easily be construed upon the part of the Emperor as an attempt at tutelage.

As a recent example of direct influence being exerted by the Imperial Chancellor along a channel which ran counter to the will and the influence of the Emperor, it is possible here to point to the attitude of Prince Bismarck in the matter of the Rhenish-Westphalian strike. The belief had spread that the Emperor had had the intention of bringing the dead weight of his authority to bear primarily against the striking workmen. This appears, from good information, not to have been the case. Although the language of the German Emperor towards the workmen was grave and decided, although the supreme lord was resolved to apply the pressure of his personal appearance on the scene in order to bring the labour question quickly back to an ordered condition compatible with the interests of the community, yet his feelings as the father of his country and his goodwill were on the side of the workmen. On the employers concerned, on the other hand, his Imperial displeasure fell in so full a measure that the Emperor wished by his personal intervention to put them to rout and compel them to accept conditions of settlement very onerous for them. If the language which the Emperor actually employed before the employers was stern and grave, it would —had Emperor William followed his original intentions— have sounded infinitely harder and more coercive. It was only the grave representations of the Chancellor, who pointed out to the Emperor that there was no constitutional authority for the action which he was proposing to take, action more or less resembling the decision of a supreme court of appeal, and that he had no legal authority to intervene with an arbitrary decision in controversial private relationships, that succeeded in deterring the Emperor from following his intended course and induced him to give his address the form in which it was made public.

On the general subject of the activities of the Imperial Chancellor in his office and his demeanour as first servant of the State in the German Empire, I have only heard this much, that, in contrast with past days, he is now very gentle and quiet in his demeanour and dealings, and displays in his whole nature a clarity and balance which only those attain who have been able to rise out of the conflict of affairs and circumstances and to place themselves above them. . . .

As is both natural and right, the Emperor stands in the centre of the situation. There his individuality grows more and more accentuated. It is of great interest attentively to follow the development of his individuality, which is now of critical importance for so much and for things of such importance, and will be so in a still higher degree in the future. This observation is becoming all the more necessary since it is to be supposed that the individuality of the Emperor— in the course of further development—will become substantially further consolidated in its inner texture, and in logical consequence will acquire a very greatly increased significance through its proportionately growing recognition.

The powerful individuality of the German Emperor can be a matter of indifference to no one. In inclination or in distaste—in love or in hate—the weight of the Emperor's personality is already felt everywhere. The feeling of this is so coming to the fore at present, and at the time it is so gaining predominance, that without doubt there is already today in Germany less talk of the Imperial Chancellor Prince Bismarck than under William I and Frederick III.

I should be entering into contradiction with myself were I not to ascribe this partial silence and forgetfulness *in part* to the voluntary withdrawal—thoroughly discussed above— of the great Chancellor. But the other part of this relative silence certainly springs from the impression created by the weighty personality of the German Emperor.

EMPEROR WILLIAM II TO EMPEROR FRANCIS JOSEPH I.

MONZA, 20.10.1889.

DEAR COUSIN,

Unfortunately I was unable to give you a description, as I wanted to, before I went away of my impressions of the Tsar's visit; so I am doing it now.

Of the externals you will have learned enough from the newspaper accounts and I will pass those over, merely mentioning that the Berliners behaved very well in public and to my astonishment gave the Tsar so much warmer a greeting than I expected or the descriptions mentioned. As to the essence of the matter, it was somewhat as follows: (Prince Bismarck and I subsequently thoroughly compared impressions.) The Tsar came to Berlin with a heart heavy-laden with cares and apprehensions. He had again been hotly attacked in the past year, and the two months in Fredensborg had not been allowed to pass unutilized by the high womenfolk assembled there. Item from his questions, which he put from his tortured heart to the Chancellor, who had been commanded at once to the audience, it transpired that he had been given the precious information that I had joined with you, Humbert and the Queen of England—the Sultan ought to come in too, in order very soon to unite in suddenly falling on the Tsar, destroying his Empire and annihilating himself and house!! The Prince, in his quiet and clear and conciliatory way, succeeded then in such a masterly manner in disposing of every point of this nonsense and on top of that giving a view of European policy in general, that the Tsar was quite gratified and said to me afterwards, *"Ah, je suis tout à fait soulagé maintenant, et la conversation du Prince de Bismarck m'a dissipé toutes mes craintes, ce qui me laisse entièrement satisfait."* He has also been told personally many lies about me personally, to make him as suspicious as possible, but all that was got rid of with a magician's wand. He was cheerful, satisfied, felt at home, and at breakfast with the Alexander Regiment was so lively that he gave a German toast and drank with almost all his lieutenants. Vorontsov told me this was the first time for 25 years that he had heard the Tsar speak in public in German. He started his homeward journey in the best of spirits and invited me to his grand manœuvres at Krasnoye Selo next year, a result that came quite as a surprise to the Chancellor, but a very pleasant one. Anyhow we have peace secure for the present for a year to come, and let us hope more still, if God wills. That is how things turned out, as I am venturing to tell you. With many sincere greetings to the Empress I remain always

Your true friend and cousin

WILHELM.

P.S. Journey good so far.

A LAST MESSAGE FOR MY SON
AND MY PEOPLE!
HONOUR THE TRUTH!

NOTES CONCERNING
THE RETIREMENT OF PRINCE BISMARCK
IN THE FORM OF A LETTER TO THE EMPEROR FRANCIS JOSEPH
DICTATED TO AIDE-DE-CAMP VON SCHOLL
3. IV. 1890

1. Copy hereof is in the possession of the Queen of England.
2. Copy in the possession of the Emperor Francis Joseph.

TO BE PUBLISHED AFTER MY DEATH.

WILHELM
I.R.

BERLIN, 3.4.90.

MY DEAR FRIEND,

In view of the close and warm relations of friendship which unite our countries and above all our two selves, and of the great trust which you especially have always shown in me, I feel it my duty to give you in confidence a plain and unreserved summary of the developments which led up to the retirement of Prince von Bismarck.

I am all the more glad to do this since for an observer at a distance it is almost an impossibility to extract from beneath the husks of Press conjectures and hashed-up stories, mixed up with semi-official and demi-semi-official announcements, a kernel of definite and comprehensible fact. My account will only be a simple description or stringing together of facts, without polemic or criticism, which I am transmitting to you alone. I will say at once in advance that it is no question of foreign policy that produced differences of opinion between the Prince and myself, but purely divergences of view in regard to home affairs and tactics.

When the coal strike broke out last May, soon attaining the great dimensions that menaced the whole State in all its internal industrial life, enquiry was naturally made, after the usual measures had been taken for security by movements of troops and so on, into the causes of the outbreak. There were discussions in the Ministry of State, in which I took no interest at the time; I had had information collected and investigations made by my friends, especially my tutor, Privy Councillor Hinzpeter, who is a Westphalian and was living in the midst of the disturbed area, concerning the relations between employers and workers, the industrial situation, and so on. Soon, however, the Ministers asked me to attend the discussions, as the Prince was entirely intractable and the negotiations were not making any progress at all.

I attended and took part. It became clear at once that the Prince was taking up a position diametrically opposed to that of myself and the Ministers. He wanted the strike to be allowed to rage unhindered throughout the country and thoroughly burn itself out. He rejected every idea of intervention by the forces of the State, considering that it was the industry's business, and that it must be left to fight out its private feud. My view, on the contrary, was that this movement had already exceeded the bounds of a private quarrel in the industry, and I found the whole Ministry of State with me in the view that, if this matter were not taken in hand with the utmost promptitude by the King, the country would suffer infinite loss and injury. Accordingly, the old officials who had been losing their heads and had made the confusion worse confounded, were removed from office and replaced by fresh and able and thoroughly expert men. As soon as that had been done, I received deputations from the mineowners and workmen with the result which you know already. This effort also met with the Prince's disapproval, and plainly he was moving more and more to the side of the big industrialists, and looking on the workmen's movement as in part revolutionary and totally unjustified, needing for its arrest and cure simply "blood and iron," that is grape-shot and machine guns.

At the end of this affair the Prince withdrew to the country, where he remained eight to nine months, until January 25 last. During this period he had next to no contact with home affairs, and in regard to the movement for labour protection was only in communication with old Kommerzienrat Baare, one of our biggest employers and the most mortal enemy of this idea. I was using the time also to get material collected on the question of labour protection, was having information sent to me from all quarters on the situation of the workers, their possible and impossible demands, consulting the Reichstag through the party leaders, and so on. In the autumn I arrived at the clear realization and conviction that time was precious and imperiously demanded an early beginning with the labour legislation if the Social Democrats were not to forestall us and inscribe it on their banners, as, according to reliable information, they intended to do. Accordingly I began by asking the Prince in the course of the autumn and on three separate occasions right on to January—first asking, then reminding, and finally intimating my desire—that he should take in hand the preparation of an Amending Bill concerning labour protection, and submit it to me for the publication of an Order. Three times he refused very curtly—said he did not intend to do it, and finally said that he was fundamentally opposed to it, and that was all he had to say about it.

On that I sat down and worked out in two nights a memorandum which gave in historical form a narrative of the conditions of our industries, and added a list of main points which by general agreement embraced the worst evils which needed drastic legislative treatment without delay. As soon as I had finished the work I summoned my Council of Ministers and the Prince from Friedrichsruh. At this time the debates on the Socialist Bill were proceeding in the Reichstag; they were very unedifying, and the unbending obstinacy of the Chancellor was driving the Cartel parties into opposition. They had undertaken to pass the

Bill for him if he would only declare that the deportation Article would be "taken into consideration," not actually dropped.

On January 25 I held the Council, developed my views through my memorandum, and closed with the desire that the Ministry, with the Prince presiding, should thoroughly discuss the points, including that of the summoning of an international conference, and should then submit to me two proclamations for publication. A discussion then began, the Prince immediately showing once more his hostile attitude of the previous spring, and describing the whole business as impracticable. The Ministers were in such fear of him that not one of them ventured to speak on the subject. Finally I came to the deportation Article in the Socialist Bill, which stood to be passed or rejected on the following day, and most earnestly asked the Prince to make the path smooth for the Government parties, and to save the Reichstag from a regrettable ending on a discordant note, by holding out the prospect, on the occasion of the final vote, of taking the Article "into consideration." I mentioned at the same time that I had been directly approached by men who were loyal to the King and Government and had been urgently begged that this should be done. His reply to this was to cast his resignation at my feet, curtly and with a minimum of deference. The Ministry remained silent and left me in the lurch. Naturally I did not accept his resignation, the Prince had his way, the Bill fell through, and the Reichstag dissolved amid general dissatisfaction and repressed indignation, of which I heard plenty of echoes in such phrases as slackness and so on—an indignation and dissatisfaction which was then spread over the country by way of preparation for the General Election. We now see the direct consequences in front of us in fullest measure. You will imagine my deep regret when I now had to recognize that the Prince was determined not to work with me.

A difficult time now began for me. While the proclamations were under discussion the Prince tried to introduce all sorts of other things, and continually irritated the Ministers. When at last he brought me the two proclamations he declared to me that he was entirely opposed to them, they would bring evil and ruin to the fatherland, and he advised me to drop them. If in spite of all I signed them, he would only cooperate in this policy so long as he was able to reconcile it with his views, and if that became no longer possible he would go. The proclamations were published, and their enormous success showed the Prince, to his thorough astonishment, that he had been entirely on the wrong track, that his whole opposition had been purposeless and that I had been in the right. Now there came the preparations for the summoning of the conference and the assembling of the Council of State under my presidency. The Prince at once began a backstairs war against me, not always carried on by honourable methods, which deeply upset me; but I took no notice of it. On the one hand I was too proud to take up the challenge; on the other, I still had too much love for the man whom I venerated. Soon, however, more conflicts came in every direction. The Prince suddenly prevented the Ministers from directly seeking an audience from me by resuscitating a buried and forgotten order of thirty years ago. He took away all the work of the Imperial Secretaries of State, and determined to do everything and countersign everything himself. Meanwhile his health grew worse every week, he was no longer able to sleep, and his nerves were giving way. He was affected with hysterics at night and sometimes during an audience. His doctor said that if this situation continued another three weeks the Prince would die of a stroke. At last, towards the end of February, the Prince declared to me during an audience that he could no longer go on in view of his nerves and his bad health, and asked for partial relief from his duties. I asked him to make proposals to me entirely as he thought best and desired, and said that I wanted to avoid even the appearance of dismissing him or desiring him to go. After long discussions

with the Head of my Civil Cabinet, on whom he had called
for the purpose, he agreed with him that he should give up
the presidency of the Ministry of State and only desired to
retain the Chancellorship, and the Foreign Ministry. After
a few weeks he would then give up that as well, and retire
altogether about February 20 or the beginning of March.
With a heavy heart I agreed to his proposals, and an Order
was accordingly drafted on the lines he suggested, and held
ready until a date which he wished himself to fix. He himself expressed himself to me as entirely satisfied with this
solution, and told me that he would now communicate this
fact to the Cabinet. Two days later he presented himself
and declared curtly, to my great astonishment, that he had
no intention whatever of going, he was remaining. To the
question I put him, in my amazement, as to his reason, he
answered that he had informed the Ministry of State of his
impending retirement and had not at once been asked,
whatever he did, not to go, and that the gentlemen had
openly shown pleasure at his going. He had inferred from
that that the gentlemen wanted to be rid of him, and that
had reawakened in him his old spirit of opposition, and he
would now certainly remain, "just to rile the Ministers."
That is all he said.

I could only answer that I was very glad to know that
he would continue at my side, but hoped that the increasing
burden of work and excitement would do no injury to his
health. Well, from that day on the battle raged. At every
audience the Prince sought to discredit the Ministry. The
gentlemen whom he had himself selected twelve years
before, he now abused in unmeasured terms, and he tried to
make me dismiss the whole lot of them, but I would not do
so.—The time was approaching for the conference, the assembling of which he did his best to prevent by all the means
of diplomacy. The sittings of the Council of State were a
splendid success, and the results gave striking evidence that
I had taken the right course with my memorandum mentioned above and its points; the consequence was that he was

overmastered by jealousy of his young Emperor, whose successes he determined to destroy. He tried first to get some of the diplomats to report home against the conference, and finally he tried to persuade the Swiss one to request the Berne Government not to give up its conference in favour of mine, so that my conference should fall through. The Swiss, a decent, honest chap—who happens also to be well known to me—was outraged at such treacherous, unpatriotic conduct against the German Emperor, and telegraphed at once to the Berne Government; if within twelve hours the official cancellation of the Swiss conference was not in his hands, he would at once demand his recall, but he would also say why. Next morning the desired announcement arrived, and my conference was saved.—

This plan having failed, the Prince turned to another. The new Reichstag had been elected, he was in a rage over the election results, and he meant to destroy it as soon as he could. The Socialist Bill was to serve this purpose. He proposed to me to bring in a new Bill, still more stringent, this the Reichstag would reject and he would then dissolve it. The people were already in a ferment, the Socialists in their wrath would organise *putsche,* there would be revolutionary outbreaks, and then I must simply shoot into their midst and bring guns and rifles into play. As a result—this was his secret purpose—there would naturally be an end of the conference and the labour protection Bill, and their prospects destroyed for a long time as Utopian or a mere election dodge. I refused to agree to this, and declared in plain language that this was an impossible line to suggest to a young King at the very outset of his career—a King "already under all sorts of suspicions"—to meet the petitions and aspirations of his subjects with grape-shot and quick-firing guns. This made him very wild. He declared that it would have to come to shooting and the sooner the better, and if I did not agree he hereby resigned. There I was once more face to face with a crisis. I sent for the Cartel party leaders and asked them whether I should bring in a Socialist Bill and smash up the Reichstag or not. Unanimously they declared against it. They said that the proclamations and the results attained by the Council of State were already relieving the situation, and the conference equally so. There was no question of risings or revolutionary movements, and the labour legislation would go swimmingly through the Reichstag, and if the Bills brought forward were not all-too drastic it would be perfectly sensible. They authorized me to convey this to the Prince as the view of their constituents, and to warn him against any flying in their face with a Socialist Bill, as he would not get a single vote for it. The Prince came, and, full of anxiety as to how the conversation would end, I made plain to him that I could not agree to his proposal to bring in the Bill. To this he replied that he had no interest in the whole matter, and if I would not introduce the Bill that settled it. He had already entirely forgotten the position which he had taken up a few days before in the matter. And a business over which he had kept the Ministers and myself and the Government parties in the greatest agitation for four weeks, over which he had been proposing to dismiss Ministers and raise up conflicts, he let drop as though it were a trifle.

These machinations and intrigues, this friction and quarrelling in every possible direction, together with the failure of his little ambuscades, had brought the Prince to a pitch of excitement beyond parallel. The Ministers had had to put up with outbursts of rage, insults of the worst sort, until they refused to go on working. Business was coming to a stop, papers piling up, nothing more was getting settled, no project, no matter how urgent, could be submitted to me, since direct approach to me had (behind my back) been forbidden to Ministers. Everything was to be submitted to him, and anything to which he objected he simply negatived and refused to allow to get through to me. There came general dissatisfaction among the officials, extending even into Parliamentary circles. On top of this I learned from my physician in ordinary of Schweninger's great anxiety about the Prince; he was getting into such a state that he was in danger of an early and complete breakdown, which might end with nervous fever and a stroke. All my efforts to make things easier in any way for the Prince, by taking a more active part in affairs, he took for attempts to squeeze him out. If I sent for any gentlemen and officials in order to discuss affairs with them, they fell into disfavour with him and became suspected of intriguing with me against him. Finally things came to bursting-point. The stored-up electricity was discharged over my guilty head. The Prince, full of fight, and guided by the motives mentioned above, made secret preparations, to the horror of those who were aware of them, in spite of my commands to the contrary for a campaign against the new Reichstag. All sides were to be provoked and belaboured. First the Cartel parties were to be outplayed, and then the Socialists maddened, until the whole Reichstag exploded and His Majesty would at last be compelled *nolens volens* to shoot. On top of this there came the interview with Windthorst, arranged by the Jew Bleichröder, which let loose a storm of indignation in the country, and which was semi-officially surrounded with a mystery which permitted of any interpretation whatever. Not only that, but the attempt was made to make it appear that I had been aware of it and had approved of it. I only learned the facts three days later through the newspapers and questions which were addressed to me in dismay from every quarter. On the third day after this affair, the repercussions of which were continually extending, and which was beginning to have a very unpleasant look for the Prince, I met him; he brought the conversation round to Windthorst's visit, representing it as though Windthorst had virtually appeared unexpectedly in his anteroom and had taken him by surprise.

I had learned definitely, however, that Bleichröder had arranged this interview for him, with his consent. I told the Prince this, and asked him in future at least to let me know of any such important matter, by any sort of note or verbal communication from his Secretary. Then the storm broke. Abandoning all manners and all reserve, he told me he was not going to be led by me in leading-strings, once for all he would have nothing of that sort from me, I had no notion of Parliamentary life, it was not my place to order him about in such matters, and so on, and so on. When at last he had poured out all his rage, I tried to make clear to him that this was not a question of commands, but that in important steps of this sort, which might involve me in binding decisions from which it would be impossible for me to withdraw, it was of importance to me not merely to get my information after the event through the Press, but to hear of them from him, so that thereafter I might at least have some idea what it was all about. All this was of no use, and when I went on to show him the upset and confusion that this visit had produced among the people, who were still under the excitement of the elections, and to say that that surely could not be what he wanted, this pregnant reply escaped him: "On the contrary, it is just what I want, there must be such confusion and such a *tohu bohu* in the country that nobody any longer knows what the Emperor is after with his policy." To this I replied that that was not my purpose at all; my policy must be open and as clear as day to my subjects; he said he had nothing more to say, and roughly threw his resignation at me. I let this third scene in six weeks pass without remark, and passed on to the Cabinet and the Order which he had issued preventing direct reports by Ministers. He declared that he had no trust in "his" Ministers, they had brought things to me behind his back, things with which he disagreed, and he had given them a lesson in consequence. I pointed out to him that it amounted to a deep affront to me, who had cooperated loyally with him as his Sovereign, to accuse me of secretly intriguing against him behind his back; this he would not admit. However, if I demanded it, he would send me his cancellation Order at once, in the course of the day, after all it made no difference to him. Then once more, merely with a view to relieving him, in his evident grave illness and nervous over-excitement, of part of his work and anxieties, I asked him to let me take a greater share in business and to initiate me and include me in important decisions, but he refused with decision, saying that he must have made up his mind before-hand as to his decisions before he came to me. I was deeply hurt and wounded to the heart, and saw clearly that the great man was possessed of the devil of lust for power, and that he was using every occasion, of whatever nature, for working against the Emperor. He intended to do every-thing and rule alone and not even allow the Emperor to collaborate. That moment it was clear to me that we must part, if everything was not to go morally to ruin and de-struction in my house. God is my witness how I wrestled for hours in prayer to soften this man's heart and to spare me the fearful ending of having to send him away from me. But it was not to be. Two days later the Order for cancella-tion had still not arrived, and I sent to him to ask whether he was not going to send it. He replied that he had not the slightest intention of doing so, he needed it against his Min-isters. At that I lost patience, the old Hohenzollern family pride mounted up. The only thing to do now was to make the old pighead knuckle under or else to complete the sep-aration, for now the question was simply whether Emperor or Chancellor was to be top dog. I had a request sent once more to him to cancel the Order, and to accomodate him-self to my desires and requests already intimated. This he flatly refused to do. That ended the drama. The rest you know.——

The man whom all my life I have looked up to as a demi-god, for whom I had endured in my parent's home a moral persecution like the pains of hell, the man for whom, after the death of the Emperor William, I had thrown my-self alone into the breach in order to retain him, bringing upon myself the anger of my dying father and the inextin-guishable hatred of my mother, was looking on all this as nothing, striding past and ignoring me, because I was not ready to bow to his will. His boundless contempt of humanity, which he had for all, even those who were working themselves to death for him, did him a bad turn here, when he took his master for a nobody and tried to degrade him to a retainer. When he took his leave he charged me with having chased him away with insults; to this I naturally made no reply.

From this long *Opus* you may gauge what sort of a winter I have passed through, and whether I acted wrongly. The Grand Duke of Baden stood by me in the last trying days as a true and loyal friend, and my conduct had his entire approval. The new Chancellor is the greatest German we have after Prince Bismarck, a man loyal and devoted to me, and one who in his character is a tower of strength.

WILHELM.

Begun April 3, ended April 5, 1890.

SPEECH OF COUNT DOUGLAS, DEPUTY,

AT ASCHERSLEBEN, OCTOBER 4, 1888

From the full summary in the *Neue Preussische (Kreuz-) Zeitung,* Evening Edition, October 6, 1888.

There has been an inclination to describe the existing situation as unclear and uncertain. The success of the foreign policy of our youthful Emperor has certainly had to be recognised by the whole of the Press, including that of the Opposition. The successes which Emperor William has registered during the short period of his reign in regard to the consolidation of peace have been manifest, and it is significant that the Bourse has reacted to the accession of our Emperor, who has so erroneously been attributed warlike qualities, with a very considerable rise in all securities. It continues to this day in its whole trend to manifest the firmest confidence in the peaceful policy of his Government. It is, perhaps, not generally known that two years ago the

Emperor undertook with the happiest success the role of mediator in face of Russia's policy, which had been giving rise to fears that peace was in danger. As a Prince he had already, with splendid application, learnt the rudimentary elements of the Russian language. This unusual accomplishment and the charm of his personality won him all hearts in Russia at the time, and the incomparable northern cruise which the Emperor took soon after ascending the throne has just completed the work with which he had already made a successful beginning.

The young Emperor has been called the Cartel Emperor—certainly with injustice if by that is meant that he is merely an Emperor for those of his subjects who belong to the so-called Cartel parties. He is an Emperor and King for all his subjects without distinction, and will see that right and justice are administered equally for all. But if the question is who it is that stands for the Imperial programme, and from whom may our Emperor hope for the furtherance of his policy as I have just described it, then surely the answer is those parties which have at last begun to realize that what we need is unity and harmonious working together, free from petty party wrangling. The summoning, at the personal instance of our Emperor, of Herr von Benningsen, the leader of the National Liberal party, to a high office in the State, is not only a personal recognition of sterling political and other services; it is above all a demonstration of the Emperor's determination to call to the service of his Government all those who are fundamentally at one with him, without regard to special party nuances, and if today the Centre party, the Liberals, and others, a thing of which there is unfortunately little prospect, take up the same position in regard to the questions of fundamental concern to the State, they too will meet with unreserved recognition of their patriotic feeling, regardless of their particular views. You know how a meeting in the presence of Count Waldersee, the present Chief of Staff, in which the then Prince William took part, was exploited in order to throw suspicion on the Prince in the eyes of the public, and to identify him with the partisan political efforts of those in high places in the church, in particular with those of the Court preacher Herr Stöcker.

All these efforts to attribute to the Emperor a personal position in favour of particular party views rest on a positive distortion of the truth. My honoured friend von Benda, the National Liberal Deputy, who was present at that meeting, noted down immediately afterwards everything he thought of significance that had happened. His notes run as follows:

"The Prince expressly pointed out that what he was interested in was an effort kept apart from any sort of one-sided religious standpoint. This is an authentic unambiguous answer to all those foolish or malicious rumours. It disposes also of the open gossip, especially in view of the fact that Emperor Frederick authorized the then Crown Princess, our gracious Empress, by a special Cabinet Order to place herself at the head of the charitable work of which the first beginnings were planned in that meeting. Nevertheless I consider it desirable to state, in direct reply to the surreptitious attacks which are still made against our Emperor on the strength of that meeting, that the relations between Emperor William and Pastor Stöcker were only of very transient duration, and confined purely to that genuinely humane, because genuinely Christian effort to render practical aid to the lower classes in view of their distress, an effort which every Christian man and every lover of the people is bound warmly to welcome, and for which Pastor Stöcker must be accorded unreserved thanks and recognition. Beyond that there was no association with Pastor Stöcker, and our Emperor is the last man to subscribe to the extreme political and sectarian party views which are generally associated with the name of this Deputy. There is no possible question as to that. And if any attempt is made to connect the Emperor actually with the anti-Semitic movement, this too is an impertinence which I can dispose of in the most definite possible way. The Emperor is aware that in this respect also he stands at a higher level than the pinnacle of party, and that the Prussians of the Jewish faith are just as much his subjects as the Christian Prussians. It follows that he will extend and is determined to extend his royal protection to the former in the same way as to the latter. In this connexion I may quote a communication made by a trustworthy informant to the *Berliner Börsenzeitung*. According to this informant the Emperor, in a conversation, expressed his views somewhat as follows:

" 'I only know of friends of the fatherland and enemies of our healthy development. No one would attribute to me any desire to turn back the wheel of time. On the contrary, it is the pride of the Hohenzollerns to rule over the noblest, the most advanced, and the most moral of nations. And in this eulogy I include all Germany. The whole of our legislation is dictated by considerations of fundamental humanity. Anyone who fails to recognise this and who introduces dissension among the people, to whatever party or group he may belong, must not count on my approval. There is in truth more serious work to do.' "

I am able to give you the assurance that His Majesty, after reading this statement attributed to him, remarked that he no longer remembered the words, but had no objection to declaring his agreement with the views expressed.

REFERENCES IN THE PRESS TO EMPEROR WILLIAM II, 1888-1890

19.6.1888   FREISINNIGE ZEITUNG [1]

The proclamation may be described as a sincere reference to the deceased Emperor and as an announcement of

[1] The quotations from the newspapers named in ordinary type are given as reproduced in those of which the names are printed in capitals. Those for which only a date is given are from the newspapers named in capitals. The quotations from English newspapers are retranslations, with the exception of those from the *Times*.

trust in the people in the same strain as that of Emperor Frederick. The proclamation is without any particular political colour.—Emperor William, too, binds himself to protect the peace.

Times

It may be taken for granted that Germany [1] desires peace and will continue to desire it so long as peace can be had on terms consistent with the dignity, welfare, and stability of the Empire. If the peace of Europe is broken, it will not be because Germany has ceased to desire it, but because other Powers are less peacefully disposed than she is.

22.6.1888   *Nationalliberale Korrespondenz*

Emperor William comes as heir to the great boons which the older among us fought to win. His glorious father lived in the midst of that heroic period. Emperor William had no part in that great past, he has still to earn what he has inherited. It is to be expected that as a genuine Hohenzollern he will show himself equal to deal with the approaching perplexities.

1.7.1888   *Bauhütte,* no. 26

The Emperor has an invincible prejudice against the Freemasons' lodges.

Reichsbote, on the foregoing

In all Christian quarters of Germany this news will be welcomed with great relief. Emperor William is performing a moral service if he now makes an end of the traditional relationship between his house and Freemasonry.

BERLINER VOLKSBLATT (later VORWÄRTS)

This paper made no criticism or comment, simply quoting from other newspapers.

[1] The *Freisinnige Zeitung* has "Emperor William" instead of "Germany."—Trans.

16.6.1888   BERLINER TAGEBLATT

He has not yet completed his thirtieth year, and already Fate lays on him one of the heaviest burdens that ever a man bore. He will be able to bear it, and the whole people will rejoice to help him, if, in a free and unprejudiced spirit and with confidence in himself and in the people, he strives to proceed further along the shining path which Emperor William and Emperor Frederick trod.—We feel that we may hope under Emperor William to find a régime blest by peace. Our youthful Emperor has solemnly announced that he appreciates these blessings in their whole significance, and so, supported by our strength, our friends and our love of peace, we will hope that the transfer of the powers to the son of Emperor Frederick will enable his heir Emperor William II to prove a *Mehrer des Reichs,* a widener of the realm, of the welfare of the citizens of the fatherland.

17.6.1888   *Vaterland,* Vienna

A younger generation has been called to the throne, entering into the heritage of power with innocent hands, and with the duty of voluntary expiation. Woe to the new heir if he enters into the uncleansed heritage! With the blessing attached to heroic deeds he takes over the still prolific curse of unexpiated crimes.

18.6.1888   Levysohn's Political Survey of the
                      Week

To have no past is, perhaps, a special advantage for the new generation in enabling it to go lightheartedly to work, though the adventurousness and excess of daring which are natural to youth may well be modified in Emperor William II by the circumstance that he has at his side the aged adviser of his father and grandfather, Prince Bismarck. So long as this Imperial Chancellor remains with the youthful Monarch, so long his régime will be preserved at home and abroad from any lack of continuity in its principles of government.

19.6.1888   Speech of Professor Dernburg

The youthful, upward-striving Germany has received a youthful master. May he guide her to the welfare and prosperity of his subjects and of the country. Well, youth, they say, has luck.

Figaro

A Prince who is an enthusiast for his army is naturally also an enthusiast for war. But it is unlikely that international difficulties will arise before he has got used to his supreme power and holds the many threads of government in his hands.

Times

It is rather to the addresses to the Army and Navy that we must look for the more spontaneous sentiments of the new Emperor [than to the proclamation to the people].

Standard

The proclamations recall past declarations of the new Kaiser's; they are entirely free from any direct threat, but breathe an unmistakable spirit of militarism.

20.6.1888   *Temps*

The manifesto is reassuring only for Germany.—Dwells on the "protection of peace," which no one proposes to disturb, which at most needs to be maintained.

Liberté

laughs at the mysticism of the proclamation.

Cocarde (Boulangist)

prophesies woe for Germany under the new régime.

21.6.1888

The supreme administration of the Press in Russia has strictly forbidden any expression of pessimism concerning Russo-German relations in references to the succession to the throne.

23.6.1888

The circumstance that Emperor William addressed his first public utterance to the army and navy was bound to have the result of giving increased authority in the eyes of anti-German elements abroad to the news of the supposed warlike temperament of the new Monarch, especially in France and Russia.

26.6.1888

No Parliamentary assembly within human memory has rendered such unambiguous, candid and emphatic homage to peace as was done yesterday in our youthful Kaiser's speech from the throne before the German Reichstag.

Novoye Vremya

counts on Emperor William II exerting a particularly friendly influence on Russia's behalf, as he is in a better position than others to appreciate the evil that the development of the Bulgarian question might bring to Germany.

26.6.1888 (Evg.) *Neue Freie Presse,* Vienna

Blessed be Emperor William's accession! His speech from the throne brings a happy omen for all men.

Tribuna,

referring to the warm sympathies which the Italians felt for Emperor Frederick, writes:

The treaties and alliances will remain in being, but the halo of sympathy which was beginning to surround them is destroyed and, we fear, for ever.

Daily Chronicle

The omission of any reference to England in the speech from the throne is a welcome sign that England is not involved in the Triple Alliance.

Gaulois

rejoices that England shows no excitement, which proves that she is neither formally nor materially associated with the Triple Alliance.

13.7.1888 (Evg.)   *Riforma*
(Crispi organ)

Official Italy and the whole of the Italian people have welcomed the new German Emperor with great sympathy.

ALLGEMEINE ZEITUNG, Munich
Neue Freie Presse, Vienna

Since the army has become a pillar of the State, Emperor William directed to it his first utterance. Consequently it is impossible not to admit a certain logic in the circumstance that the army command preceded the proclamation to the nation.

21.6.1888   *Pester Lloyd*

According to the proclamation the young Kaiser has a profound sense of his mission and will reign in such a manner as to please God. But there is no satisfactory answer to be obtained from the proclamation to the question how the worldly or definitely political claims of the German nation will be satisfied. There are very regrettable echoes of the Christian-Social programme.—Where are now the great national and political interests on behalf of which a whole generation poured out its blood on the field of battle? What has become of the great interests of culture and progress?—This cannot be Emperor William's last word, there must be more to follow.

17.6.1888   VOSSISCHE ZEITUNG

Only a few pages of the new Emperor's book of life
have yet been entered up, but what has been written in them
is pleasing to read. We know that he is a man true to his
word, zealous above all in the profession which is naturally
the first one for a Hohenzollern ruler, the profession of the
warrior, that he has taken his duties seriously in great things
and small alike. We know that a serious outlook on life is
natural to him, and that he has a deep and broad conception
of the duties which have fallen on his shoulders.

18.6.1888   *Justice, Soleil, Autorité, Radical,*
Lanterne, Intransigeant

point out that William II's aim is primarily to be the leader
of the army, not the ruler of the nation, and that the reference to the glory of the arms of his forefathers is not calculated to revive the slender hopes of peace.

19.6.1888

The words which King William II speaks to the Prussian people can only win their full significance from further
manifestos. They are a fine and noble shell the contents of
which are as yet hidden from view.

Temps

Emperor William II has not seen fit to renew the pacific
assurances which were a striking element in the address of
Emperor Frederick III to his nation.—Everything is calculated to give us food for thought; a heavy responsibility
would lie on those who failed to draw from those events the
moral which they contain.

26.6.1888   *Budapester Tageblatt*
(Opposition)

The new Kaiser is alive, every line, every word of the
speech from the throne lives. One might say that William

II has jumped with both feet into the vacated place, but one must add that he completely fills it.

16.6.1888 KÖLNISCHE ZEITUNG
République Française

It is not without concern that Europe finds herself faced with the coming of William II to the throne. The new ruler firmly intends to follow in the footsteps of his father and grandfather, but he is only thirty years old. There is no guarantee that Bismarck's policy under William II will be quite the same as under William I. Let us, then, be on our guard, fearless but cautious.

Mot d'Ordre

We must be prepared for anything. For us Frenchmen a very grave hour is striking. Let us hold ourselves ready! All other considerations must give way before the imperative duty of national defence.

Figaro

Certainly we must be more on the alert than ever; but we have every reason for assuming that Emperor William will remain pacific and prudent. Thus, for the moment we have no reason for alarm.

16.6.1888
NEUE PREUSSISCHE (KREUZ-) ZEITUNG
Nationalzeitung

Extreme Left-wing elements brought pressure on the Monarch who has just died; extremists of the Right brought pressure on the present ruler even before he became Crown Prince, with the arrogant intention of representing him in advance as the holder of one-sided views, in order so to isolate him and gain him for these views.—We are confident that Emperor William II, who gave a plain enough public repudiation at the beginning of the present year of the intrigues of the other extreme, will disappoint the expectations of the Right.

Hannoverscher Kurier

Opposition has been shown to the views of Crown Prince William, to whom there has been ascribed an inclination towards the principles of the *Kreuzzeitung* party and religious orthodoxy. Our readers will understand it if we regard these tactlessnesses of the National Liberal newspapers in front of the still open coffin of the deceased Emperor as not worth replying to.

19.6.1888

It is only a few short words that the King and supreme commander of the army has spoken, but they suffice to reveal a complete picture of the young ruler in place of the hearsay of the past, and this picture is that of a great man.—The main thing remains the impression of purposeful strength of will which has been received by everyone at home and abroad. This impression, however, must serve peace in every sense.—The messages have done everything that could be expected; they have done more—they have brought glad surprise.

26.6.1888

The words in which the Imperial message is clothed are the masterpiece of a cool head reinforced by a warm heart. Everything is said which could win and nothing which could wound.—They contain loyalty to the Imperial Constitution. There is thus no reason to fear a misuse of power. Anyone who is nevertheless anxious about that will have to find the answer from his own evil conscience.

8.7.1888   FREISINNIGE ZEITUNG
(On the Imperial journey to Petersburg)

Emperor William is giving proof of friendliness to the other Monarchs through his journeys; he will certainly also bring back friendly impressions from the capitals of our neighbour countries. On the other hand, the political significance of such journeys should not be overestimated. We should greatly welcome it if the meeting of the Emperors were to bring assured results in one sphere, where the interests of Germany and Russia are not opposed, namely the economic sphere.

19.7.1888 *Königsberger Hartung'sche Zeitung*

When his father was last in Königsberg, Emperor William visited the quarters of the Freemasons' lodges there on one occasion, and in connexion with the visit made a joking remark about the lodge; but it was entirely harmless and conveyed no sort of hostility to Freemasonry.

20.7.1888 *Norddeutsche Allgemeine Zeitung*

Germany policy has never allowed itself to be led astray from its firmly pacific policy by the provocative and revolutionary Russian Press. These convictions also guide the Emperor William II, and move him to make his accession visit to his neighbour in Petersburg with no sort of demands or claims. It would be difficult for us to say what we have not and Russia could provide for us. We have no knowledge of any Russian demands which Germany would not at any time have conceded—irrespective of the shameless vainglory of some of the Russian newspapers.

26.7.1888   *Journal de St. Petersbourg*

The current of mutual sympathy was confirmed at the farewell on board the yacht *Hohenzollern*. Emperor William's visit springs from his desire to create at once relations of confidence which will serve the friendship of the two Empires and consolidate confidence in European peace.

Frankfurter Journal
(Report from Schweinburg)

The Petersburg Press insists that Emperor William is going to support the Russian claims in the Balkan peninsula.

27.7.1888 *Standard*

A German proposal was made concerning the Bulgarian question, which Russia accepted: Russia was patiently to wait until the Coburg Prince makes his further presence in Bulgaria impossible. Then Russia will resume relations with the new Bulgarian Government.

31.7.1888 *Politische Correspondenz,*
Vienna

The Russian journey has only prepared the ground for disposing of the critical situation. No positive decisions could be arrived at before the meeting between Emperor Francis Joseph and Emperor William, as an agreement must first be come to between Austria-Hungary and Russia.

Nord (Russian semi-official organ in Brussels)

At the meeting between the Emperors no formal agreements were concluded, but the friendship between Germany and Russia received a definite confirmation.

BERLINER VOLKSBLATT (later **VORWÄRTS**) has no comment on the journey to Petersburg so far as the Kaiser is concerned.

21.7.1888   BERLINER TAGEBLATT
Soleil (Orleanist)

Emperor William's journey to Petersburg is a last German effort to propitiate Russia, and a great success for Russian diplomacy, revealing the German Emperor as a vassal of his powerful Russian neighbour.

21.7.1888 (Evg.)   *Novoye Vremya*

The interview will not result in any alliance, which would fail to win public approval in Russia; while maintaining Russia's freedom of action, it will remove all the existing misunderstandings between the two States.

Journal de St. Petersbourg

One may count on an era of friendly relations, which will be a secure pledge for the maintenance of the general peace.

23.7.1888 (Evg.)

NEUE PREUSSISCHE (KREUZ-) ZEITUNG

Nothing could better illumine the winning and captivating nature of the personality of our Emperor and King than the fact that since His Majesty appeared on Russian soil even the section of Russian public opinion which is unfavourably inclined towards Germany has shown itself won over.

27.7.1888 (Evg.)

With the youthful gaiety and love of enjoyment that suit him so well, winning hearts everywhere by his open and manly approach, the German Emperor is acquitting himself of his countless duties in representation of his country with astonishing endurance.

18.9.1888   KÖLNISCHE ZEITUNG

While Ultramontanes, German Liberals, and the rest of the following of that company are trying to throw contempt on the National Liberals over the appointment of Herr von Bennigsen to be merely an *Oberpräsident* while Herr von Maltzahn, the Conservative, has become Secretary of the Treasury, we have found in the ranks of our political friends only general satisfaction at the fact that our leader for so many years has been preserved to Parliamentary life and consequently also to his party.

22.9.1888

The appointment of Professor Harnack to the theological faculty of the University of Berlin must be regarded, in view of the accompanying circumstances, as a very gratifying and significant event. The intolerance of the high church party has suffered a severe reverse; that is the gratifying element in the upshot of the Harnack case.

17.9.1888
NEUE PREUSSISCHE (KREUZ-) ZEITUNG
Indépendance Belge

It would indeed be strange if, after the Kaiser had given so much scope to the younger element in the army, and had so plainly indicated his intention of general rejuvenation, he had allowed things to remain as they were in the Government. This also explains the rumour that there is a difference of opinion between the Chancellor and his Sovereign.—William II as Kaiser certainly admires the Chancellor just as he did as Prince of Prussia and Crown Prince. But William II as Kaiser is not bound like William I by an irrevocable "Never." William II is 28 years old, and for so young a Prince, Prince Bismarck is an adviser of inconvenient age.

18.9.1888

The *Berliner Tageblatt* endeavours to show from the circumstance that Herr von Bennigsen has been appointed *Oberpräsident* of Hannover and Baron von Maltzahn-Gültz Secretary of the Treasury that we are approaching an era of Parliamentarism.—That, however, is an illusion. The selection of these two politicians undoubtedly amounts to a recognition of the attitude of the parties which they represent, but it does not in any way bear the character of a permanent obligation such as characterizes a Parliamentary system.—The moment the Opposition has to be considered because it has the necessary number of votes, there is an end of the monarchical principle.

21.9.1888 (Evg.)   *Nationalzeitung*

The Harnack case is nothing less than a demonstration of the general policy which is being pursued under the new ruler.

Post

The settlement of this case has symptomatic importance.

21.9.1888 (Evg.)

The attack of the *Post* and its National Liberal contemporaries last December against "Stöckerism and Cant" were the tactless preparations for the still greater tactlessness with which they claimed His Majesty the Emperor at every opportunity during the elections actually as an ally in their purely party machinations. We rejected this attempt, as we also did the recent impudent attempt of the *Magdeburgische Zeitung* to claim His Majesty the King as at one with its view. These newspapers seem totally blind to the absolutely insulting implications of these continual efforts to use the person of our royal master as a shield for their own enmity towards the church, the very shadow of which is so sinister in the sight of the *Nationalzeitung*.

7.1.1889   BERLINER TAGEBLATT
Levysohn's Survey

In the stoppage of the proceedings against Professor Geffcken the home and foreign Press sees not merely an ordinary decision of the courts but—rightly or wrongly—a smashing defeat for the German Imperial Chancellor.—The legalist's pen which wrote the Chancellor's direct report of our Emperor deserves, in any case, no thanks from the friends of the fatherland.

10.1.1889   *Deutsches Wochenblatt*

If in spite of all the allowances which we must make the Geffcken case has become a defeat for Prince Bismarck, the whole responsibility for this lies with the publication of the direct report to the Emperor.—The paper complains of the bad legal advice given to the Chancellor, as on other occasions to the Kaiser; the prosecution instituted by H.M. the Emperor in the diary case against the *Freisinnige Zeitung* and the *Kieler Zeitung* also had to be withdrawn.

10.1.1889

We consider that, before the Monarch can be advised to take proceedings, the most conscientious investigation is needed whether the action can be carried through to success and the winning of the case depended on. It does nothing to increase the authority of the Monarch if an action brought by the Emperor is lost or withdrawn. To us it is a matter of shame that the Emperor's action had to be withdrawn. The Emperor should never have been brought into such a position.

9.1.1889   *Berliner Volksblatt*
                     (later *Vorwärts*)

The release of Geffcken and the ignominious despatch of the libellers of Morier and the late German Emperor are events of high political import.—They are two heavy blows that have fallen, certainly with no chance simultaneity, on the German Chancellor and his eldest son and putative successor.

7.1.1889 (Evg.)

VOSSISCHE ZEITUNG

Daily Telegraph

Even in despotically governed countries a worse mistake has rarely been made by an angered statesman or an irresponsible executive than the arrest and detention of Geffcken.

9.1.1889 (Evg.)   *Weser Zeitung*

Prince Bismarck, whose direct report to the Emperor was, as is well known, responsible for the prosecution of Geffcken at the instance of Emperor William II, incorporated in the documents a long memorandum in which he laid special stress on the assertion that the defendant had disturbed the relations between Germany and the Cabinets of England, Luxemburg and Belgium by the publication of the diary of Emperor Frederick III. This contention Geffcken was able at once to dispose of through the speech of Emperor William II from the throne, which contained the express statement that Germany's relations with the other European States were of the best and most undisturbed nature.

Dresdner Nachrichten

It will be remembered that Chief Justice Dr. Simson received the Order of the Black Eagle from Emperor Frederick; at the ceremony, however, of laying the foundation stone of the Courts of Justice he was not spoken to by Emperor William II.

7.1.1889

NEUE PREUSSISCHE (KREUZ-) ZEITUNG

The purpose of the Chancellor's direct report to H.M. the Emperor was in the first place to ascertain the person immediately responsible, and further to discover who were behind him and threatening to bring down the Chancellor through their intrigue.—He does not say a word about the latter in his direct report. If one recalls the sittings of the Reichstag in which Bismarck rejected the insinuation of the Liberals that he was seeking shelter behind the person of his Imperial master—rejected it with the utmost indignation—this fact is so obvious that there can be no justification for regarding its opposite as even possible.

8.1.1889 *Wiener Tagblatt*

discusses the relations between father and son and seeks to undermine the supreme authority in the State. Concludes: The dead man is unconquerable.

Wiener Allgemeine Zeitung

attacks Emperor William II's decisions as the outcome of the wildest reaction. It would be possible to overlook these outrages . . . if one were not well aware who the people are who are at the back of this document, and if one did not recognize at once the systematic and determined way in which this activity has been carried on since the first public appearance of Emperor William—everywhere, not only in Vienna. During the newspaper feud of last November between Germany and Austria we pointed out that that great destructive power——Greater Jewry—has its hand in every disturbance. We were charged with tactlessness, because we had dared to spurn insolent attacks on the person of our Emperor. The same persons who wrote those articles stand at the centre of the international movement for Jewish domination . . . which unites in Paris and London with a current which has its source only in envy and uncharitableness towards the fame and power of the German Empire and its Christian Emperor.

20.1.1889 KLADDERADATSCH

The German Liberals are in luck with the darling of their choice. With what pride they can now gaze once more on the noble martyr Geffcken, who made a name through a contemptible breach of confidence towards the deceased Emperor Frederick.

19.4.1889 BERLINER TAGEBLATT

Reichsbote

We want no favouring or pampering of positive church circles at the hands of the Government; nursed by Court and State, the Christian life easily develops unhealthy and unnatural excrescences; Christendom thrives only in the pure freshness of God's air. This confession is suggestive of the fox finding the grapes of Court favour sour because they are to be hung further out of reach.

24.4.1889

Might not a mass of confusion and agitation have been avoided and our country spared the spread of a wretchedly misguided agitation which the late Emperor Frederick branded once for all as a disgrace? If to-day the Court preacher-demagogue is reprehensible and dangerous, why was he not years ago? And has not this tolerance favoured and pampered what to-day it is considered a duty to remove?

24.4.1889 (Evg.)
Kölnische Volkszeitung

In our view the decision in the Stöcker case represents a sort of compromise between the political standpoint taken up by Prince Bismarck and the princely considerations which are supported in influential Court circles. Stöcker has decided to retain his office at Court, subject to the condition of avoidance of political agitation, and it is said that in this he was guided by the influence of Count Waldersee or even a much higher influence. It is said that the Emperor himself desired that Stöcker should remain Court Chaplain.

24.4.1889
Vossische Zeitung

The semi-official attacks of which Herr Stöcker has lately been the victim have nothing in common with the dislike of anti-Semitism or of the "Berlin movement," but have been aimed at the Court Chaplain merely as a tool of influential circles which are becoming dangerous to the

Chancellor's position.—The fate of Herr Stöcker is merely a stage in the struggle which is being carried on between much more powerful persons than the Court Chaplain and the pastor of the Golgotha Church.

The *Schlesische Zeitung*

attaches special importance to the fact that on Good Friday the Kaiser attended early morning service in the Cathedral, Court Chaplain Stöcker officiating. "It must be more than three months since the Emperor was last present at a service conducted by this priest. One may take this as a sign that the Emperor approves the present solution, apart from any question of what share the Emperor may himself have had in the matter."

25.4.1889 (Evg.)   *Germania*

believes that before Stöcker's withdrawal from the political arena there was a stage in which he tried to secure release from his post, but was induced by persuasion from "a high quarter" to remain at it. "On Good Friday the Imperial family attended his service in the Cathedral, and directly afterwards he set off for the South of Europe. From this it would appear that Herr Stöcker has had enough of the attempt to cut a figure in politics, and quickly abandoned this ambition in face of a more important consideration when he found that 'a high quarter' had had enough of his vanity."

26.4.1889

The Emperor himself prevented Stöcker from retiring from his post at Court, according to the *Liberale Korrespondenz,* and visited Herr Stöcker for this purpose.—Herr Stöcker's influence in certain important directions seems to have been consolidated by those who were out to get rid of an awkward opponent.

21.4.1889

BERLINER VOLKSBLATT (later VORWÄRTS)

A lot of newspapers (especially Conservative ones) are going thoroughly every day into the question of Stöcker and his fate. What the end may be is of little concern to us.

26.4.1889

It is one of the little ironies of world history that Stöcker, the doughty and much-fêted Socialist-killer, should have to sink his political activities and vanish from the scene at the very moment in which the German Social Democracy is preparing for an election campaign which promises it such successes as it has never before achieved.

24 4.1889   KLADDERADATSCH

The man on the shelf

Jacta est alea! The brave and bold,
The warrior who had towered o'er the melée,
Disgruntled, growling, and with looks that scold
Has put his buckler and his sword away.

The tempest threatened, brewed, piled up, and burst,
It crashed and howled and hurtled round his head,
And now—Ye Hebrews, fear no more the worst!—
The preacher lives, the agitator's dead.

(There follow three more strophes with the same refrain.)

In the South

A million violets waft their scent around him,
And all around the nightingales are piping;
Amid the groves of southern myrtles strides the
Magnificent Stöcker.

Radiant with bliss his cheeks so smooth and rosy;
Peace dwells within his bosom, and forgiveness;
Softly he whispers, smiling, "Donnerwetter!
May the devil take them!"

Stöcker at the Crossroads

Herr Stöcker is to retire "for the present" from the arena of party politics, and is to devote the next ten days to thinking out, far from Berlin, how long he can stick it.

26.1.1890   BERLINER TAGEBLATT
(On the dissolution of the Reichstag)

We are so little spoiled that it can only surprise us and fill us with some satisfaction when we find that Emperor William II expressly and repeatedly mentions the good service that the Reichstag has done in watching over the maintenance of peace at home and abroad.—There would certainly have been satisfaction and rejoicing in the camp of the Cartel if the Emperor's speech had contained a sentence or even a word that could have been exploited in any way in the election campaign. But it would seem that the Monarch has too strong a sense of constitutionalism to lend an ear to any suggestions of that sort that might reach the throne.—The noble, cool, and wise reserve which has protected the wearer of the crown from placing an unbridgeable gulf between himself and the great majority of the voters in the Empire, may surely be taken as a sign that Emperor William II is filled with truly constitutional feelings. And as he gives no hint of concern with the issue of the coming elections, it is certainly no overdrawn inference to conclude that the Emperor desires to ascertain in free elections the result of an unfalsified expression of the public opinion of all the citizens of the State.

27.1.1890   Levysohn's Survey

All those imputations against the personality of the young Emperor which have been made by those who envy and hate the name of Germany, have been exposed as lies and slanders by the things William II has done or forborne from doing.—The absolutist inclinations attributed to the new Sovereign in certain quarters have shown not the slightest sign of existence. Thus the German people has learnt to look up to the holder of the kingly office with sincere trust, just as he himself omits no opportunity of showing the nation his full trust as its Emperor.—Emperor William II often goes his own way, which is not always that of those who would be glad to prescribe bureaucratic standards for the wearer of the crown. The speech from the throne (at the dissolution of the Reichstag) also gives evidence of the characteristic independence of views which is so often brought to bear by our Emperor.

1.2.1890
(On the appointment of Berlepsch as Minister of Commerce)

Of late the Emperor has frequently had memoranda prepared for him, over the heads of Ministers, by Herren Berlepsch and Hinzpeter, the latter a pronounced friend of the workers. It would also appear that the Emperor is inclined further to reduce the influence of the Imperial Chancellor at least in one field, and that one of the most important, that of labour legislation.

6.2.1890   (On the Kaiser's Messages)

With these few words a step of enormous importance has been taken, showing us that the Monarch is alive to the demands of the present day.—He is placing himself in the centre of the pulsing present, and holds the view that, if the worker renders unto Cæsar that which is Cæsar's, the Kaiser is also bound to give the worker that which is the worker's.—In any case the suggestions which Emperor William II has seen fit to make to the Chancellor and to the Prussian Minister of Commerce, Industry and Public Works, will find wide acceptance. We Liberals may rejoice that we prepared the way for this initiative on the part of the Monarch.—With this proclamation of her ruler, Germany places herself at the head of the new and true civilisation.

6.2.1890 (Evg.)

Our Emperor has himself inscribed on his standard the International Conference on the labour question, and now our opponents also find the idea entirely excellent. We rejoice at this conversion, and are grateful to the Emperor for having effected it.

7.2.1890   *Post*

Industrialists familiar with conditions among the workers and also friendly towards them see in the setting up of committees of the workers a serious danger, especially in the direction of their easy development into an organization of the Social Democrats. This view is shared by Herr Stumm, the great leader of industry, whose narrow ideas Emperor William is said only lately to have energetically combated at the Bismarck dinner.

St. James's Gazette
The two messages are a significant sign of the times.

Pall Mall Gazette
The Kaiser's declarations are entirely admirable. The messages are one of the most important events in modern European history.

7.2.1890 (Evg.)   *Kölnische Zeitung*

The energetic application of the German Imperial power to the practical interests of the workers will awaken many high-flown aspirations, which will be bound to be followed by disappointments, and will increase the sense of power of the working masses and their itch to become a Great Power.

Fremdenblatt, Vienna
Emperor William has given unforgettable proof of his great-hearted, truly philanthropic intentions. More lasting

than brass will be the memory of this in the feelings of all and its record in history.

Wiener Tagblatt

The messages announce a new world era. It will add to the fame of the German Emperor that with his powerful hand he intends to push through the solution of the labour question.

8.2.1890 (Evg.)   *Journal des Débats*

The messages are one of the most important events in the economic history of the present time.

Rheinisch-Westfälische Zeitung

The messages will certainly increase the persistence of the working classes.

9.2.1890

William II intends to be, like his great predecessors, another Widener of the Realm in all the gifts and goods of peace.—Emperor William II has also inherited the courage and daring of his forefathers. (He does not conceal from himself the difficulties in the way of the international regulation of the labour question, but he faces them and goes on to wrestle with them.)

Reichsbote

In the preparation of the messages the Emperor was faced with objections, but did not allow himself to be deterred by them; he pointed to the duty of the Monarchy to protect the economically weak, expressed in the familiar title of honour given to King Frederick I—"King of the Poor."

10.2.1890   Levysohn's Survey

The Liberals are joyfully and enthusiastically acclaiming the Emperor's programme; the Cartel parties are largely holding aloof in dudgeon or agreeing with a sour expression, while the little group of those ultra-Conservatives against whom the Government Press has just declared a determined feud have given unreserved praise to the Monarch's decisions.

10.2.1890 (Evg.)   *Nord*
        (Brussels—semi-official Russian organ)
The messages are true harbingers of peace, shouting down the noise of arms in Europe.

11.2.1890   *Tägliche Rundschau*
The principal clauses in the Imperial manifesto are the work of the Emperor himself.

15.2.1890
The Emperor's speech is mainly welcomed by the Press of almost every political shade with the same satisfaction as the messages, the policy of which is also that of this latest pronouncement of the Emperor's.

17.2.1890   Levysohn's Survey
Prince Bismarck's prophetic words are finding their fulfillment in his own lifetime: The day will come when this Emperor will be his own Chancellor.—One may with justification entertain the hope that the Emperor's far-reaching step will succeed, in spite of all the secret and open resistance from the Cartel parties (which will be overcome), in producing at least a relative recovery of the health of our body politic.—While the Emperor is plainly listening with close attention to the political and social pulse of the nation (and yet will have nothing to do with any attempt artificially to quicken or retard it through influencing the elections by means of the administrative machinery or an official election address), he has the satisfaction of seeing that his suggestions in social politics are mainly finding unreserved acceptance abroad, at least from the Governments.

19.2.1890 (Evg.)

Hamburgische Nachrichten

As to the difference between Emperor and Chancellor before the publication of the messages as to their contents, a difference which is said to have resulted in a modification of the messages, this has probably been ascribed an exaggerated importance. The Emperor and Chancellor have, at all events, at no time differed in their view as to the ultimate purpose of all the measures to be adopted.

24.2.1890   Levysohn's Survey

The non-prolongation of the Socialist law, the retirement of Prince Bismarck from the Ministry of Commerce, and the Emperor's two messages on social reform were the external manifestations of an independent way of thinking of the Monarch's, which is leading far from the paths hitherto trodden by Prince Bismarck.—Emperor William II feels in a modern enough way to realize the impossibility of guiding a Government along tracks which are the antithesis of the expressed will of the nation.

26.2.1890 (Evg.)

The Imperial messages have now to bear the brunt of the blame for the electoral defeat of the Cartel and of Prince Bismarck. The *Norddeutsche Allgemeine Zeitung* has the brazenness to attribute the fiasco of the Cartel and the Socialist victories almost undisguisedly to the messages. The *Schlesische Zeitung* also writes that many have given reason to suppose that they voted on the lines of the "Labour Kaiser," by depositing their ballot papers for the Labour candidate. The same thing is declared by the *Hamburgische Korrespondenz* to be stated to have been observed, especially in rural districts.—It looks, therefore, as if at a given signal the Cartel Press intends to make the messages, and therewith the Emperor himself, responsible for the triumph of the Socialists.

27.2.1890 (Evg.)   *Strassburger Post*

If the Emperor finds in the new Reichstag a serviceable majority for the work of taxation reform, which up to now has been more than well protracted, then it may and, if, as we believe, we read the Kaiser's mind aright, will, be a matter of indifference to him by what parties the majority is formed.

28.2.1890

Emperor William is, indeed, initiating a rigid régime, for every régime must be so or it is none at all. The Emperor intends to introduce a rigid social ordering, and in his view that is only possible through international socio-political arrangements.—The Emperor sees in the workman a citizen of the State with the same rights as every other citizen. That being so, the Emperor sees his highest task in assisting the workman to his social rights, as his forefathers did the burghers.—But he is far from meaning to favour one class of the population at the expense of the others; by his socio-political efforts he wants to strengthen the idea of the State, and for that very reason the Emperor is showing himself to be the representative of the whole of the people and not the representative of a class.

3.3.1890   Levysohn's Survey

Worthy of note that the news that a Chancellor crisis has been surmounted leaves the public cold. The feeling is beginning to spread in the country that, now that the nation has been twenty years in the saddle, it has itself learnt to ride; consequently the German people would not lose its equanimity if yet another Chancellor crisis were to come. The nation is aware that the ship of state is safe in the good, strong hands of the Emperor, and looks forward with confidence to the days when there will no longer be a Bismarck.

5.3.1890 (Evg.)

Augsburger Postzeitung

(Baron von Fechenbach on the Messages)

'At Germany's head there stands our young Emperor, intellectually and physically strong; he had already won our hearts in his earliest youth and filled us with trust, love and hope. It is by no means impossible that under him an epoch is beginning from which history will name his time, an epoch which will establish for the whole civilized world a new economic order, which will possess its own sign manual, and will closely unite the fame, the greatness and the prosperity of the German nation for centuries with the name of William II. All the prerequisites are present, the rest lies with God and remains open to a clear and strong will.

10.3.1890　　Levysohn's Survey

The Emperor's speech at the banquet of the Brandenburg Provincial Diet contains a very painful warning for all those who had imagined that they alone were entitled to take a hand in governing. (" . . . I shall destroy.")—It is an open secret that in certain high regions there is a scarcely suppressed dislike of the Emperor's reform ideas (depreciatory judgment of the Emperor's socio-political ideas, of his great peace tours) ; it may, therefore, appear desirable to the Sovereign to make an unmistakable declaration of his power and so remind those members of exalted and super-exalted circles who are seized with political alarm that they have no reason to give way to black care, and that they must keep in mind the difference which has always existed between a Hohenzollern and a Bourbon.—In any case a division is beginning to be more and more definitely marked between old and new. The new in the person of the Emperor is even today taking some of the place hitherto occupied alone by the gigantic figure of the Chancellor.

7.3.1890 (Evg.)

Hamburgische Nachrichten

We say nothing as to whether the old Chancellor, in spite of his services and qualities that make mock of all standards, is beginning to fade in the political consciousness of the nation before the splendour of the young and active Emperor, representative of a new era and irradiated with new tasks. Were that the case, it would explain the fact that the foremost statesman has persisted in such great seclusion that scarcely any political influence is any longer felt. The absent always suffer.—The Emperor is a man of extraordinary comprehension, great independence, who as such is justified in wishing to apply his gifts as ruler over so mighty a realm with such great and difficult problems.—The old times in which the Chancellor looked after everything in political life, and the Emperor remained more in the background, are certainly gone for ever.

18.3.1890 (Bismarck's Retirement)

Emperor William II belongs to a different generation to the aged Chancellor, who, as the Samoa affair and the Wohlgemuth question have shown, has begun to lose that strength and sureness to which he had owed in the past his principal successes—even in the domain which was most peculiarly his own, that of foreign politics. The tasks of government were an unwritten page to Emperor William when he came to the throne, and to his astonishment and regret he found that he was expected to take over all the traditions, all the methods of government, all the grudges in which the adviser of his grandfather for so many years had grown grey. That was the fundamental reason which made impossible in the long run any fruitful collaboration between the two men.

19.3.1890

The Emperor is attributed this line of thought: If one has to do only with bad elements and enemies of the coun-

try, one may certainly assure one's self against painful sur-
prises by such legislation as the Socialist law and the Septennat. But if one is to count on the independent cooperation of the good and honourable section of the population,
then the trust for which one asks calls for the trust which
one gives.—Such an attribution is incompatible with the
mistrust in political opponents which in Bismarck's case
had become an instrument of government.

1.2.1890   VOSSISCHE ZEITUNG

If the information published by the *Kölnische Zeitung*
and the *Hamburgische Korrespondenz* is correct, the
change of Ministers is a sort of compromise between the
Emperor and the Chancellor. The Emperor seems to be in
favour of the Labour Protection Bill unanimously passed
by the Reichstag. Apparently Prince Bismarck is giving
way in regard to this. The Chancellor, however, seems to
have secured, in opposition to the views which the Emperor
put forward to the representatives of the mineowners last
May, that a firmly negative attitude shall be adopted towards the demands of the miners.

1.2.1890 (Evg.)
Rheinisch-Westfälische Zeitung

The very fact of the appointment of Baron von Berlepsch seems to us to point unmistakably to the intention of
the Government of our Emperor and King to adopt to
begin with in the home country, which has most suffered
from strikes, such measures as it will be possible to describe
as "pro-Labour."

6.2.1890

In view of Tuesday's messages from the Emperor and
King it will be impossible for anyone any longer to con-
tend that Prince Bismarck's resignation of the Prussian

Ministry of Commerce has no political significance. The appointment of Herr von Berlepsch in place of the Prince is more than a change of individuals, it is an entire change of system, which we can now gladly welcome.—The messages show in many places an unmistakable similarity with the Emperor's speech of May 16 to the mineowners. They are, on the other hand, unmistakably irreconcilable with the views which Prince Bismarck expressed.—If the Emperor secures international agreement as to the possibility of meeting the needs and desires of the workers, he will be carrying into execution a plan which Prince Bismarck has opposed in the past.—The position which the Emperor has hitherto taken up in regard to the labour question excludes the possibility of any suspicion that the messages mentioned above are no more than electoral window-dressing.—The Emperor has thus announced his purpose, and we hope that the future will show that in this instance also where there is a firm will there will prove also to be a way.

6.2.1890 (Evg.)

In past instances Prince Bismarck has agreed to the publication of royal decisions in the *Staatsanzeiger*, even if only subject to conditions.—Today messages can appear which a little while ago would undoubtedly have resulted in the Chancellor's resignation.

7.2.1890 (Evg.)

We hope the day may come when it will be possible to have the satisfaction of saying that the Emperor's message to the Chancellor has been entirely brought to fruition. But we are under no illusion as to the length of time which must first elapse.

Presse, Vienna

This is a political action of the first importance, and one which will be epoch-making in its influence on the social

question in Europe for a long time to come.—The undertaking of an international protection of labour through the
German Emperor is in itself a spreading of the idea of
peace, which extends itself through international treatment
to the idea of international peace.

Pesti Naplo

The Emperor has set before himself a splendid programme. Whether it is realizable, we will not enquire; the
mere fact that a Monarch who has millions of bayonets at
his disposal is striving not after the bloody laurels of war
but to improve the lot of the poor and heavy-laden, is in
any case one which will bring him more fame than any
warlike deeds.

Neues Pester Journal

The Kaiser's proposal should be certain of the full approval of all who have human feelings.—Today he is perhaps more popular than the Iron Chancellor ever was.

Moniteur Universel and Figaro

consider that Prince Bismarck has played his part, and that
Emperor William will himself be Bismarck's successor, as
Louis XIV was Mazarin's.

10.2.1890 (Evg.)

Hamburgische Korrespondenz

The difference between the bases of the Emperor's social
policy and of that hitherto followed by the Government in
regard to labour legislation is unmistakable, but not in the
same measure in regard to the organization of the workers.

The difference between Emperor and Chancellor in this
latter point is not unmistakable "in the same measure." But
here too it is probably too readily assumed that their views
were the same.

15.2.1890

The fact that the Emperor's messages represent a sort of compromise with the Chancellor is confirmed by the opening speech to the Council of State.

17.2.1890 (Evg.)   *Deutsche Revue*

Letter from Cardinal Manning, Archbishop of Westminster:

I regard this act of the Kaiser's as the wisest and worthiest which has proceeded from any Sovereign of our time. The situation in which the wage-earners of all European States exist is a grave danger for every State in Europe. . . . Home life is made an impossibility for them (through the long working hours), and yet the whole ordering of the State rests on family life. . . . Emperor William has thus shown himself to be a true and farsighted statesman.

18.3.1890

It is always a mistake to pour new wine into old bottles. Much as the Emperor may venerate the great statesman, he has himself too pronounced an individuality to be able to subordinate himself to the Chancellor's guidance.—Today the crisis is upon us, and—a sign of the times, and also a sign of the loyalty of the Chancellor's party—not a finger has been lifted, not a pen taken up, so far as individuals and journals in an independent position are concerned, to advocate Prince Bismarck's continuance in office.—The Iron Chancellor had lost his sureness of touch, he had begun to vacillate, while the will of the youthful and energetic ruler was coming more and more strongly into play. It was as the child of another time, guided by another outlook on the world, filled with ideas which ran diametrically counter to those of the aged Minister, that Emperor William came to his task. Since his first day of rule there has no longer been entire unity in the conduct of the State. And how could there have been? On one side stood the Chancellor, child of the pre-1848 days, brought up in the system of Metternich; on the other the Emperor, who has imbibed the spirit of the days since the uplifting years of war! On one side there was deliberation, caution, devotion to tradition; on the other boldness and enterprise, self-confidence and confidence in others! On one side the memory of personal feuds, on the other an unencumbered impartiality to all parties! There was no lack of friction, and often Prince Bismarck was victor; but they were Pyrrhic victories, and today he finds himself checkmated.

19.3.1890 *Kölnische Zeitung*

Prince Bismarck had acquired the mentality of one who had enjoyed unlimited power in a position of supreme authority. Now there stood at his side an Emperor of full manly stature, with a will of his own, a Monarch who intended himself to rule.—Prince Bismarck often found himself in a situation in which he believed that the moment had come for reining in, while the Emperor was for plunging on.

19.3.1890 (Evg.) *Soleil*

The sentinel of European peace has been dismissed, the German Emperor now conducts the Government himself. From now onwards he ceases to be under Bismarck's tutelage. But his rule is an unknown element.

Justice

No one can know what the young Kaiser, who at present is an adherent of Christian Socialism, will do.

Fremdenblatt, Vienna

Emperor William will follow his predecessors in not departing from the strict maintenance of the path of the lover of peace, and will hold to the alliances which have been concluded for the benefit of the three States.—Emperor William's deep insight and sense of duty add to the guarantees of a policy of peace. The thing which inspires confidence above all is the Emperor's gifts, his strength of character, and his restless activity, the patriotism of the German Princes, the nation's readiness for sacrifice, and the great spirit which begins to infuse it.

21.3.1890

The German Emperor in his messages has expressed to the great man who for a whole generation has held the reins of the chariot of State in his strong hand, the feelings which inspire not only himself but the overwhelming majority of the Germans. The separation has come without recrimination, without bitterness. The thanks of the fatherland to Prince Bismarck will never be lacking; but it will be impossible to escape the recognition that in the internal politics of the German Empire a thoroughgoing change had long been needed, and had ultimately become inevitable.

24.3.1890 (Evg.)

It will be recalled that even before Prince Bismarck had submitted his request to be allowed to retire, there had been kites flown in the Press from semi-official sources, with the evident intention of inducing the Emperor to refuse the request. Now that the decision has disappointed these expectations, the whole weight of the responsibility for it is being thrown on the Monarch. Every suggestion that Prince Bismarck could have had any share in this responsibility is being demonstratively rejected.

Norddeutsche Allgemeine Zeitung

The *Hamburgische Korrespondenz* shows itself incompletely informed when it maintains that there was no lack of attempts to persuade the Prince to continue to keep control of foreign policy. Such attempts may have been made in the Prussian Ministry of State; but there were no personal steps of the Emperor's or of influential federal Princes.

Hamburgische Nachrichten

It will be safe to assume broadly that the programme of the future is to be found in an amalgamation of Cabinet rule in the sense of Frederick the Great with parliamentarism, that the Emperor intends himself to decide everything of primary importance and will regard the Ministers as merely the executants of his will.

Times

These incidents are merely variants of one and the same explanation. The Emperor has determined to be his own Chancellor. The Emperor and his new Chancellor have in front of them a blank sheet of paper on which to write history. The world will watch anxiously to see what manner of history it will be.

25.3.1890

The Emperor will *not* be his own Chancellor. He is not in a position everywhere to mediate between the natural particularism of the various administrations. He needs a leading statesman to take over this work himself. The Emperor cannot conduct or supervise the business of the State so closely as to smooth away all friction; he would have to go so deeply into all the details of the work of the various departments that his strength, however robust, would soon be overtaxed.—Geffcken says that the freedom from responsibility of the head of the State is secured only when it is covered by the responsibility of the Ministers.—For all that, there is a grain of truth in the assertion that the Emperor wants to be his own Chancellor. The Parliamentary system is probably not being introduced. But the system of sole Ministerial responsibility extending even over the Crown, which while denying the British conditions for the position of the Premier, yet claims that position, is being broken: Prince Bismarck sawed that bough off while he was sitting on it, when he tried to limit the freedom of the

Crown.—In future what Prince Bismarck described as essential, although it was not in existence, is being carried out: the Emperor will not actually rule in detail, but rule he will.

27.3.1890 (Evg.)

If the change of Chancellors has made any difference, it is in the point at which, in the eyes of the public, the prestige and the service of a policy of peace are centred; from now on this will be the business of the German Emperor: such is his intention.—The Emperor's firm resolve to hold to the past peaceful policy will be able to compensate for the loss, all the more since the edifice of peace has not to be built up from the foundation but stands already in a solid frame before the eyes of all the world.

6.2.1890 (Evg.)

NEUE PREUSSISCHE (KREUZ-) ZEITUNG
(On the Kaiser's Messages)

We have to give expression to our deepest and most joyful thanks to H.M. our Emperor and King, who has shown once more to his people and to the whole world the comprehensive view and the devoted care with which he is tackling the solution of the great problems which dominate our time. The aim and purpose of the Emperor's desires are so clear that to add a word would only obscure their significance.

9.2.1890

We Conservatives, with our programme of both Christian and social character, have a better right than any other party to maintain that the contents of the messages are entirely in harmony with our own efforts for many years past.

15.3.1890

Amid astonishment and admiration, and envy in some quarters, the recognition is forcing its way that Germany, in the person of her Emperor, has taken over the leadership in a direction which, if steadily maintained, may well guide the development of the nations into entirely new and peaceful paths.

19.3.1890

Our Emperor and lord has from the first omitted no opportunity of bearing public witness to the great value which he places on the imperishable services of the Imperial Chancellor, and the warmth with which he feels personally bound to him. If now, in spite of all, he has parted from him, the reasons which have led to this resolve and—we say it openly—were bound to lead to it, have for some time past not been concealed from the unprejudiced observer.—Just, however, as the anxiety which showed itself in the past in Germany as to what would happen when the Chancellor, the joint founder of the German Empire, was no longer with us, has given place to the firm confidence that our young Emperor and lord, with his wide outlook, clear intelligence and strong hand, has acquired his heritage and will keep a strong hold of it, so foreign opinion is aware that Germany's Princes and races are showing unshakable loyalty to the Empire, whose Emperor has devoted his thoughts and actions to the work of reconciliation and peace, but is also skilled in handling the sharp sword and in keeping its edge keen. Looking up joyfully to our Emperor, whom may God's grace and help never fail in his work, Germany will be able to look forward calmly and hopefully to the future, whatever internal and external storms it may conceal in its lap.

30.3.1890 *Deutsches Tageblatt*

If Emperor William II offers in his person the best conceivable guarantees that the destiny of the German fatherland will continue to be guided in the same spirit, the impression and the feeling in German hearts will be ineffaceable that an injustice such as could not conceivably be more unmerited has been done to Germany's first great statesman. For the idea that Prince Bismarck could voluntarily lay down his offices is considered absolutely out of the question. Men lusting for power might, perhaps, have tried to delude the Emperor as to the heavy burden on the national consciousness which would lie in the dispensing with the support and advice of a political sage such as Prince Bismarck is, before the decree of God commands it. We regard it, however, as entirely incredible and thoroughly impossible that Emperor William II should entertain such advice even for one moment. This very day he will have made up his mind that there is only one solution of the crisis which can calm the nation, namely that he shall repeat the reply which his grandfather gave to Bismarck's request for permission to resign—"Never."

Neue Freie Presse, Vienna

Prince Bismarck is retiring, young hands are seizing on the helm of the State, a wide gap has opened and one looks round in vain for men who shall fill it.

20.3.1890 (Evg.) *Grashdanin*

The retirement of Prince Bismarck is a spectacle which may become for Germany a drama. Any play with Socialists is dangerous; the parting with the Prince contains a still greater danger for the Kaiser. An interesting personal struggle is going on between the young and inexperienced Monarch, unfamiliar with the business of State but filled with fervid aspirations, plans and dreams, and the experienced old man, familiar with all forms of human intrigue, and rich in memories and well learned lessons. The Kaiser proposes to divest Bismarck of power in order to liberate himself from his tutelage, for he has an impatient character and is unable to await the natural end of the great founder of the German colossus. But it is no more possible by a stroke of the pen to command a Bismarck to pass out of existence than by an Imperial ukase to make anyone into a

Bismarck. There are probably but few Germans for whom the Prince and Germany are not one and the same thing. It may therefore come to pass that the Kaiser will remain isolated with the Socialists, while Bismarck, with a Germany taking his part, retires into the background. Then the young David will say to the old Goliath: "Here, take the Socialists and give me Germany back again."

23.3.1890

Bismarck's retirement from office, although it is exciting very deep emotion all over the world, has in practice taken place as quietly and with as little disturbance as though it were nothing more than an ordinary change of Ministers.— The German people has firm confidence in the German Emperor and his first new adviser, and is confident that their powers will be equal to their intentions; accordingly it looks forward to the future calmly and with resignation; the change has come under much happier conditions than was widely expected. Where there's a will there's a way.

7.2.1890

BERLINER VOLKSBLATT (later VORWÄRTS)

(On the Kaiser's Messages)

The change of front in the Empire's social policy is a defeat for the Chancellor. This defeat of the Chancellor is a victory for the Social Democracy. The indications given by the Emperor in his messages all have reference to old Social Democratic demands put forward years ago. It follows that the workers must vote Social Democrat wherever they can at the coming elections if the labour legislation now to be inaugurated is really to correspond to their needs and interests.

21.3.1890   (On the fall of Bismarck)

We were and still are opponents of the Imperial Chancellor on principle, and have suffered severely under his

policy; but we count ourselves among the respectable politicians, and for the sake of our reputation we shall not join
in the chorus of the professional sycophants and faultfinders.

(No reference to the Kaiser.)

INDEX OF NAMES

283

SUBJECT INDEX